BOYS
WILL BE
GIRLS

CLAUDIA NELSON

BOYS WILL BE GIRLS

The Feminine Ethic and British Children's Fiction, 1857–1917

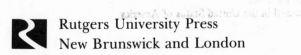

Rutgers University Press
New Brunswick and London

To my parents,

David Aldrich Nelson

Mary Dickson Nelson,

with love

Contents

List of Illustrations

Acknowledgments

My grateful thanks must go first to Mary Burgan of Indiana University, whose commentary and encouragement were invaluable to the dissertation upon which this book is based, and to the members of my doctoral committee, Patrick Brantlinger, Alfred David, and Donald Gray. I am also indebted to the Charlotte W. Newcombe Foundation, whose fellowship enabled me to spend 1988–1989 in Oxford, and to the helpful staffs of the Indiana University Library, the Lilly Library, the Kinsey Institute, the Bodleian Library, and the British Library. Special acknowledgment is owed to Alison Roberts and Nick Barton for their gracious hospitality in Oxford, and to friends and colleagues—chief among them Cynthia Patton—who let me tell them more about Victorian boys' books than they may have wanted to know. I also thank Leslie Mitchner and Gregory Suriano of Rutgers University Press.

Some of the material in Chapter Two appeared in a slightly different form in "Sex and the Single Boy: Ideals of Manliness and Sexuality in Victorian Literature for Boys" (*Victorian Studies* 32 [Summer 1989], 525–550), and is reprinted here by permission of *Victorian Studies* and the Indiana University Board of Trustees.

Boys
will be
Girls

Introduction: Manliness and the Angel in the House

Children's books in England came into being less to delight than to instruct. And when children's fiction began its golden age in the mid-nineteenth century, entertainment may have formed its limbs and outward flourishes, but didacticism remained its backbone. It was not, however, a didacticism of facts. Just as early writings for children, from etiquette manuals to books on holy dying, had stressed behavior above all else, the education Victorian children's fiction sought to provide for its readers was primarily an emotional education. Covertly or overtly, the novels as a body promise to bestow upon their consumers not a talent for business or a knowledge of geography, but something more precious still: manliness or womanliness.

In the inquiry (now in its second century) into the position of women in the Victorian era, we have often assumed that, at least for the Victorians, manliness and womanliness are separate and potentially conflicting sets of qualities rather than one ideal with two genders. And certainly, in the nineteenth century, male and female are not so much different sexes as different species. But maleness and femaleness are functions of biology, manliness and womanliness of ideology—and for the greater part of the century, until science began to invade religion's territory in the popular mind, biology and ideology were at cross purposes. Until the last quarter of the century, most commentators saw femaleness and womanliness as similar, maleness and manliness as conflicting. Or more accurately, perhaps, most mid-Victorian commentators saw womanliness as so powerful that it controlled the nature of femaleness, while manliness had a harder struggle against maleness. This three-cornered relationship of femininity, maleness, and manliness is a central subject for Victorian novelists, and particularly for Victorian children's novelists, whose primary responsibility was in many ways the socializing of gender.

Nineteenth-century explicators of manliness and womanliness used similar terms to define their subjects: self-control, self-sacrifice, selflessness. The chief difference between the two was merely one of presentation. While womanliness had a single incarnation as the Angel in the House, who carried her domestic halo even on missions to London slums or Crimean battlefields, manliness could not be organized into one image of Soldier or Knight. It was her association with the private sphere that gave the Angel her power; forced by unkind nature to operate primarily in public life, man had no mythic role to draw on. Firmly rooted in the home, shaper of memory and personality, women became archetypes, while men could only hope to be adults. For this reason, mid-Victorian novels explaining the nature of manliness do so, eagerly or reluctantly, in terms of the characteristics of the Angel.

Despite what many historians see as the unusually strong gender distinctions within Victorian childhood,[1] the Victorian stereotype of childhood had much in common with the feminine ideal. Because in the traditional great chain children possessed less worldly power even than women, the preadolescent of either sex took on many of the qualities of the Angel, for whom separation from public concerns meant strength. For all his father's efforts, Paul Dombey of Dickens's novel can no more be assimilated into the adult masculine world than can Little Nell; like women, children serve as an instructive contrast to the limited status quo, standing outside and "pointing upward." And because in evangelical theory worldly power hinders spiritual growth, both children and women accomplish real good in a literature whose roots are largely religious. By the mid-Victorian years, the forceful innocence of the good child, like that of the good woman, was an article of faith. The evangelicals' insistence that the sparrow's importance at least equaled the hawk's gave children as much power as fathers—but it was a different kind of power, and it derived from mothers.

Our own century's interpretations of that power are as many as the number of interpreters; before we can find the Angel within the childish ideal, we must define her. In "Professions for Women" (1931), Virginia Woolf depicted her as stiflingly pure and hypocritically sweet, maintaining her own existence at the expense of women's self-expression. Simone de Beauvoir saw femininity as a masculine evocation of the Other to which women assented at their peril, the Angel as a will-o'-the-wisp luring her followers into a patri-archal quicksand. Later, Patricia Meyer Spacks implied in *The Female Imagination* (1972) that women who accept the Angel easily are deny-ing an inescapable hidden anger, for selflessness is really "self-cast-igation" and passivity's power really deviousness. Marilyn Butler's *Jane Austen and the War of Ideas* (1975) posited a conflict between the sentimentalist/"jacobin" tradition and its opposite, in which literary men constructed a canon around those novels that upheld their own ideas of women's sensibilities; conditioned to underrate the noncan-onical, we may ignore what women have to say. Sandra Gilbert and Susan Gubar likewise explored a double tradition in *The Madwoman in the Attic* (1979), wherein the Angel is the façade holding back a "demonic" creativity and pallid heroines foil raging authors: patri-archy, that peculiar institution, imprisons princess and witch within one body. And to Nina Auerbach in *Woman and the Demon* (1982), angel-woman and demon-woman express identical revolutionary ar-dor, so that the myth empowered rather than stifled the goddesslike ideal that dominates Victorian literature. We've come a long way from Woolf here.

Similarly, social historians often see the Angel as a symbol of con-spicuous bourgeois consumption, a status possession for middle-class men—but sometimes view her instead as the catalyst for Victorian social change. Thus Joan Burstyn argues in *Victorian Education and the Ideal of Womanhood* (1980) that sex stereotypes result primarily from Victorian male anxieties over rank, but Carol Dyhouse's *Girls Growing Up in Late Victorian and Edwardian England* (1981) empha-sizes not only the great divide between the genders but also the ways in which reformers depended upon the Angel to expand women's educational and professional options. Catherine Gallagher's *The In-dustrial Reformation of English Fiction* (1985) likewise proposes the family as the chief source for reform within the novel tradition, wherein woman is the head and man only the hand; the family met-aphor offered Victorian society its hope of reunification. And Nancy Armstrong asserts in *Desire and Domestic Fiction* (1987) that in her role as novelistic heroine, the Angel undermined male hierarchies by replacing money with morality, lineage with love, as authors re-defined the desirable. It was in reaction to the complacent Augustan exaltation of aristocratic masculine rationalism, Ian Bradley's *The Call to Seriousness* (1976) suggests, that the Evangelical Revival occurred in the late eighteenth century, and in turn it was the early-nineteenth-century dominance of evangelical values such as altru-ism, domesticity, and emotion that provided and defined the Angel's power.[2]

For the Victorians as for the critics of our own day, the Angel was less an individual than an Angelic host; because she existed, it seems, it was necessary constantly to reinvent her. Her grounding in the religious revolution—the effort to create a new community to replace man-eat-man individualism, the assertion of the worth of the powerless, the insistence on right feeling over mere knowledge— tied her also to the evangelical precept that each Christian has not only the right but the responsiblity to come to an individual understanding of doctrine. Every woman, and every man, had to create a unique version of society's rules; each was obligated not to let convention blur truth. Thus the Angel could not only shrink into a Victorian version of Marabel Morgan's "total woman," but expand into a semisecular Virgin Mary. Her ultimate role was as the instrument of Victorian society's subversive quest to heal itself by undermining the precepts of aggression, selfishness, and competition upon which the male world depended.

It is this incarnation of the Angel to which feminists today often owe a debt they may be loath to acknowledge; it is this incarnation with which I shall concern myself. Untainted by nineteenth-century capitalism, the Angel imaged an alternative society that valued gentleness, feeling, community, mutual respect, and spiritual equality. Victorian men might control money, but Victorian women could control life. Thus when modern feminists such as Barbara Ehrenreich and Deirdre English complain that this Mammon-versus-Mamma worldview, pitting marketplace against home, was "by its nature committed to lies and evasion" because it refused to confront the flaws of the patriarchy,[3] they underrate the strength of the Victorian womanly ideal. Surely one reason we must take the Angel seriously is precisely her willingness to criticize the market's values. From John Ruskin and his queens in their gardens and John Stuart Mill and his geniuses in their cages to Eliza Lynn Linton rebuking the "girl of the period" for commercializing love and Emily Davies arguing that women offer society its best chance for salvation, countless Victorian writers of both sexes re-create Coventry Patmore's insipid icon as a weapon for deconstructing the dominant male ideology— not only among women but among men. The same code of selflessness, emotional warmth, purity, and concern for others that typifies the ideal of the Victorian woman also consistently appears in works explaining manliness, as if those not born Angels might still have Angelhood thrust upon them. For the primary motivation behind the emotional didacticism of many Victorian authors for children is implicitly the desire to rebuild society, not by changing human laws but by changing human nature. The closer men could approximate the Angel, the better for humankind.

This book is about the novelistic mechanism by which the ideals of womanliness were presented to Victorian boys as the ideals of manliness, and about some of the reasons that mechanism gradually stopped working. To discuss these topics intelligently, we must examine not only the four major genres within the boys' fiction of the period—the school story, the adventure, the historical tale, and the fantasy—but also the theories of sexuality that necessarily informed depictions of gender, and the traditions from which boys' fiction arose. Paradoxically, it seems most appropriate to begin exploring middle-class boys' fiction between 1857 and 1917 (the years and the audience for which the manliness question was most thoroughly explicated) by looking at what stood outside it: earlier children's fiction for both affluent and working classes, parallel girls' fiction, and non-fiction commentary on the nature of childhood and womanliness. We shall encounter a related series of recurring questions. How far do the ethical messages contained in these works resemble the "feminine" ideal? What visions of the commercial adult world—or, perhaps, of a world that might be preferable to it—do the writings typically present? And do these messages and visions vary significantly with author's gender or book's genre? Finally, with the passage of time, what changes do we see taking place? In each case, the answers are linked to the varying distances in Victorian and Edwardian society between manliness, womanliness—and maleness.

• ONE •

Forerunners, Feminism, and Girls' Books

The development of children's fiction is best viewed in tandem with the development of adult ideas of childhood, which in turn has much in common in the nineteenth century with the development of ideas of true womanhood. Powerless at first, the womanly woman and the childish child made a virtue of their separateness, as under religious pressures conformity to the standards of adult males came to seem less important than conformity to the standards of God. The gradual romanticization of childhood went hand in hand with the romanticization of womanhood; both visions of unworldiness signaled the opinion-makers' discontent with the world as it was. The preeminent Angelic quality, the power to influence others for good, came to be attributed in sentimental writing to children as well as to women, as novelists depicted this "influence" creating utopia after utopia. The ultimate utopia, of course, is heaven, the Angel's ultimate home. Thus in much midcentury fiction, bodily weakness is both a sign and a source of virtue, serving to cut young heroines and heroes off from earthly contamination. As time went on, however, the world reasserted itself; even girls' fiction came to distrust some of the elements of the Angelic stereotype, and in doing so, harked back to the eighteenth-century rationalist stories that form a significant part of the history of children's fiction.

The stress in such stories is on the world as it is. Secure in the knowledge that adult civilization was daily going from good to better, eighteenth-century rationalist writers felt no urge to portray their young protagonists as in any way more powerful morally than their adult preceptors. The occasional parent might be frivolous or inattentive, but the offspring of such bad stock would invariably fail as well, doomed by bad upbringing to early death or at least humiliation. For example, Tommy Merton of Thomas Day's *The History of Sandford and Merton* (1783) is a spoiled and stupid sprig of a regrettable aristocracy and may be improved only by finding an alternative father in wise, middle-class Mr. Barlow. Likewise, we can actually see Maria Edgeworth's Rosamund learning sense in *Early Lessons* (1801): the child may have to walk slipshod for a season because she has asked her alarmingly sensible mother for a purple jar instead of shoes, but having discovered through ownership that the enticing jar is only, in Harvey Darton's phrase, "coloured water and a smell,"[1] she knows better than to press her request for a marble pear in a subsequent story. And her mother, of course, knew better all along.

In this orderly world, children are differentiated not so much into boy and girl as into well brought up and poorly brought up. The single most important characteristic in separating sensible sheep from foolish goats is obedience; children who insist on having their own way, or on taking their own way behind their parents' backs, invariably live—or often, do not live—to regret it. Nor are we left in any doubt as to the source of their manifold misfortunes. As A London Lady describes him in *A Cup of Sweets That Can Never Cloy; Delightful Tales for Good Children* (1804), Henry has "one very disagreeable fault, which was, that he did not like to be directed or advised." Thinking that "he was certainly big enough to take care of himself," he procures some gunpowder, blows up himself and his sister, loses an eye, and learns the valuable lesson that "children would avoid a great many accidents . . . if they would listen to the advice of their elders, and not fancy they are capable of conducting themselves without being directed."[2] The adult world is the unquestioned ideal.

Another youthful Guy Fawkes, Tom Tindall in *Tales Uniting Instruction with Amusement* (ca. 1810), having blinded and killed his father, "wishes he had followed his poor father's good advice. If he had done so, he might now have been at a genteel boarding school, with both his eyes safe, instead of being a chimney-sweeper, and blind of one eye";[3] the stress, again, is on exterior, practical values such as social status and bodily health. Obedience prepares one for adult worldly success. In such tales the sorts of mischief boys and girls can fall into may differ; Mrs. Trimmer's heroine Julia Sandford, for instance, commits a specifically feminine act of disobedience in swallowing the ends of her embroidery thread, to perish from strangled intestines.[4] But the moral is always the same: "From that moment the children unanimously agreed strictly to attend to their father's orders, and never in the slightest instance act in opposition to his will."[5] Nancy Armstrong's point that in the mid-eighteenth century instructional children's books shared the behavioral ideals of women's conduct manuals and ladies' magazines, so that this ideal directed the "social control" of girls and boys alike,[6] still holds true around the turn of the nineteenth century; it is "feminine" decorousness, not "masculine" inventiveness, that these authors wish to inculcate. Yet the goal of overweening obedience forbids the implication that children may in any way positively affect their environment; their world neither asks nor needs any help from them.

Early-nineteenth-century religious writers such as Mary Martha Sherwood, as David Grylls has observed, likewise make little distinction between boy and girl characters;[7] in Sherwood's *The Fairchild Family* (1818–1847) obedience is again a key virtue. But here the emphasis has shifted slightly, so that we see that obedience (to God) is required even of parents. Children owe a filial duty because God has so commanded, and because to recognize any higher authority is useful in learning to be faithful to the Supreme Authority. We are not to assume, however, that the senior Fairchilds are morally better than their offspring. To be sure, in the Fairchild family Father certainly knows best; his pronouncements and prescriptions in moral matters are always right, and we never glimpse any cracks in his impressive self-control. At the same time, we are constantly aware that his wisdom is not innate but acquired—and acquired through long obedience to divine laws. Unwilling to depict weakness in the head of the family, who must "stand in the place of God" to his children, Sherwood nevertheless hints that such weakness is inevitable. She does so by allowing us a brief look at the inner struggles of *Mrs.* Fairchild, who explains to her children that all humanity is flawed and that even parents forever need to exercise self-discipline to keep down their baser natures. The major lesson of the books, that "without God's help nobody can be good," applies to male and female, parent and child, without exception; obedience is for everyone.[8]

The effect of the doctrine that before the Lord all souls are equal—or equally bad—is to establish beside the earthly hierarchies of age, sex, and rank a spiritual antihierarchy in which only humility brings power. In this framework children may be bound for heaven or hell, depending on the degree of their obedience to divine authority. But it is always evident that they deserve full respect as the moral peers of adults.[9] From here it is but a step to the suggestion that the child may effect the adult's conversion; earnestness is ageless.

The issue in religious children's books, then, is not so much behavior (at which children must always be at a disadvantage) as the state of one's soul. Given enough self-knowledge and its inevitable consequence, humility, a child can be saved where an adult may be damned. This is not because adult sins are necessarily more highly colored than childish ones, for Sherwood observes that stealing an apple or squabbling with a sibling may well be enough to tip the scale toward perdition, but because the circumstances of a child's life may offer more opportunities for remembering the need for humility and discipline and thus fewer opportunities for committing Satan's sin of spiritual pride. As early as 1672, James Janeway's *A Token for Children* had presented the holy deathbeds of godly infants (all of them secure in a sense of sin) as an object lesson of particularly useful moral value; by the early decades of the nineteenth century this doctrine found both challenge and, oddly, reinforcement in a Rousseauan influence that likewise saw the world as a place of moral danger.

The tradition the early Victorians inherited thus emphasized on the one hand that children's gender was comparatively unimportant, since both boys and girls should be obedient, courteous, self-disciplined, honest, sensible, and neither foolishly timid nor recklessly brave, and on the other that the "feminine" knowledge of one's own powerlessness in this world may be the best way to ensure entry into the next. The latter point appears over and over in "antifeminist"—a better term might be "femininst"—writings in the mid-nineteenth century by women for women, which as we shall see find their counterparts in children's literature. As a usefully explicit laying-out of the theme, it is worth taking a brief look at Sarah Stickney Ellis's *The Daughters of England* (1843). This work plays on the hidden power of humility, making the characteristic point that woman's temporal inferiority does not detract from her spiritual authority, but adds to it.

Ellis spends much of the book ostentatiously underlining women's inferiority with one hand while quietly erasing it with the other. Certainly, she explains to her female audience, women are "inferior in mental power, in the same proportion that you are inferior in bodily strength," and often woman's inability to deal with powerlessness makes it irrelevant that "in the softer touches of mental and spiritual beauty, her character may present a lovelier page" than man's. In fact, however, we suspect that woman's greater capacity to feel pain and pleasure may mark her superior to her coarser mate—especially since this heightened feeling and perception apparently enable woman "not to live for herself, so much as for others; but, above all, not to live for this world so much as for eternity."[10]

The underlying message is clear: men, working away in "the strife, the tumult, the perpetual discord which constant occupation in the midst of material things so inevitably produces," are unconsciously playing grasshopper to women's ant, and come the wintry day of judgment, heaven will be predominantly female. Willing and able to waste his moral substance on "his worldly interests, his public character, his ambition, his competition with other men," man is incapable of the "almost superhuman eminence" of the pure, selfless, Edenic love that comprises all of a woman's life—and, we assume, enables her joyfully to devote herself to the crass males around her. And despite man's ostensible superiority, Ellis directs her chapter of advice to the lovelorn almost entirely to warning her readers against falling in love with men of inferior character. By the climax of the book, indeed, she is implicitly comparing women to Christ, the only man ever to exhibit the feminine self-sacrifice, pure devotion, and "capacity for exquisite and intense enjoyment."[11] Ellis thus chimes harmoniously with Nina Auerbach's suggestion that what I term femininism is "less a passive withdrawal from life than an active displacement by female of male religious icons."[12]

It is important to note here that even as she makes obvious woman's real superiority, Ellis is never willing to state flatly that women are better than men. Indeed, when she is discussing worldly themes she is eager to make plain that the opposite is true—that is, men have an unquestioned right to all their legal advantages. But her point is that men's strength is their misfortune, since "these restrictions imposed upon our sex" are directly responsible for "the high moral standing of the women of England." With such a premise, it would indeed be a major error to resort to blunt argument rather than to the gentle influence she identifies as woman's power; the whole book goes to show that he who asserts himself is lost. Even her preface illustrates this point, for she finds it advisable to explain that one should not take her role as author to imply that she wishes to impose her own views on others, but rather that as the response to her previous work proves, she has accidentally become the conduit for a vast surge of majority opinion: "Such are the circumstances under which 'The Women of England' has been received by the public, with a degree of favour, which the merits of the work alone would never have procured for it."[13]

By 1858, when Dinah Mulock Craik's A Woman's Thoughts About Women appeared in Chambers's Journal, the suggestion that "what they [men] expend for wealth and ambition, shall not we offer for duty and love—the love of our fellow-creatures, or, far higher, the love of God" has become a matter of course. So sure is Craik that her readers will take as natural law the idea that to err is male, to be female divine, that she has no hesitation in implying before a mixed audience not only that the real world is the world of home, which woman rules as of right, but that men are only an annoying intrusion. She remarks in a tone of tolerant patronage that

> A house where "papa" or the "boys" are always "pottering about," popping in and out at all hours, everlastingly wanting something, or finding fault with something else, is a considerable trial to even feminine patience. And I beg to ask my sex generally—in confidence, of course—if it is not the greatest comfort possible when, the masculine half of the family being cleared out for the day, the house settles down into regular work and orderly quietness until evening?

Like Ellis, Craik pays lip service to the idea that the business of the marketplace, which most women are incompetent to do, may be "as honourable, as difficult" as woman's role of living for others.[14] At the same time, however, she leaves her audience aware that to give men more than their meed of credit in this way is simply part of being a true and selfless woman. As Elaine Showalter has noted, Craik's writing thus unites "didacticism and subversive feminism" in encoded form.[15]

Not surprisingly, this exaltation of powerlessness as the truest road to power seemed tailor-made not only for women but for children, whose "seen-but-not-heard" etiquette so heavily stressed antiegotism. Simultaneously, children's humble status frequently denoted innate virtue instead of importance. Certain Nonconformist excesses to the contrary, early-Victorian British Christianity was gradually decreasing the Puritan emphasis on original sin and reinterpreting scripture to conform to Romantic "child-idealisation." In other words, texts urging us to become as little children were now about innocence rather than, as in Puritan dogma, about obedience—since prevailing opinion held that society, and not Adam's fall, was the source of corruption.[16] This being so, distanced like the ideal woman from worldly contamination, children had only to accept their economic marginalization to find themselves central to moral culture. It was thus not only possible but common in the early nineteenth century to write Sunday-school novels for young readers demonstrating the real spiritual force that an egoless child could wield in the domestic and future worlds. Such novels typically present self-effacement as the most effective means of getting not one's own way but God's way.

A good illustration of the strength of submissiveness as a social force is Miss Grierson's popular tract *Lily Douglas*, published circa 1821 and in its seventh edition by 1824. While Sherwood sees the quest for individual salvation as lifelong, Grierson's work reads more like a fictionalized version of Ellis's: the battle for humility need rage only once, after which the victors may set about implementing their new spiritual authority for the good of society at large. To Sherwood and Grierson alike, however, the salvation of the soul is more important than that of the body; it is the ultimate fate of Lazarus and Dives, not their degree of comfort while alive, that matters.

Hence Grierson doesn't want to improve the gruesome physical world her working-class characters occupy, since even well-meaning attention to the damage the marketplace wreaks might represent an offense against God's wish that we "keep ourselves unspotted from the world." Where Christian middle-class influence will prove most lastingly effective is not in charity to the body, but charity to the soul. The local benevolent society is therefore right to respond to the Douglas family's starving and fever-struck destitution with tracts and prayers instead of with food and medicines; perhaps due to their efforts, "all the fruit [of the Douglases' afflictions] seemed to be to take away sin."[17] Hitherto liable to egotistical error in rebelling against outside authority and outside system, little Lily goes to Sunday school and achieves a sense of sin. Humility not only turns her into a womanly woman, but integrates her into the larger feminine community by enabling her to form spiritual bonds with the pious older women in the story. And with her new strength, she saves not only her own soul but the souls around her, so that after her fruitless early anger at her wretched situation, Lily has finally found her real power in influence. What Grierson is recounting is the submergence of Lily's originally separate (and hence frustrated and useless) ego in the larger, anonymous, and communal Christian feminine force that, the tale suggests, is the one true hope for a society full of economic and worldly injustices.

Accordingly, Grierson frowns upon every evidence of female individuality or self-assertion. Even to have a name brands one as unregenerate. Lily's grumbling great-aunt is identified as Mrs. Macfarlane; her separation from the Douglas family surname seems akin to her refusal to be grateful for leftover salt herring and to her strangeness in living alone. Lily's mother, who is saved, has no name but that of her husband, while after Lily's conversion the name Lily clearly becomes not the label of an individual but an emblem of general (and feminine) Christian purity. And while a model child who dies young has a name so that we can better remember and emulate her, other models do not—including the author, whose name appears nowhere in her work. While the modern reader may complain that this practice makes the already difficult task of differentiating the characters even harder, the point seems to be that the ideal woman is just that: undifferentiated. By the end of the story, for instance, Lily has effectively become the narrator in both precept and practice; we last see her succoring an impoverished and ailing old woman, in imitation of the first actions of the narrator herself.

But Lily's task is already easier than that of the narrator because her "client" has from the start brought her own ego under evangelical control and is calm and happy despite bodily misery. From this and similar clues we may conclude that accepting worldly impotence is indeed an effective anodyne for suffering; to turn one's back on the world is to turn one's face toward heaven. Furthermore, we see that like Ellis, Grierson is willing to practice what she preaches, giving no explicit credit to her sex for the changes they are effecting. She presents both typical tract writer and typical tract reader as male; the Christian convert, she says, proves *him*self "by piety, diligence, and charity—by the calm and unruffled tenor of his temper—the purity of his thoughts and affections—the gentleness and kindness of his words and actions—and by the good works and almsdeeds which he is enabled to do."[18] But since the characters she depicts as behaving in this way are all women, and since her purpose as stated in her preface is "to exhibit the character of a . . . GOOD GIRL," clearly the persona she describes is feminine. (Men, indeed, hardly exist here, Lily's father being dead and the industrial tyrants responsible for the town's problems invisible.) By pretending through judicious pronouns that influence is male, despite the evidence of the story, the author demonstrates her own willingness to do without worldly praise for her own actions and those of her sex. She thereby provides one more example of self-abnegation for young readers to follow in order that their influence may be the purer and the more effective. Paradoxically, this striving for nonbeing is ultimately a stratagem for ensuring that the last shall be first.

One of the relatively few differences between the early evangelical literature intended for girls and that aimed at boys is that, while both preach the necessity of eradicating such ego-linked sins as pride, laziness, and the questioning of rightful authority, boys' books less frequently show the perfected hero's perfect integration into the Christian community.[19] Heroines like Lily Douglas achieve happy endings by becoming interchangeable with mothers, teachers, and authors; their male counterparts are more likely to win from their class superiors a respect that is wholehearted but never quite brotherly. The title character of Hannah More's *The Shepherd of Salisbury Plain* (1795), for example, who delights in the suffering a merciful Providence inflicts upon him because he knows God intends each hurt to help, awes his middle-class interlocutor and improves his own social and financial standing through displaying virtuous stoicism. This patience (atypical, Gillian Avery observes, for a More cottager)[20] presumably accounted for the tract's popularity among such Victorians as Charlotte Yonge, who would have seen in it an image of Christ's presence on earth. But although More's purpose in writing was to create a "good shepherd" to inspire similar behavior in her working-class readers of all ages, so that the community of doubly humble men might exist in fact if not in fiction, there is no sense within the story that the shepherd is gathering around himself a group of like-minded men. On the contrary, his success results from the uniqueness of his virtue.

Predictably, evangelical fictions commonly trace the lack of a male Christian network to the corrupting influence of the adult male world. With the spread of the Romantic view of childhood, however, the adult heirs of More's shepherd begin to find it possible to meet other males on terms not of respect alone but also of empathic identification and love—if these other males happen to be prepubescent boys. The first of Frederick Marryat's novels to aim specifically at a juvenile audience, the 1841 *Masterman Ready,* centers upon the instinctive bond between the pious and elderly title character and twelve-year-old William Seagrave as each attempts to help the shipwrecked Seagrave family adapt to life on an unknown island, exiled from a world that the novel consistently criticizes as besotted with commerce.

Of the group, only Ready is present on the island voluntarily, having declined to make his escape via the last place in the lifeboat the ship's selfish crew preempted—as he tells Mr. Seagrave, "I think much more of your children than I do for myself." This proof of unworldliness is underscored not only by Ready's unfailing ability to deal with all aspects of life on the island (where all the Seagraves but William are helpless), but by reminiscences in which he confesses his incompetence to deal with life elsewhere. Through his boyhood arrogance, overconfidence, and lack of consideration for others, he has long since squandered every worldly advantage. With such a background of repentance and reform, Ready is supremely qualified to become the party's moral advisor, explaining to Mr. Seagrave that the children may be lucky to be castaways, since none can know "what might have happened if you had arrived at Sydney, and had followed up your worldly concerns. . . . Who knows but what this visitation upon them may have preserved them from wickedness."[21] Nevertheless, he professes embarrassment over his role as guide. Both practical and spiritual power are functions of Ready's practical and spiritual humility; his handiness results from his years before the mast, while his moral teachings invariably follow an acknowledgment that by rights he should not presume to try to improve his audience, who must know better than he since God has placed them in a higher position.

But Marryat requires readers to understand that the sailor's respect for his class superiors illustrates not the Seagraves' grandeur but Ready's virtue. As Mr. Seagrave points out in a gloss on Ready's autobiography, "riches and prosperity in this world prove often the greatest of temptations; it is adversity that chastens and amends us, and which draws us to our God." And while the elder Seagraves are as good as one may expect adults of their rank to be, the real effect of their combined age and social status is to exclude them from the spiritual communion of Ready and William. When Ready spies a ship that may take them back to civilization, for instance, he can confide the news only to the child, since if the ship overlooks them, "it would be too cruel a disappointment to your father and mother"—they miss the world far more than William does. (As for Ready himself, he says, "I would willingly remain upon the island for the remainder of my days.") Similarly, it is William who receives the bulk of Ready's moral homilies, since the sailor feels too shy to tackle the adults' improvement with words. Indeed, the project of influencing the elders must be undertaken not only wordlessly but lifelessly, when Ready's sacrifice of his life for the family leads Mr. Seagrave to exclaim that "by his example, sinful as I must ever be, I have become, I trust, a better man."[22] In the literal unworldliness of death, Ready achieves both the ultimate self-effacement and the ultimate influence—and clearly the one depends on the other.

Beside this paragon William inevitably appears nondescript. His chief characteristics are filial piety and a willingness to expose his own ignorance and unimportance by asking questions of his mentor or his erudite father. But these proofs of humility are enough to establish a firm companionship between hero and boy, so that William spends far more of his time on the island with Ready than with his father—and, significantly, sees much more of it than does Mr. Seagrave, who sticks close to the relatively civilized campsite. Even their titles suggest a bond: that William, to Ready, is always Master William permits us to read Ready's own cognomen not as Masterman, after the wealthy and unprepossessing godfather whom he never joined in the marketplace, but as Master Man, the adult whose worldly powerlessness allows him, enviably, to participate in the pure and isolated (island) world of childhood.

Beset by sharks and savages, the island demonstrates the body's vulnerability. But life in the European world endangers the soul; the close-knit community of the castaways is impossible in a civilization whose motto is "Every man for himself." Ready's autobiography exposes the un-Christian error of the "civilized" world. His past teems with men unable to see that the true use of authority is to help and guide others: ironically, Ready's godfather cheated the youth and his widowed mother out of their small fortune, while Ready himself spent his boyhood fleeing one abuser of power after another. Regaining his money, he nearly lost his soul by misusing his position and scorning his friends, and it is explicitly the loss of his worldly goods to which he attributes his salvation.

Thus while Ready is not only a full member of the island family, but its leader, both he and the reader sense the hollowness of the elder Seagraves' assurances that should the group be rescued Ready will still have a (tangential) place in their home: civilization is simply too divisive to permit community. It is a foregone conclusion that the sailor will die on the island, since the world of adult men is so inimical to his own. Indeed, having had to leave the besieged stockade to fetch water because little Tommy Seagrave had squandered the group's supply, Ready succumbs to a savage's spear thrust just as the Western rescuers invade; the timing seems no coincidence. Given the circumstances, we may conclude that the reason he asks that Tommy be kept in ignorance of his crime is not merely a rejection of grisly Sherwoodian principles of infant accountability, but an acknowledgment that death on the island may be preferable to life in England. Mr. Seagrave instinctively exclaims of Ready's death and its immediate cause, "What a lesson it will be to Tommy"; Ready's shielding of Tommy from guilt extends the lesson to the entire adult world.[23]

Male and female alike, mid-Victorian commentators on childhood were eager to profit by Ready's example. Steeped in the theories of

Rousseau and seeing childhood as an island of innocence in the savagery of commercial adult civilization, child-rearing experts insisted that children should live as separately as possible from the adult world, while reviewers of children's books warned parents against juvenile literature that bore signs of adult contamination. Writing anonymously in the *Quarterly Review* in 1842, for example, Lady Eastlake inveighs against American authors who create a spurious child-speech in which to talk to their young readers; who try to sneak facts into stories, as if children should be developing their brains and not their hearts; who attempt to induce piety by appealing to the child's reason rather than to the child's faith and succeed only in vulgarizing God; and who insist on expressing ideals of family affection with financial metaphors. Such writers are not fit to preach to those enjoying "the only truly enviable part of life."[24] Clearly their unsuitability as mentors arises from their ignorance that children are different from adults and that this difference is valuable. Made precocious by their reading, American children are merely miniature adults.

Lack of appreciation for childhood, Lady Eastlake implies, is not characteristic of British authors; and indeed the most cursory glance at British adult periodicals from the first half of Victoria's reign (and even earlier) containing articles on childhood will reveal author after author well aware of how much more Angelic one is at five than at fifty. The author of "Childhood," published in *Blackwood's Magazine* in 1822, is eloquent on the subject of "the yet guiltless inhabitants of Eden":

> There is in childhood a holy ignorance—a beautiful credulity—
> a sort of sanctity that one cannot contemplate without some-
> thing of the reverential feeling with which one should approach
> beings of celestial nature. The impress of the Divine nature is,
> as it were, fresh on the infant spirit—fresh and unsullied by
> contact with this withering world. . . . Ay, which of us—of the
> wisest amongst us, may not stoop to receive instruction and re-
> buke from the character of a little child? Which of us, by com-
> parison with its sublime simplicity, has not reason to blush for
> the littleness—the insincerity—the worldliness—the degener-
> acy, of his own?[25]

Male and female children are one here—and they behave like women. More than forty years later, *Chambers's Journal* was to run a lead article almost identical in spirit: "Children" likewise separates the adult and juvenile worlds and gives the advantage to the latter, with the pithy beginning, "It is a bad world, we say, this world of men: full of evils of all sorts and sizes; overrun with selfishness and its prolific brood. . . . Still, here are *children* in it." And in their innocence and helplessness is our hope, for "children . . . exert an influence with respect to the work of men, the importance of which can hardly be exaggerated." Not only do they elicit soft feelings in the hardest of men, but they encourage male selflessness by ensuring that men will work for the benefit of their children and not themselves.[26] The Edgeworthian brand of didacticism is long gone; in the early-Victorian ethos it is Rosamund who teaches and her parents who respectfully attend.

Given this sense of two spheres—one idyllically prelapsarian, the other sterile and contaminated—it is not surprising that the chief issue in mid-Victorian children's fiction should be the avoidance of the guilt of adult men. Domestic fiction (usually written by women for a predominantly female audience) proposed two solutions: forbidding the child hero to enter the adult world, putting an end either to the story or to the child before the danger became imminent; and inculcating in the child character the traits approved for women rather than those likely to bring worldly success.

To the former strategy we owe the wildly popular sagas of innocence adrift and confused in an unsympathetic masculine world, such as Hesba Stretton's *Jessica's First Prayer* (1867), which reputedly sold an incredible 1.5 million copies.[27] A starving street waif, daughter of an alcoholic actress of easy virtue, Jessica knows nothing of religion and right conduct. But all her disadvantages only make it easier for us to see her innate goodness—and the wicked hypocrisy of those worldly authorities who, in their nonconcern for the souls of such as Jessica, only damn themselves. Thus Jessica's own salvation is never in real doubt, since we can see from her acceptance of unimportance and destitution that she images unwitting Christian humility. The true focus of the story is on how Jessica saves the soul of the snobbish, miserly, and "respectable" pharisee who befriends her. The irony of "Jessica's first prayer"—"O God! I want to know about you. And please pay Mr. Dan'el for all the warm coffee he's give me"—is that Jessica has instinctively put her finger on the difference between herself and her friend: she worships God, he Mammon. Nor has the good but ineffectual minister ever brought Daniel's sin home to him; it remains for Jessica to accomplish this feat through a series of transparently innocent questions, which, Daniel explains to the minister, "have gone quicker and deeper down to my conscience than all your sermons."[28] That the minister and Daniel eventually integrate Jessica into congregation and coffee-stall is insignificant beside her action in allowing them to enter the Christian community of which she is the unconscious center.

As the century continued, middle-class children too might serve as moral guides to elderly men of straying soul. Both Frances Hodgson Burnett's Little Lord Fauntleroy and Florence Montgomery's Gilbert Ramsay (in *Transformed*, 1886) are the epitomes of innocent influence, their very inability to fathom the contaminated characters of (respectively) grandfather and uncle proving their strongest weapon in their war to purify the strongholds and strongboxes of adult power. Not wishing to lose Fauntleroy's love, the earl of Dorincourt becomes a model landlord and learns that kind hearts are more than coronets. This lesson—translatable not only as "the persistent criticism of adult values from the standpoint of the child,"[29] but as the criticism of male values from the standpoint of the woman—made *Little Lord Fauntleroy* (1885) a best-seller. Likewise, consciously attempting to find happiness by becoming as a little child, John Ramsay discovers the delights of giving and the power of passivity and is finally reintegrated into the family he had abandoned for tycoonship.

Largely indifferent to money except as a means of benefiting others, the Angelic heroes of this brand of fiction run no risk of turning into tycoons themselves; their innocence is proof against the best the marketplace may offer. Early moralists of the Sherwood stripe would presumably have been horrified at this belittling of the strength of worldly temptation; writing in the *Quarterly Review* in 1896, Alexander Innes Shand pertinently observes that "when the Fairchilds unexpectedly come in for a fortune, we are inclined to sympathise with the victims of prosperity" and have ample cause to fear for little Henry [Fairchild]'s soul.[30] But in a school of fiction that owes its view of human nature far more to Rousseau than to Sherwood, the only "victim of prosperity" is the adult male.

Hence the moral struggles in these stories of the child-as-innocent invariably belong to the man being influenced, as he gradually learns to divest himself of the pride, forcefulness, and business sense that keep him from true happiness in this world or the next. Another strand of domestic fiction, however, seeks à la Sherwood to show the turmoil in the soul of the child, suggesting that it is never easy to become a moral influence. In sharp contrast to authors of *Fauntleroy*-like idylls of innocence, Yonge (chief exemplar of this second, darker category) never hesitates to warn readers of the dangers of power. Her version of the Cinderella story, the 1862 *Countess Kate*, shows the near-loss of Kate's soul on acceding to a title and to the feelings of self-importance that naturally accompany the acquisition; only through feminine humility and love, by coming to a sense of her lack of grace and her need to belong to a family, can Kate find salvation. Yonge consistently uses the circumscribed feminine lot to chastise the egotistical and to teach the earnest of both sexes, as a necessary prelude to creating what Catherine Sandbach-Dahlström calls "an ideal androgynous community ruled by the Christian values that women have often made their own." As Sandbach-Dahlström shrewdly points out, these values are opposed to the "masculine" qualities of "the contemporary secular world," so that the ultimate accomplishment of Yonge's fiction is its attempt to rebuild society along feminine lines.[31] And like Grierson with *Lily Douglas*, Yonge sees ordinary power not as an advantage in the feminine struggle but as a nearly insurmountable hindrance; women's "inferiority" is something to cherish.

But Yonge doesn't pretend that this truth is, or even should be, easy to accept. The best moral lessons come the hardest, and Providence is always willing to drop difficulties in a woman's way. The feminine lot is the more frustrating because representatives of the patriarchy in Yonge's work are so frequently blind to subtle shades of character that have nothing to do with social success but everything to do with salvation. Thus Mr. Edmonstone in *The Heir of Redclyffe* (1853) can easily persuade himself of Guy's supposed villainy; Dr. May in *The Daisy Chain* (1856) is quick-tempered and irresponsible and lacks real insight into his children; and even the upstanding Colonel Keith in *The Clever Woman of the Family* (1865) can't see the buried good in Rachel, so evident to Ermine and to the feminized Alick. This flaw at the top of the earthly power structure seems to be a deliberate effort on God's part to save women's souls, since the "manly man's" obtuseness often opens the way to spiritual humility and self-discipline in Yonge's protagonists, whose talents might otherwise make them impatient.

In *The Daisy Chain*, for instance, the perfect Mrs. May's accidental death (she selflessly allowed her boyish husband to drive her behind his dangerous new horse) proves a blessing in disguise for most of the older children, who in attempting to fill her place learn the importance of Angelhood. The true worth of the plodding Richard, hitherto a cipher in a family that had by and large prized cleverness above kindness, becomes apparent, while the brilliant Norman discovers that his aspirations toward glory are mistaken: genuine glory means becoming a missionary. Forced to give up competing with

Norman in Greek because the day no longer holds enough hours, Ethel gradually gains true womanliness—indeed, in the 1864 sequel, *The Trial,* she has succeeded (quite against her natural bent) in becoming her mother: "'You have got your mother's voice, and some of her ways, since you have grown older and more sedate.' 'Oh, I am so glad!' said Ethel, who had been led to view her likeness to her father as natural, that to her mother as acquired."[32] Ethel's achievement in quelling her natural self makes her the hub of the family, raises her status to that of helpmate to her father, and brings her the only power worth aspiring toward, the power of influence—although appropriately, "she knew not that she had personal influence at all, but went on in her own straightforward humility." It is she who saves the hero's soul in *The Trial.* As for Margaret, who might seem to have been perfect before the accident paralyzes her, "she knew the temptation of her character had been to be the ruler and manager of everything, and she saw it had been well for her to have been thus assigned the part of Mary, rather than of Martha."[33]

Margaret's injury and eventual inspirational death are a characteristic means of spiritual education in mid-Victorian domestic fiction, in which pain and enforced separation from the world often act as the refiner's fire, suggesting to the reader that as far as the body is concerned, it's better to be sorry than safe. Writers for adults might venture to depict invalids as incurably spiteful, selfish, and even murderous—like Emily Brontë's Linton Heathcliff or, more comically, Wilkie Collins's Frederick Fairlie—but writers for girls typically find in illness the surest road to spiritual health. (Death, of course, could be better still, and in sharp contrast to the horrid ends so favored by the writers of the early cautionary tales, mid- and late-Victorian authors are wont to punish their villains by leaving them alive. If saintly children were often too good for this world, their antitheses were apparently too bad for any other.) Novel after novel amplifies the idea expressed by Marianne Farningham (Mary Anne Hearne) in 1869 that "a sick daughter is often as an angel in the house" in influencing others and demonstrating the truth of religion.[34] In addition, many also make clear that sickness might be the only force strong enough to bring out the latent virtue in boisterous children. Juliana Ewing's *The Story of a Short Life* (1885) is typical.

Like Yonge in *Clever Woman,* Ewing draws a parallel between the boudoir and the encampment, suggesting that heroic denizens of both go overworked and underappreciated as they exist nobly in low positions and forgo glory for discipline. At the outset, however, little Leonard prefers the glory; the first thing we know about him—as

1. *The Invalid as Hero.* Leonard's crutches form the bond between him and his martyred Cavalier ancestor, Rupert, whose so-called "effeminate" features underscore rather than undermine a "more than common" manhood. Illustration by Gordon Browne to Juliana Ewing's *The Story of a Short Life* (1885).

his father exclaims, "Most annoying!"—is that he repudiates self-effacement. Skilled in "the art of being troublesome to the verge of expulsion," Leonard is a spoiled brat. He adores things martial but has no chance fully to understand the military life until his mis-behavior while watching soldiers on parade injures his spine. Nor does enlightenment come easily even then, for "the poor child was absolutely unaccustomed to prompt obedience, and disputed the doctor's orders as he had been accustomed to dispute all others." But at length his mother, herself a semi-invalid, determines that even though "it was not the trumpet's sound that summoned him to fortitude," she cannot accept "that her son should be a coward." A maternal lecture converts the eight-year-old into an instant soldier; he endures his fate silently and obediently, "for if the high, ambitious spirit, the ardent imagination, the vigorous will, which fired the boy's fancy for soldiers and soldier-life, had thus led to his calamity, they found in that sympathy with men of hardihood and lives of discipline . . . a constant incentive to . . . courage and patience."[35] Leonard's other incentive is his family motto, *Laetus sorte mea* (Happy with my lot), which Ewing associates at once with the fate of the soldier dying for queen and country and with the fate of the in-valid—or woman—living frustrated and confined. Both, she suggests, demonstrate a heroism not possible to men in everyday life.

This harping on the superiority of selfless feminine heroism over flamboyant male courage is a common theme in literature for girls in the 1880s. Alongside articles and stories recommending commit-ment to the unspectacular altruism possible in daily life (sewing for the poor or accepting paid employment in order to send a brother through school), the *Girl's Own Paper* profiled self-sacrificing hero-ines in fact and fiction. Even handwriting offered an opportunity for the quelling of self; penmanship being an index of character, readers were exhorted to match the Spencerian models the paper occasionally reprinted, just as they were expected to take the hero-ines endorsed by the editors as role models for life in general. Girls who "cultivate the qualities we point out in every number of this publication," the editors advised, would always have God on their side whatever their worldly disadvantages[36]—and whatever the dis-agreeable worldly consequences of such selflessness. Thus the paper made much of such historical prototypes as Catherine Douglas, the medieval maid of honor who bought time for the fleeing James II of Scotland by sliding her arm through the rings to bolt the door; the combination of patriotism, egolessness, and mutilation (when James's enemies forced the door open) proved irresistible.

Short stories and long serials in the *Girl's Own Paper* stressed similar points, as in the aptly titled "Beauty on Crutches": Anne Jelakel
dislikes her cousins' adaptation of her name into "Angelical"—"for I
am *not* fit to be" an angel—but the reader understands that this de-
murral is just Anne's modesty. Our first sight of the heroine, her
crutches seeming "more as slender pedestals supporting some delicate figure, than symbols of weakness or deformity," alerts us that
"God has made the little hump on my back the bearer of so many
mercies that I would kiss it if I could stretch my lips back." We
hardly need to hear in the denouement that Anne won her deformity at the age of ten in saving one of her infant cousins from a
burning house, and that the hump is "a glorious one—as grand as a
Waterloo hero's scars!"[37] Still more than the saving of the baby, the
injury elevates Anne above male firefighters.

Likewise, the heroine of the twenty-one-part serial *Wild Kathleen,*
which ran in the same periodical between March and September of
1880, is notable not only for her fey humor and madcap antics, but
also for her willingness to lay down her life to save her friends from
danger. It is this selflessness that eventually dominates her personality, since "bold and brave, and saucily independent as Kathleen
was, deep in her heart was . . . sweet, pure womanliness." Her womanliness emerges imperfectly in her mistaken love for the artist Cyril
Wynch, who despite his profession is too conventional to appreciate
her (he sketches her as Undine instead of as Angel); we finally see it
in its pure form when Kathleen saves Cyril so that he can marry her
well-named friend Dolly. Forgetting his prior commitment, Cyril be-
latedly comprehends Kathleen's worth and proposes, but by that
time she is too good and too moribund to respond to earthly love:
"In truth Kathleen Crofton was far on the upward path, far advanced beyond those friends she cared for so affectionately; she was
too filled with the highest, holiest love, too near that land where they
neither marry nor are given in marriage to well understand for herself any other love."[38] In 1880, the physical and the spiritual are antitheses.

In his article "What Girls Read" in the *Nineteenth Century* (October
1886), Edward G. Salmon professes himself unable to understand
what he sees as the moral underlying most books for girls: "If you
are wicked you must reform, and when you have reformed you will
die!" Comparing the sorts of protagonists we have been examining
with their twin sister, Little Nell, Salmon asks, "If she was too good
for the world, why was she ever brought into it; if she was not, why,
in the midst of the sin, the misery, the suffering of mankind, were

her sunny presence and beneficent influence removed so soon?" As we have seen, the answer is inherent in a point Salmon makes elsewhere in his article: women typically display "the greatest heroism, the noblest devotion, the highest purpose, the longest suffering, the harshest and cruellest of human trials . . . courage of the first order," far superior to the mere physical courage of the male. "The one is devotion, human, spiritual, Christian; the other is pluck, animal-like in its character, desperate in its instincts," and apt to consist more of show than of substance.[39] If women have little to do with the "animal-like" sphere of male aggression, writers may logically suggest that the animal dimension of women's existence is comparatively unimportant beside the spiritual influence that is as immortal as the soul. Given that the essence of womanly virtue is the sacrifice of self, which alone can save society from masculine egocentrism, dying may be the ultimate social duty. Thus it is reasonable that the protagonists of girls' fiction should so frequently perish: what is death, if not the perfect symbolic manifestation of selflessness?

But it is significant that a male commentator of 1886 is reluctant to see this point, for as we shall discover, mid-Victorian fiction for boys often uses images of sickness and death in precisely the same ways that girls' fiction does throughout the century. Obviously the preferred male models are shifting from *Masterman Ready;* by the standards of the 1880s both Ready's courage and his fate are apparently starting to seem inappropriate for his gender and genre. Indeed, the Angel came increasingly to seem an inappropriate model even for feminine behavior. In girls' books if not always in boys', it was not her assumption of moral superiority that drew questions, but the tradition that this superiority depended on her separation from the masculine world. As fears about national decadence increased, ill health became unpatriotic, an indication that women were lax in not understanding that strong mothers bore strong soldiers for "'the Empire and the Race.'"[40] Simultaneously, Anna Davin observes, sanitary progress created a feeling that "not to learn and obey the laws of health was a sin; mothers were responsible to God for the lives of their children"[41]—a major shift in emphasis from the heyday of evangelicalism, in which parents' major divine responsibility was for their children's souls. In the 1890s, Grant Allen's "New Hedonism" argued that "Self-development is better than self-sacrifice"—not because it is more pleasant, but because it is more altruistic: to heed physical matters is to benefit the race, emotionally and eugenically.[42] Darwinism had made the body respectable (even Angelic) for women as for men. And besides giving birth to little empire-builders, women were to use their new vitality in part to equip themselves to enter the male realm on its own terms, the better to sweep out corners of the Augean stables that influence had never reached. A key argument in favor of woman suffrage was that it would enable women to legislate against "male immorality."[43]

As it became commonplace for unmarried middle-class women to work outside the home for money rather than for the sheer joy of serving, and for girls to leave their families for school just when the "home influence" was most crucial, the boyish heroine became a fixture in girls' fiction. (Angela Brazil introduced the hockey-playing heroine in 1906.) Simultaneously, the excessively feminine girl became a figure to distrust; authors depicted her as an embarrassing reminder of female physical inferiority, or as a shallow and overindulged teacher's pet whose popularity with adults typically came from betraying natural childhood in order to conform to the unrealistic ideals of the grown-up world. For all her assumption of virtue, such a girl was invariably selfish. The choice of sin here is revealing, inasmuch as it demonstrates a new feeling: not that the ideals of Angelhood were flawed, but that the Angel herself did not live up to them, only hypocritically pretending for her own advantage. In other words, the spuriously "good" girl had sold out in an attempt to achieve power in the adult world, when she might better have kept to her own sphere—as the Angel, were she sincere, would have been the first to point out.

One of the classic examples of this turn-of-the-century argument that Victorian prescriptions for childhood self-sacrifice would only lead to the very sins they were trying to eradicate is Burnett's *The Secret Garden* (1911), which turns *Fauntleroy* inside out. Theoretically, Mary Lennox and Colin Craven ought to be both good and agreeable; both have been brought up in such complete separation from the adult world (Mary in India, where she barely sees her parents, Colin in a room forbidden to most of the servants, where his father rarely ventures) that their existence is only a matter of rumor. Colin has the added advantage of invalidism, and no one expects that he will live to grow up. But in fact the cousins are remarkably spoiled, selfish, and unlikable, and only when first Mary and then Colin begin systematically to break adult rules and overcome adult expectations can they become healthy, happy children who will assuredly live to grow up because they have something other than their own misery to focus on.

Their new interests center on the "secret garden" that represents Colin's parents' love and that has been kept locked ever since Colin's mother fell from a breaking branch, went into premature labor, and died. Mary, who has been forbidden to go anywhere without adult approval, rightly regards as arbitrary the restrictions that surround her and consistently seeks to expand her environment, first exploring the grounds of the manor house, next examining the house itself, then finding Colin (of whom her guardians have kept her ignorant), and finally discovering the way into the garden. As Mary and Colin, under the tutelage of the Yorkshire "angel" Dickon,[44] watch spring regenerating the garden, the two children also bloom. Mary becomes as pretty as her social-butterfly mother; Colin's illness turns out to be imaginary, needing only healthy thoughts and strengthening exercises to come right. (Shortly before writing the book, Burnett had become a Christian Scientist.)

The interpretation of the garden is obviously crucial to interpreting the novel. Pushing an arcadian mythic reading, for instance, Humphrey Carpenter argues that the garden is a version of T. S. Eliot's Waste Land: "Its dead state seems profoundly related to the sickness of Colin, who is a kind of wounded Fisher King."[45] But while the story undoubtedly revolves around fertility, this implication that masculinity is the key to the mystery misses the point. The image of the garden traditionally relates to feminine sexuality, and it is suggestive that Mary is the one—in an exploration that has been progressively more interior—who first finds her way into the forbidden space, saying defiantly, "They're letting it die, all shut in by itself. . . . I'm the only one in the world who wants it to be alive."[46] While Mary's statement applies not only to the garden but to Colin, he and it aren't synonymous; if the garden represents any human, it is the "earth mother" typified by the dead Lilias Craven and the living and fecund Susan Sowerby. And as Phyllis Bixler observes, this all-female triad connects *The Secret Garden* to Burnett's adult novels, which often "gave a divine aura to female power."[47]

The femininity of the garden, its life-in-death sexuality, and its hidden power are inextricably linked, so that most readers will distrust the ending, which focuses on Colin rather than on Mary; much more than the boy, the girl seems to have a right to the garden and to center stage. That she ends up playing second fiddle recapitulates the very mid-Victorian lessons about the dangers of the ego that the novel ostensibly rejects. The introspection of evangelicalism has gone too far and betrayed itself into self-centeredness; in a fascinating twist, Burnett has replaced it by redefining sexuality, and physicality in general, as selfless and good. The Angel is still present, despite all denials, but she has become fertile.

The "they" who are killing the garden by imprisoning it are apparently the members of the oppressive, rigidly caste- and propriety-conscious adult society, personified in this novel by the aptly named housekeeper Mrs. Medlock, who meddles in Mary's explorations by forbidding her to enter locked gardens and locked rooms, and by Colin's physician and uncle, Dr. Craven, whose inheritance depends on Colin's death. Lewis Carroll once wrote a poem concluding with the "Moral: You mustn't"; Medlock and Craven might have stepped straight from its stanzas with their continual reminders about proper rules of territory, behavior, diet, and even speech. (Yorkshire dialect, here the language of vitality, is "too common" to be respectable; one of the symptoms of the children's regeneration is that they learn to speak it, "as if it was French.")[48] Health lies in loosening up, in thinking of the natural instead of the prescribed—in bringing the "strong, glad, positive qualities [of the garden] which were driven from the man's business world" into "the new public life of an ideal social order,"[49] which will partake not of oppressive "adult" propriety but of freedom. To save themselves, the children must defy Victorian mores; following the negative rules of society only creates spoiled, unproductive, confined, and sterile offenses against nature, while following instinct will create the sort of natural child who is genuinely capable of thinking for others. So we have come full circle, back to the _Lily Douglas_-like ideals of a humble and unselfish feminine community that can radically change society. The twist is that the society to be thus altered is a ladylike world of propriety, asexual purity, and the obedient doing of whatever doesn't come naturally.

· TWO ·

Asexuality and Virility as Social Ideals

While the early Victorians believed that Nature is what we are put in this world to rise above, by the end of the century—two generations after the *Origin of Species*—overruling Nature seemed neither possible nor desirable. Over the course of the century, too, ideas of the right and the proper came to focus less and less on the exceptional, on the tract heroes who could achieve a saintliness beyond the reach of ordinary mortals. With increasing emphasis, glory fell instead on the normal. In their wholesomeness and freedom from morbid soul-searching, John and Jane Bull were better than saints—they were British. To be average—once cause to strive for improvement—gradually became reason for self-congratulation.

Given the perceived importance of children's literature in socializing the country's future adults, this radical change in the pattern adult inevitably affected juvenile fiction. As we have seen, childish virtue became less a matter of superhuman effort than of what one might term the superhuman effortlessness of a Jessica or a Fauntleroy: to be good was simply to be artless. And if the typical mid-Victorian children's book brings its hero or heroine to spiritual perfection through feminizing processes of illness, humiliation, or powerlessness, its Edwardian counterpart scorns both process and product as "muffish." The carefully taught Victorian ideals of goodness had come to seem effeminate. As early as the 1880s the ideal child had become the "normal" child, enterprising, adventurous, and even innocently destructive due to a "natural" lack of comprehension of the workings and subterfuges of the "civilized" adult world. The conscience-laden struggles of Sherwood's Fairchild family and F. W.

Farrar's Eric gave way to the free wanderings of Rudyard Kipling's Mowgli and E. Nesbit's Bastables. Once only to be gained through prayer, virtue could now be achieved through vigorous outdoor play; muscles had more to do with the new hero than Christianity.

This trend was contemporaneous with another that I have already noted: the increased differentiation of genders. Unlike so many of his Victorian forebears, the typical fictional Edwardian boy can never be mistaken for a girl in breeches; even Peter Pan is the most masculine of androgynes. The conjunction of the idealizing of normalcy and the insistence upon strict demarcations of gender suggest that these trends may have roots not only in Darwinism and in the decline of religious faith, but also in evolving cultural constructions of sexuality. Because the purity of the Angel is her most obvious characteristic, the change in nineteenth-century thought on sexuality (as sex moved inexorably out of the domain of the clergy and into that of the scientist) is crucial to any examination of why Angelic qualities became increasingly problematic. And to view Victorian mores through the lens of ideals of boyhood, we must examine why chastity became undesirable and "normalcy" edged out godliness. Only then can we understand why Angelhood slowly grew antithetical to "manliness" as midcentury definitions of the terms (such as *Tom Brown's Schooldays*, 1857) gave way to new and vastly different versions.

Victorianism has long been popularly associated with a hypocritical and even prurient silence on sexuality; Captain Marryat's amused report to his compatriots that Americans were so overfastidious as to dress piano "limbs" in ruffled pantalettes has ironically been transformed by tradition into the quintessence of solemn British practice. In fact, however, Michel Foucault's characterization of the era as one in which discourse about sex was not forbidden but mandatory comes nearer the mark. Before Victoria's reign was half over, both men and women were writing voluminous treatments, fictional and nonfictional, in medical tomes and family magazines and sixpenny pamphlets, of prostitution and venereal disease, birth control and masturbation, until by the end of the century the discourse itself had become a subject for discourse: as *Reynolds' News* asked plaintively in April 1895, "What does all this perpetual discussion of sex mean? Wherefore this constant analysis of the passions? How comes it that the novels of today are filled with nothing but sex, sex, sex?"[1]

While the feeling that sexuality somehow threatened society remained fairly constant throughout the Victorian period, opinion on what its dangers might be (and on how concerned citizens might combat them) did not. At midcentury consensus located the problem in the male, the solution in the female: men were better able to feel and less able to control their lower natures than women. That the sexual urge was in fact part of a "lower nature" was rarely questioned. Raised on the stern early-Victorian credo that whatever came naturally was morally suspect, Thomas Hughes's contemporaries recommended self-discipline as a means of controlling, if not necessarily eradicating, desire. Thus even those early Victorians who refuse to discuss sexuality when discussion might seem appropriate may be proposing a solution—not through speech but through refusal to speak. Not to discuss may be to practice rather than to preach, since the theory ran that the body could not be brought under control before the mind; if one would be pure in deed, one must be pure also in thought. Silence, therefore, was golden.

But so, in man's fallen state, was remonstrance. Many mid-Victorians saw sexual control as crucial to social improvement because it offered a universal chance for sacrifice: men in all walks of life could subordinate their base desires to self-discipline and judgment. Meanwhile, without such subordination, the sexual instinct sometimes seemed to be the root of half of Britain's problems. Infant mortality or debility could be traced to fathers who had spent sperm unprofitably or had infected their wives with syphilis; women's premature deaths might be blamed on the moral and physical exhaustion insatiable husbands inflicted; prostitutes were fast threatening to rival "decent" women in number—and their clients, perhaps, outnumbered decent men. The problem, then, was how to restrain men from giving in to the promptings of animal instinct.

The obvious solution in the cases of prostitution and venereal disease—legislation—was a dismal failure; just as evangelical children's writers might have predicted, laws could not minister to a soul diseased. To cure society, it seemed, one must cure the individual soul, as even some lawmakers appear to have accepted. Thus William Ewart Gladstone, whose government displayed no particular support for the legislation against the white-slave trade,[2] spent many nights over many years trying to reclaim prostitutes, one soul at a time. Where Parliament led, public furor followed. The Contagious Diseases Acts of 1864, 1866, and 1869, designed to protect the health of British soldiers in garrison towns by quarantining women who were suspected of being prostitutes and of being afflicted with venereal disease, were less a thrown gauntlet than a dropped brick. Protest was strong, not only because mere suspicion was sufficient to imprison women without trial, but because, as Josephine Butler put it, the acts would encourage men to vice "by accustoming them to think that vice is so natural, so necessary, that no one expects them to be virtuous; for they must see that those who framed these Acts despaired of ever improving mankind."[3]

In this case the government could not sustain its attempt to make the double standard law. The 1883 suspension and 1886 repeal of the acts upheld Butler's dictum that society must adhere to a single standard of morality, that of the Angel: "The essence of right and wrong is in no way dependent upon sex, and shall demand of men precisely the same chastity as it demands of women," she preached.[4] Even to male social-purity reformers, the history of this legislation demonstrated the superiority of feminine virtue to masculine power; as Rev. J. Hirst Hollowell described the acts in 1889, "They were one of the many blunders of professional authority and scientific egotism."[5] Politics and science, Hollowell suggested, had proven incapable of creating utopia, and it was time to replace masculine values with their antiegotistic feminine counterparts. And it is this solution to the problem—attempting to bring men to a womanly standard of virtue—that held sway for most of Victoria's reign.

A similar viewpoint informed the attitude of the Victorian medical establishment toward birth control. Most doctors kept silent on this subject; nineteenth-century society's ongoing desire to approach reform by attacking cause rather than effect encouraged reticence, since the real problem seemed not unwanted pregnancy but uncontrolled sexuality. If birth control were accessible, one writer warned in 1829, it "might be then used to escape the punishment ordained by God for sexual misdemeanours."[6] Indeed, such medical men as C.H.F. Routh claimed as late as 1879 that God had suitable punishments also for birth control, among them hyperaesthesia of the genitals, nymphomania, sterility, cancer, and suicide.[7] Women who adhered to lax male standards of sexuality, then, would lose their womanly purity, their ability to mother children (so much a part of that purity), and even their lives. Likewise, through the first three-quarters of the century, those doctors who did support contraception generally justified their stance on essentially femininist, antisexual grounds, claiming that safe sex would lessen immorality—especially male immorality—by making prostitution and masturbation less tempting.[8]

With this sort of controversy in mind, much mid-nineteenth-century writing about sex concentrated on just how handicapped men might be in the contest for social purity. The usual conclusion was that woman's hypertrophied morals went hand in hand with her atrophied sexuality. Even prostitutes were often portrayed as naturally good rather than as victims of their own lust. Instead of being super-sexed and subhuman, they turned out to be once-respectable women who had been brought low by upper-class rakes, by social injustices that gave working-class women the stark choice between selling their bodies and starving, or—most disturbingly—by their innate female virtue.

In his famous *Westminster Review* article on prostitution (1850), for instance, W. R. Greg argues that while in men "the sexual desire is inherent and spontaneous" from puberty on, in women "the desire is dormant, if not non-existent, till excited." Thus even prostitutes have rarely fallen due to the "desires in which they do not share," but rather because of the "strange and sublime unselfishness, . . . [the] positive love of self-sacrifice" natural to their gender; and so horrible is their subsequent life to them that without gin many would have "gone mad from mental horrors." Indeed, Greg hints that since middle-class women happily "pass through life without ever being cognizant of the promptings of the senses," it may be only society's approval that keeps respectably married women from similar disgust: "As a most virtuous and sensible lady once said, 'It is not a quarter-of-an-hour's ceremony in a church that can make *that* welcome or tolerable to pure and delicate feelings, which would otherwise outrage their whole previous notions, and their whole natural and moral sense.'"[9]

Biologists and medical doctors often (although not always, as M. Jeanne Peterson reminds us)[10] concurred with the virtuous lady's feeling that "*that*" was an activity few women would take to naturally. William Acton's view in 1857 was that "the majority of women (happily for society) are not very much troubled with sexual feeling of any kind. What men are habitually, women are only exceptionally." Generally, as Greg had also argued, women endure sex only out of unselfishness or a longing for children, and Acton's "perfect ideal of an English wife and mother" is "so pure-hearted as to be utterly ignorant of and averse to any sensual indulgence."[11] Though Acton was frequently criticized by his medical peers, who "expressed grave reservations about his opinions, and indeed his competence," his writings nevertheless enjoyed "widespread popularity" in lay circles.[12]

If science was willing to consider *femina sensualis*, society in general was not. Thus a reviewer for one of Acton's books in the *London Medical Review* for September 1862 takes issue with the suggestion "that venereal pleasure is almost entirely on the side of the male. Now, this is unphysiological in the first place, and moreover, experience proves the contrary."[13] In contrast, even late in the century, more popular writers regularly quote Acton's pronouncement on women's sexual anesthesia, treating him as a respected and sensible authority. A booklet of quotations on the value of continence published by the Social Purity Alliance in 1889, for instance, features him prominently and asserts that "the professional standing of the authors selected is so high as to be quite unquestionable."[14] Despite Acton's difficulties with one wing of the medical party, he expressed what a large segment of the public wanted to hear.

Not that all medical and scientific practitioners disagreed with Acton. Thus an American doctor, George Napheys, sought to squelch the "vulgar opinion" that women "are creatures of like passions with ourselves; that they experience desires as ardent, and often as ungovernable, as those which lead to so much evil in our sex. . . . Nothing is more utterly untrue. Only in very rare instances do women experience one tithe of the sexual feeling which is familiar to most men."[15] Even in 1897, after more and more writers had "discovered" women's sexuality, the biologists Patrick Geddes and J. Arthur Thomson could trace the "stronger lust and passion of males" to differences at the cellular level (male cells disperse energy, female cells store it); the innate chastity of the female is inseparable from her greater altruism and patience.[16]

So strong was the public belief in feminine purity (whatever individuals may have known to the contrary) that a sexual woman was often regarded as a criminal or a maniac—not because of the intrinsic hatred of a patriarchy for womankind, Jean L'Esperance argues, but because of society's longing to locate virtue in its own opposite.[17] Therefore, by providing (for instance) that a husband could divorce his wife for adultery, but a wife her husband only on grounds of "incestuous adultery, or of bigamy with adultery, or of rape, or of sodomy or bestiality, or of adultery coupled with" unreasonable cruelty or desertion,[18] the Matrimonial Causes Act of 1857 in effect decreed that while to dissolve a marriage the wife had to prove that her husband's sexuality was abnormal, the husband need only complain that his wife's sexuality was improper. As one anonymous expert claimed in the *Journal of Mental Science* in 1872, a woman's adultery was indeed evidence of her insanity, since obviously "a woman who, for the gratification of a lust, risks or abandons all that most persons hold dear, has a strong tendency in her to be either mad or bad—badly mad or madly bad."[19] And from the Continent, the leader of the new Victorian discipline of sexology, Richard von Krafft-Ebing, confirmed in 1886 the general suspicion that women interested in sex were sick: "Since woman has less sexual need than man, a predominating sexual desire in her arouses a suspicion of its pathological significance."[20]

Because it seemed obvious that woman's sexuality was—or should be—entirely bound up in reproduction, in the 1860s Dr. Isaac Baker Brown introduced the clitoridectomy as a solution not only to such manifestations of undesirable sexuality as nymphomania and masturbation, but to a variety of disorders ranging from epilepsy to hysteria. His explanation, that "the clitoris is not an essential part of the generative system, [so that] the expression 'mutilation of the person,' so freely employed, may be passed over as possessing no meaning," leaves no place in women's lives for nonreproductive sex.[21] Brown was eventually struck from the medical register, but he may be viewed less as an anomaly than as an extremist who carried contemporary ideas about women's sexuality to their illogical conclusion.

In female frigidity, many mid-Victorians found, lay male salvation. The good wife's silent revulsion at her marital task, Smith H. Platt suggested in *Queenly Womanhood* (1875), will cause the good husband, unable to "behold such sacrifice for *him* without feeling the noblest instincts of his manhood stirred to their profoundest depths," to "nullify to the last possible degree the necessary infliction . . . [on] the noble woman who not only has given herself to him, but *given herself for him*."[22]

By adopting feminine patterns of sexual behavior, the husband improves his own lot. Through the first half of the century quack literature overwhelmingly concentrated on advertising "cures" for debility resulting from sexual overindulgence.[23] And more reputable doctors often shared the quacks' views on the dangers of sex; Thomas Laycock, for instance, links ataxia to "the effects of *hyperstimulation* of the erotic nerves . . . such as results from very frequently repeated, perhaps, bridal congress, and not merely from masturbation."[24] Quoting a variety of medical authorities on the healthfulness of chastity, even as late as 1884 Alfred S. Dyer is contending not only that the excessive exercise of sexual desire within marriage is unhealthy, but that sexual desire itself—the "abuse of the imagination"—is too.[25] Health requires not merely restraint in deed, but a feminine restraint in thought.

Acton's belief that God made women cold in order to discourage men from using up their natural heat had wide currency in the mid-Victorian years. In the widely disseminated work of the American

J. H. Kellogg (who draws extensively on Acton and on other British sources, both popular and medical), the idea appears as follows:

> While it is true . . . that men have stronger passions than women, in general, and that many men demand of their wives a degree of sexual indulgence which is . . . even impossible for them to grant without doing themselves the greatest wrong, it is by no means proven either that these demands are imperative, that they are natural, or that they are not injurious to the man as well as the woman. . . . On the contrary, there is as great a weight of evidence as could be required that restraint, self-control, and moderation in the exercise of the sexual instinct, are in the highest degree beneficial to man, as well as to woman, and are necessary for his highest development.

Women's insistence that men adopt feminine standards of virtue will prove the means by which "society shall rise to higher levels."[26]

This tactic, on the part of a male authority, of assigning to women the primary impetus in sexuality's repression may strike modern feminists as offensive scapegoating. In fact, however, women had every reason to distrust sex, not only because men would have felt comparatively little pressure toward skill, but because sexual risks and discomforts were so considerable. Although Victoria had given the royal imprimatur to chloroform in childbirth in 1853, both mortality and agony levels remained high. (One notices that the great majority of dead mothers in Victorian children's fiction lost their lives consequent to giving birth.) Moreover, venereal disease was sufficiently openly discussed, even before the Contagious Diseases Acts, that women knew that men consorting with prostitutes—even years before marriage—might bring incurable infection into the conjugal bed. Christabel Pankhurst's accusation in *The Great Scourge and How to End It* (1913)—"Women are not naturally invalids, as they have been taught to believe. They are invalids because they are the victims of . . . syphilis and gonorrhoea"[27]—is not the expression of a new idea but the unusually forthright statement of a long-held suspicion. Finally, Nancy Cott argues in a American context that "passionlessness served women's larger interests by downplaying altogether their sexual characterization, which was the cause of their exclusion from significant 'human' (i.e., male) pursuits."[28] The antisexual revolution was less an expression of patriarchal control over women than of women's rejection of that control.

Men too were thought to benefit from accepting a feminine asexuality. For as Dr. Lionel S. Beale and the Edinburgh-educated

American physician James Foster Scott (among others) explain, celibate men attain genius through preserving their energies for their work: "the power of thought, of concentration of the intellect upon a definite thing, and of high devotion and self-sacrifice, appear to have in some instances attained to a maximum when the mind has not been permitted to be disturbed by thoughts of love and marriage."[29] Even within marriage "the proper subjugation of the sexual impulses, and the conservation of the complex seminal fluid, with its wonderfully invigorating influence, develop all that is best and noblest in men."[30]

If the mid-Victorians customarily saw sexual abstinence as both feminine and desirable, and androgyny (if not outright femininization) as a necessary step for humanity's purification, the ultimate androgyne was God: "He is feminine as well as masculine. It is as true and natural to pray to the God-Mother as to the God-Father," argued the American Henry C. Wright in 1854 in a work that attempted to get the minds of married people (especially husbands) off sensual gratification and onto parenthood.[31] Likewise, Hughes makes an impassioned case for Christ as androgyne, "in whom alone the love, and the tenderness, and the purity, and the strength, and the courage, and the wisdom of all these [men and women] dwell for ever and ever in perfect fulness."[32] And George MacDonald's fantasies for children usually center on a female Guide and God.

But in sex manuals and children's fiction alike, in the mid-century years the word usually chosen to encapsulate the blend of compassion and courage, gentleness and strength, self-control and native purity, was "manliness." David Newsome fixes in the 1870s the point at which "manliness" took on for Victorian boys the meaning with which we still associate the word—the hearty games-playing, stiff-upper-lip spirit that built the empire.[33] But through most of the century the term's connotations were thoroughly androgynous and thoroughly asexual; as shorthand for "humanliness," it sometimes applied to girls as well as to boys.

Thus Hughes devotes *The Manliness of Christ* (1879) not to explaining, as we might suppose having absorbed the popular opinion of Tom Brown, that Christ was good at games and no sissy, but to arguing that real manly courage involves "self-sacrifice for the welfare of another," that real manliness includes "tenderness, and thoughtfulness for others," and that both courage and manliness are possible for women as well as for men: "One of the most searching of all trials of courage and manliness [is] when a man or woman is called to stand by what approves itself to their consciences as true . . .

against all discouragement."[34] While George Worth comments cautiously that "the term could conceivably be applied to right-living girls and women as well as to right-living boys and men,"[35] his adverb is unnecessary: Hughes does so apply the term. Indeed, since one of the hallmarks of "the noblest type of true manliness" is patience,[36] like chastity generally thought by the Victorians to be a quality for which women had a natural gift, manliness may come more easily to the woman than to the man.

Likewise, arguing against contraception and its inevitable consequence of sex for sex's sake, the *British Medical Journal* juxtaposed "purity of thought and manliness of life";[37] the manly person is one to whom continence is second nature. In a discussion of prostitution that has much in common with Greg's *Westminster Review* article, Napheys agrees that to *"reform the men"* is the only way to cure social evil, and that in self-control lies true manliness. He goes on to define the ideal human dispositions, "which include in themselves what we are accustomed to define as the masculine and feminine attributes, which temper the rude force of man with the delicate sensibilities of woman, which fortify her susceptible nature with his sterner strength."[38] And in the 1880s, Rev. R. Ashington Bullen, the honorary secretary of the Social Purity Alliance (based on the premise "that the law of purity is of universal obligation on all men and women alike" and enjoining male and female members equally "to do all in [their] power to influence others to purity of life"), sketched an androgynous ideal for both children and adults, in which men shared traditional womanly virtues: *"So long as a man is unselfish he will be pure."*[39]

Idealists confident that a society thus based on manly androgyny was a real possibility were naturally interested in childhood; in the words of Alexander Pope, "As the twig is bent, the tree's inclined." The Rousseauan belief in "the natural purity of children, their innate propensity to turn out well unless besmirched by grown-ups"[40] was especially attractive in the context of the discourse about sexuality, for if only one could figure out how to keep the child from sexual contamination, the gates of Eden must reopen. The problem, of course, was maintaining this original purity; Kellogg is typical in remarking gloomily, "It is doubtless true that children raised in a perfectly natural way would have no sexual thoughts during the earlier years of life, and it would be better if it might be so"—but clearly a "perfectly natural" atmosphere seemed impossible by 1877.[41] Between the 1860s and the 1890s nearly all the elements of Freud's essay "Infantile Sexuality" (1905) had been stated or implied;[42] often with considerable reluctance, doctors were concluding that the battle for innocence might be lost well before puberty.

Earlier theorists had been slightly more hopeful. Greg suggests that licentiousness might be considerably eroded if "the education of boys were to be conducted with any degree of the same watchful attention to purity that marks that of girls."[43] And Milton Rugoff reports of Thomas Arnold that in 1835, questioned about whether worldly evils might not be evidence against the existence of God, "he solemnly declared: 'We should . . . try to feel as if they had no existence, and then in the most cases they do cease to exist after a time.' Although he meant only that one's doubts about God would go away, there is clearly the implication here that the evil itself might also be exorcised in the same way."[44] This tendency to desperate optimism may underlie the contradictions that riddle mid-Victorian statements on childhood sexuality. Acton, for instance, can write: "In a state of health no sexual impression should ever affect a child's mind or body. . . . Total ignorance of any sexual affection is, as it should always be, the rule."[45] Yet as Steven Marcus explains, Acton simultaneously communicates that "childhood sexual play and childhood masturbation were both widespread and well-known phenomena. . . . [Children] are described as constantly threatened by horrid temptations, open to stimulation and corruption, and in danger of becoming little monsters of appetite."[46]

It thus makes sense that mid-Victorian concern about childhood masturbation was linked primarily to purity rather than debility. While some writers in the middle years of the century continued to warn that masturbation destroyed the constitution and left the "self-abuser" prey to epilepsy, consumption, blindness, and a host of other ailments as varied as they were serious, majority opinion held that it was the spirit that was especially endangered. Acton's contemporary Sir James Paget, for instance, denied that masturbation or excessive fornication should be treated as matters of medical concern, since the damage resulting from these practices was not physiological but moral.[47]

Paget's view of masturbation as irrelevant to bodily health was typical; mid-Victorian doctors had gradually concluded that the true danger was to the mind (idiocy or insanity) and to the soul. For the most obvious attribute of "self-abuse" was its egocentricity—the very quality that contemporaneous writers for children found most antithetical to virtue and thus also to androgynous manliness. Solitary sexual pleasure not only distracted from such higher goals as the procreation of children or the substitution of love for lust, but made such goals more difficult to attain: masturbators risked impotence, sterility, and perhaps worst, emotional catalepsy as the sufferer learned to look inward for all satisfaction. Pathologist Henry Maudsley's comment in 1868 is typical: "The miserable sinner whose mind suffers by reason of self-abuse becomes offensively egotistic; he gets more and more closely wrapped up in his own narrow and morbid feelings, and less and less sensible of the claims of others upon him . . . his moral nature is blunted or lost." Lacking the power of restraint essential to "natural gratification," Maudsley's masturbators, for all their sexual activity, suffer from "real sexual impotence"; unable to marry, they are also unable to feel. Most offensively of all, "incapable of reforming themselves, they are quite prepared to reform a wicked world"—not by influence but by force.[48]

Thus the persona of the masturbator—selfish, indifferent to others, stupidly preferring earthly gratification today to heavenly bliss tomorrow—bears a striking resemblance to Victorian stereotypes of undiluted masculinity. That the ultimate fate of this "super-man" was to be the loss of manhood in impotence is a poetic twist. Attitudes toward the manifestations and results of childhood sexuality accordingly join the corresponding views on adult sexuality in explaining why "manliness" should, at least until the last quarter of the century (and in many cases later still), carry with it overtones of androgyny and antimasculinity. For in the context of early-nineteenth-century evangelical distrust of the "normal" self, masculinity in its most exaggerated form is just beastliness.

If parents were painfully aware that even the most carefully reared children could be corrupted by servants or playmates, they had at least the consolation that virtuous androgyny could likewise be inculcated. And since sexual stirrings before puberty were rare (Krafft-Ebing comments that "premature manifestations of sexual instinct" invariably indicate "a neuropsychopathic constitutional condition"),[49] all children were really born female. To Napheys, "It is far more accurate to say the child is mother to the woman than father to the man."[50] But we have yet to answer the crucial question of how mid-Victorian boys could be maintained in the condition of innocence that was their birthright, so that when they encountered the dangerous instincts of puberty, they could face down temptation in the calm self-control of Arnoldian androgynous manliness.

The answer is apparent in one of the classic texts of androgyny, "influence," and manliness: *Tom Brown's Schooldays*. Hughes's novel contrasts the various possibilities for male character, weighing the boyish Tom Brown and Scud East against the bully Flashman, the eccentric Martin, and the frail George Arthur. But to make the post-Victorian assumption that Tom represents the ideal is to misapprehend Hughes's message. Traditionally—and, as J. S. Bratton implies, mistakenly—the tale has been read "as a glorification of boyish simplicity" as summed up by the jolly Tom.[51] Hence the anger of such twentieth-century readers as Kenneth Allsop, who calls the novel's tone one of "thick-headed self-satisfaction" and accuses Hughes of unconsciously preaching "cruelty, conformity, and homosexuality" to glamorize "a brutalising, utilitarian system for staffing the British Empire."[52] But such an interpretation better suits novels written forty years after *Tom Brown*. In fact Hughes seems to have intended his tale as "an exposition of Arnold's method" of inculcating moral responsibility.[53] Viewing matters in this light, we must conclude that of all the boys at Rugby it is Arthur who is the most adult and the most genuinely manly.

The title refers not only to Tom's days at Rugby but to his "schooling" as a boy preparing for adulthood. For almost a quarter of the proceedings Tom is not at Rugby at all but is under the tutelage of nurses, village lads, and finally the staff of his private school. But Rugby is the main focus of the story, because there Tom learns the nature of true manliness: not—as he originally assumes—the physical toughness that comes naturally to him, but the moral toughness that he learns over a long and painful time from Arthur and from Dr. Arnold himself, first as moral courage, then as nurturance, next as self-discipline, and finally as humility. None of these qualities is natural to Tom's character, and each is androgynous or downright feminine to modern eyes. And while Henry Harrington assumes that the boyish Tom's "fear of emotional excess" is among the characteristics that Hughes is trying to inculcate in his readers,[54] in fact, Tom's growing willingness to express his deepest feelings is an important signal of his maturation. Thus, in analyzing the text it is important to realize, as Worth reminds us, that Hughes regarded manliness and muscular Christianity "in ways that are quite different from, and much subtler than, the simpleminded attitudes often ascribed to him."[55]

Tom spends the first half of the novel developing the skills that come naturally to him—independence, pluck, and athleticism—to the point where he can defeat such obvious menaces as Flashman. (In his selfish, greedy, and short-sighted amorality, Flashman closely resembles the dangerous stereotype of "masculinity" described above: he is not truly manly, but only a "flash man.") But this achievement is inadequate. The physical pluck and stoicism Tom exhibits while playing football, running marathons, or being toasted over a slow fire are not enough to make him manly, but only enough to make him think that he is. Tom allows his success to make him overconfident and sees disobedience to the masters as the manly way to behave.

Recognizing this false ethic, Arnold shakes his head over Tom and East, saying, "They make me very uneasy. . . . I shan't let them stay if I don't see them gaining character and manliness. In another year they may do great harm to all the younger boys."[56] In other words, Hughes, who "had always intended to work up to moral manliness [in this novel] by way of sturdy manliness," has brought his protagonist to a perilous halfway point; Tom has the masculine power to corrupt others but not the feminine power to influence them for good. Plainly "the values of the boy-culture," the popularity that is the reward of pluck and physical ability, may at best be tools to implement the Doctor's reforms, but they are not moral ends in themselves[57]—a point Hughes takes pains to emphasize in *The Manliness of Christ*: "Athleticism is a good thing if kept in its place, but it has come to be very much over-praised and over-valued amongst us."[58]

Tom's true moral growth cannot occur until the second half of the novel. At this time we glimpse what Arnold's idea of manliness includes when he gives Tom the charge of the delicate Arthur:

> From morning till night he had the feeling of responsibility on his mind, and even if he left Arthur in their study or in the close for an hour, was never at ease till he had him in sight again. He waited for him at the doors of the school after every lesson and every calling-over; watched that no tricks were played him, and none but the regulation questions asked; kept his eyes on his plate at dinner and breakfast, to see that no unfair depredations were made upon his viands; in short, as East remarked, cackled after him like a hen with one chick.

Manliness involves motherliness. It also requires the courage to pray openly, not an easy step to take in the days before "Arnold's manly piety had begun to leaven the school." And significantly, Arthur has the Christlike courage of his convictions even as a new boy; before Arthur's influence reaches him, Tom lacks this particularly vital form of pluck. Gradually Tom begins to take Arthur not simply as his responsibility but as his pattern, especially after Arthur's near-fatal illness invests him with the special purity and moral authority of the archetypical mid-Victorian invalid child. Lying on his sickbed looking like "a German picture of an angel . . . transparent and

2. *The Angel at Work.* Arthur's sickbed becomes a pietà as against a cruciform background he inspires Tom to lead a better life. Illustration by Louis Rhead to Harper's 1911 edition of *Tom Brown's Schooldays.*

golden and spirit-like," Arthur uses the gentle debating skill of the good woman to persuade Tom to stop using cribs in Greek and Latin.[59] Henceforth Tom will have to work in earnest to learn the lessons that interfere with cricket, for manliness requires self-discipline and self-denial.

And before taking the last step into manliness, Tom must realize his own insignificance; he must kill the masculine ego. He crosses this hurdle when he discovers that the perfectly manly and perfectly selfless Arnold has been responsible for every one of Tom's moral advances, and the boy himself has had no part in the formation of his own character. The news that real work is managed by covert influence rather than by "masculine" aggression shocks Tom, since "in his secret soul he did to a great extent believe, that the great reform in the School had been owing quite as much to himself as to any one else"; what a surprise to find that "the great Head-master had found time in those busy years to watch over the career, even of him, Tom Brown . . . and all this without taking the least credit to himself." Miss Grierson's *Lily Douglas* could not have said it better. As the scales fall from Tom's eyes, "the Doctor's victory [is] complete";[60] the boy has become a real man, gentle, pious, humble, obedient, disciplined, and ready to cry on affecting occasions—in a contemporary review, Fitzjames Stephen singled out Tom's uninhibited grief at Arnold's death as the most "manly" part of the narrative.[61] Tom's original naive assumption that manliness is the opposite of womanliness (early on he instructs his protégé never to mention "home, or your mother and sisters," and worries that "Arthur would be softened and less manly for thinking of home")[62] has been corrected to reflect the truth: in their emotionalism and feeling for community rather than self, manliness and womanliness are effectively synonymous. The friendship between the two boys may have saved Arthur's life by encouraging him to strengthen his body, but more importantly, it has saved Tom's soul and raised the tone of the Rugby community in general by teaching the androgyny of virtue.

Sexuality, as we have seen in Chapter One, is not an issue in pre- and early-Victorian children's books. In Hughes's work, however, asexuality is an explicit and essential component of the anti-masculine manliness he upholds. With regard to the 1861 sequel, *Tom Brown at Oxford*, Harrington suggests "that the ending of the novel, Tom's marriage, is also the ending of manliness" because sexuality must pierce the layers of manly repression.[63] This proposal is plausible but ultimately unconvincing; the fact is that Tom's marriage signals not the end but the culmination of manly continence.

Throughout the story Hughes has presented Tom's love for Mary (significant name!) as the means of the young man's salvation from a difficult grown-up world full of politics, class differences, and flirtatious barmaids. In a college where the best scholars "neither wished, nor were likely to gain, the slightest influence on the fast set," where "the worship of the golden calf" seems to have taken over, and where "musclemen" far outnumber muscular Christians, forming alliances with the pure in heart is Tom's only hope. His friendship with Hardy, whose hot temper alternates with "bursts of womanly tenderness" and whose poverty has kept him in the subservient position that Hughes would later call Christlike, is the logical continuation of his youthful love for Arthur.[64] But although Hardy warns Tom against the dishonor of pursuing a physically based friendship with working-class Patty, "self, the natural man, the old Adam" makes it difficult for Tom to see that in Hardy's advice lies "all true strength and nobleness and manliness." Again Tom must humble his pride, stripping himself of his unconscious belief that his rank gives him the right to behave irresponsibly toward "inferiors," before he can return to the ways of comradeship. "Natural man" is sexual man; in repression is true religion. For as Hardy asks, "Can there be any true manliness without purity?"[65]

Hughes nevertheless makes clear through Mary that purity and love are not, as Harrington might suggest, incompatible: "The delights which spring from sudden intimacy with the fairest and best part of the creation, are . . . far above those of the ordinary . . . undergraduate." While Tom's attraction to Patty was all too "ordinary" in its self-indulgence and egocentricity, his love for Mary is uncommonly fine. The two represent a choice, as he writes to Arthur, between "all sorts of devils' passions, [and] the spirit of God." The worship of God, the scorning of worldly position, and the reverencing of parents and women, are part and parcel of each other; and only Tom's acquisition of these aspects of noble humility makes him manly enough to win Mary for his wife.[66] It is not her body but her soul that he worships, and that he can wait patiently for several years without seeing her (due to her parents' misapprehension of his character) illustrates that the purity of the marriage will never be sullied by a lapse in manly self-control. Not chastity but continence, as Victorian writers on sexuality nearly unanimously agree, is what virtue demands. Thus the comradely, mutually respectful union of Tom and Mary signals not the destruction of Tom's aspirations toward androgynous manliness but their fulfillment.

The seeds of Tom's marital success were clearly sown in his earlier male friendships. While the love Tom bears for his male comrades occasionally boils up into a physical component (after ending his quarrel with Hardy, Tom "had three parts of a mind to kiss the rough face which was now working with strong emotion"),[67] the attractions to men—like the attraction to Mary—are sanctified because their root is love, not lust. But Hughes is aware of less holy feelings. In *Tom Brown's Schooldays* the chief difference between Tom's virtuous union with Arthur and the vicious parasitic alliances between strong upperclassmen and effeminate juniors is that the latter relationships have a sexual dimension. In a famous passage, the narrator contrasts the Tom-Arthur friendship with those entered into by "the miserable little pretty white-handed curly-headed boys, petted and pampered by some of the big fellows, who wrote their verses for them, taught them to drink and use bad language, and did all they could to spoil them for everything in this world and the next."[68] What "spoiling" includes is made additionally clear by the reticence of Hughes's footnote to the sentence: "There were many noble friendships between big and little boys, but I can't strike out the passage; many boys will know why it is left in." "Noble" friendships, like noble heterosexual loves, emphasize spirit, not body. But the "white-handed boys" are making no attempt at self-discipline, duty, piety, and repression of the flesh; again, they are not genuinely feminine, but masculine in the worst sense of the word.

Nevertheless, it is ultimately the influence of the white-handed boys that causes the definition of manliness to shift in such a way that its type specimen becomes Tom Brown instead of George Arthur. As the century wore on, the tendency to equate femininity (or androgyny, or manliness) with sexlessness, and to equate masculine appetite with sin, began to lose ground. Post-Darwinian thinkers discovered worth in an activity that might previously have seemed simply an embarrassing reminder of man's frailty: whether by design of God or of Nature, sex turned out to be the primary mechanism in the progress of the species. Concurrently, researchers argued with increasing conviction that far from being free from the promptings of the senses, women too had their sexual drives—and majority opinion gradually shifted to redefine feminine frigidity as illness rather than ideal.

In the mid-Victorian years most texts exposing women's secret sexuality were concerned with eradicating it. Bram Dijkstra cites the work of Nicholas Cooke around 1870 as typical of a new wave of research designed to blast the myth of the innocent virgin. But such broadsides were intended to uphold tradition rather than assist in a sexual revolution; like the majority of his predecessors, Cooke contended that female sexual apathy was "the cornerstone of a healthy society."[69] Less conservative theorists, however, saw matters differently, and it was their views that were coming to the fore. According to Annie Besant's 1877 birth-control manual, *The Law of Population*, "Man [and clearly woman too] is but the highest in the animal kingdom, not a creature apart from it." Since "celibacy is not natural to men or to women; all bodily needs require their legitimate satisfaction, and celibacy is a disregard of natural law," its practitioners are no saints, but short-lived, snappish, and disagreeable. For women to "surrender themselves where the surrender of heart and of pledged faith have led the way," Besant concludes, is far from incompatible with the new virtue.[70] That some 40,000 copies of the book were in circulation by 1880, and 175,000 by 1891, suggests that the public was eager to concur.

To some extent public sympathy with views such as Besant's was a late-century phenomenon. While George Drysdale's antichastity tome *The Elements of Social Science* (1854) had gone through a respectable twelve editions in the first twenty years of its publication, the next thirty years saw an amazing twenty-three more. Drysdale's message, that "abstinence or self-denial in the matter of sexual love is far more frequently a natural vice than a virtue"[71] and that sexual normalcy should be among the highest aspirations of humankind, was somewhat advanced for 1854. By the end of the century, however, his contention that a society that stresses female purity actually creates the abnormal sexual evils it cannot then extirpate (masturbation, homosexuality) would have seemed newly persuasive to a generation eager to encourage feminine passion. Not sex but the absence of sex might be the true social evil; the 1890s were dotted with articles like that on "The New Hedonism" by Grant Allen—author of *The Woman Who Did* (1895)—claiming the "sex-instinct" as "the origin and basis of all that is best and highest within us," and parenthood as a "moral obligation . . . on the part of the noblest, the purest, the sanest, the healthiest, the most able among us."[72]

Just as not all mid-Victorian women took pride in sexual unresponsiveness, not all late-Victorian women were eager to surrender their right to be "above" sex. Increasingly, however, theorists in the last quarter of the century criticized this stance. Stephen Kern proposes 1870 as the year commentators began to feel a benevolent interest in the female orgasm and an increasing concern about male "psychic impotence."[73] By the end of the century, indeed, Havelock Ellis could imply in his study "Auto-Erotism" (1900) that while it is

bad to masturbate too much, it may be worse not to masturbate at
all. His depiction of women who, "evidently with a considerable degree of congenital sexual anesthesia (no doubt, in some respect or
another below the standard of normal health) . . . not only do not
masturbate, but do not show any desire for normal gratification," is
clearly intended not as praise but as blame.[74] To Ellis, the erstwhile
purity of the invalid is really degeneration. Freud was not alone in
arguing that too much self-restraint creates neurosis; as the sexual
mystic Emmeline Pethick Lawrence reported in "Education in Love"
(1912), many contemporary specialists had learned to "trace back
innumerable nerve and mind disorders to sex repressions."[75] And as
the crowning irony, while mid-Victorian thinkers had recognized
and applauded the idea that piety might sublimate the sex urge,
their heirs condemned piety for precisely that reason. Not to do
what came naturally had struck most mid-Victorians as admirable
self-control. To their later counterparts it often seemed merely sick.

We may trace this shift in part to the effects of Darwin's work,
which deconstructed romance and enthroned biology in its stead;
Darwinians neither could nor would escape the body. Early evangelicals could view the salvation of the individual soul as far more crucial than the comforting of innumerable bodies; before midcentury,
as we saw in *Lily Douglas*, tract literature commonly taught that
prayers are a better response to starvation than bread. But Darwinism replaced the goal of individual spiritual salvation—possible not
only without sex but without life—with that of the biological survival
of the species. This shift in emphasis necessitated a newly approved
sexuality, since "survival depended upon sexual selection, and the
ultimate test of biological success lay in reproduction."[76] Thus late-
century writers on female sexuality such as Dr. J. Matthews Duncan,
whose *On Sterility in Woman* appeared in 1884, are increasingly apt to
consider women in the exclusively animal light of reproductive capability. Duncan, for whom Darwin is a major source, inveighs against
the "education injudiciously ascetic" so often given to women, which
inhibits normal sexual desire and therefore causes sterility. The normal woman is sexual, but not too sexual—not for moral reasons, but
because "excess of sexual desire is probably unfavourable to fertility."[77] Clearly it is not concern for ephemeral individual pleasure that
animates such works, but for the biological (and of course imperial)
survival of the British race as a whole.

To be sure, not all late-century writers—even medical writers—
professed themselves converts to Darwinism as applied to human
beings; Beale, for example, denies its usefulness in this context, pre-

ferring more traditional dicta about self-control's separation of humans from animals.[78] Nevertheless, even the social-purity writers of the 1880s, in many ways utterly opposed to evolutionary thought, were not above twisting it to their own ends. In *Plain Thoughts on Purity* (1885), for instance, Stephen Bourne concedes that since sexual desire is hereditary in males, "it is rendered more difficult for the men of our day to keep themselves pure, because they were born with dispositions stronger and very often less, perhaps, under control than they would have been if their parents had not sinned before them."[79] But it is still both possible and desirable, Bourne explains, to overcome nature. In an address the Social Purity Alliance published in the same year as Bourne's book, Rev. Richard A. Armstrong concurs that "the sins of the fathers are visited on the children many generations after," accounting for "this cruel legacy of passions abnormally virulent, tendencies to excessive lusts, which are not in the true order of nature." In the post-Darwinian generation, one can best make sex seem repellent by making it seem unnatural; it is not nature but abuses against nature with which Armstrong professes to quarrel. By just saying no, his audience can help get heredity on humanity's side: "If you will consecrate yourselves to manly purity, if you will bear your cross bravely and truly till it ceases to be a cross at all, then you will help to bring it about that the youths of the twentieth Christian century shall be freed from this torment."[80] Armstrong's feelings plainly resemble those of his midcentury predecessors, but some of his arguments—such as that animals, who are immune from lust, exemplify the divinely ordered norm for humankind—might have struck pre-Darwinians as bizarre.

But social purity was a losing cause. As more and more writers exalted erstwhile "beastliness" into a modern sacrament, sexual didacticism changed direction. Even if producing the asexual adult were possible, it had come to seem undesirable. Accordingly, toward the end of the century the "manly" boy increasingly contains an admixture of the animal, as boys' novels spend more and more time dilating on the width of the hero's shoulders and less and less on the depth of his principles. Manliness becomes less a state of mind than a state of muscle, and its new antonym is "effeminacy." The benign unnaturalness of self-controlled, responsible, asexual androgyny seems newly dangerous—degenerate, sterile, and often homoerotic. Tom Brown before his schooldays strikes the typical turn-of-the-century writer as an adequate role model for youth, with Arthur cast at best as admiring sidekick. Soul-searching is morbid; the highest accolade for the boys' book now is that it is "red-blooded" and "healthy."

Thus what we see over the last years of the nineteenth century, in sexology and boys' fiction alike, is a gradual reclassification of the attitudes and behavioral patterns considered appropriate to men, often combined with a rejection of qualities associated with femininity. Hence "purity" came sometimes to be seen as "frigidity" and "Christian humility" as "spinelessness." Similarly, no longer do commentators contrast regrettable male sexuality and laudable female asexuality; by the turn of the century the usual distinction is between good, normal heterosexuality and bad, abnormal homosexuality. With this shift in definition, the sissy becomes suspect and "androgynous manliness" turns into an oxymoron.

For Hughes the threat of the "white-handed boys" seems not to have been that they would grow up homosexual, but that introduced to sex in a context in which purity was impossible, they would grow up corrupt, to patronize prostitutes or overtax their wives. Even as late as 1887, Edward Lyttelton's chief fear about schoolboy homosexuality was that "the premature stimulus to the passions, [even if] only temporary, increases their strength in early manhood to a terrible degree"; by allowing secret vice to flourish in schools, society is raising a generation of Don Juans who will know nothing of self-control when they finally encounter women.[81] Similarly, writing in 1881, J. M. Wilson is eager to stamp out boyish experimentation in order to preclude adult libertinism in general; "the nation may be on the eve of an age of voluptuousness and reckless immorality" that only schoolboy purity can check.[82] By the end of the century, however, Darwinian sexology was concerned rather that these boys might never be sufficiently "normal" to desire women at all; according to an anonymous writer signing himself Vox in Solitudine Clamantis in 1893, "the young men of Sodom are in a more perilous plight than those who yield to the blandishments of Delilah."[83] Over the last thirty years of the century (punctuated by such widely publicized scandals of "abnormal" sex as the 1870 arrest of transvestites Ernest Boulton and F. W. Park, the 1884 Dublin Castle exposé of homosexual officialdom, the Cleveland Street homosexual brothel case of 1889, and the Wilde trials in 1895), middle-class Britons were gradually jolted out of their assumption that sex was sex. Sometimes, it seemed, sex was perversion.

And so it became vital to distinguish the kind of childhood sexual impulses that led to matrimony from the kind that led to headlines. Foucault's comment that "the sodomite had been a temporary aberration; the homosexual was now [i.e., after the 1869 coining of the term] a species"[84] has become a truism. It is nevertheless important to remember that while earlier opinion had held that homosexual acts resulted from excessive sexual energy or a jaded search for new sensations, late-Victorian sexology re-created the homosexual as separate and alien flesh, more suited to medical scrutiny than to prayer.[85] Many sexologists made it a priority to explain the warning signs that would betray the future pervert before he acted on his warped impulses; some of these experts held out hope that the instinctive homosexual could be turned toward normalcy if the reindoctrination process began sufficiently early.[86]

Careful parents, then, knew that they no longer need worry if their child showed early signs of interest in sex, so long as this interest stayed within "normal" limits. Masturbation, for instance, was no longer cause for concern but something common to all boys and most girls. But practiced in excess, it was indeed serious, because it might "enfeeble the sexual activities" to the point of passivity or signal congenital inversion. The key to the distinction between normal and abnormal was often effeminacy. Ellis's comment that "there is a distinctly general, though not universal, tendency for sexual inverts to approach the feminine type, either in psychic disposition or physical constitution, or both"[87] is typical of the turn-of-the-century equation of male androgyny and perversion. In this late-century formulation, purity is often as suspect as any other abnormality. Writing in 1898, Scott hints that the dangers facing the "delicate, soft-skinned, girlish boy" too long kept in a state of sexual ignorance are those either of "*Anaesthesia,* or absence of sexual desire, [which] is deplorable," or of its mirror image, "*Paraesthesia*" (perversion, inherited or acquired through masturbation or "other execrable sexual acts").[88]

"Girlish boys," once often approved, have come by the end of the century to be figures of contempt. In a discussion of bullying in school, for instance, J.E.C. Welldon—whose fiction reveals a distinct affinity for the androgynous—claims that the abuse has been stamped out save in the (justifiable?) case of "those curious creatures . . . who are abnormally sensitive and timid . . . who do not stand up for themselves. . . . No doubt it is a schoolmaster's duty to protect these boys, but they give him a great deal of trouble." It is apparently women's influence that is to blame; his example of the "troublesome" student is that of a "good and religious boy" whose mother unwisely persuaded him never to return a blow.[89] The mid-Victorian's hero is the late-Victorian's sissy. Even the homosexual apologist J. A. Symonds, in the essay on Greek "paiderastia" he wrote (but did not publish) in 1873, attacks the problem of justifying his subjects' actions by claiming that their love "was a powerful and masculine emotion, in which effeminacy had no part, and which by no means excluded the ordinary sexual feelings." The "Scythian disease of effeminacy . . . essentially foreign and non-Hellenic," Symonds continues, involved an "abandonment of the masculine attributes and habits . . . [an] assumption of feminine duties and costume, [that] would have been abhorrent to the Doric custom."[90] Greek homosexuality, in other words, was completely "normal" in that it was free alike from inversion and from asexuality.

The seeds of the distrust of androgyny can be found earlier in the nineteenth century; Acton, for one, had written in 1857 that the bookish boy might be peculiarly liable to sexual precocity: "For, as any one may observe, it is not the strong athletic boy, fond of healthy exercise, who thus early shows marks of sexual desire, but your puny exotic."[91] But it was not until near the end of the century, when sexologists began to publish lists of ways to detect incipient homosexuals, that the full implications of medical theory became clear. George Arthur, whom a more naive generation had held up as a saint, turns out to be a sodomite.

The abnormalities that mean purity to Hughes signal pollution to Krafft-Ebing, and a comparison of the two writers' interpretations of Arthurian traits will go a long way toward explaining the differences between mid- and late-Victorian definitions of manliness. Contrast Krafft-Ebing's profile of the typical homosexual—whose traits appear below in italics—with Hughes's characterization of the moral boy:

1. *Tendency toward passionate friendships*; according to Krafft-Ebing, "The psychical love manifest in these men is, for the most part, exaggerated and exalted in the same way as their sexual instinct is manifested in consciousness, with a strange and even compelling force."[92] Arthur's "psychical love" for his confreres is one of the strongest aspects of his personality.

2. *Signs of physical degeneracy*. Arthur's frailty is so evident that Tom immediately predicts that "this new boy . . . would be . . . always getting laughed at, and called Molly, or Jenny, or some derogatory feminine nickname."

3. *Congenital neurasthenia*. In complexion Arthur is pale and washed-out, in mien timid and shrinking; "he seems all over nerves," Tom reports.

4. *Artistic talent and/or eccentricity.* Such is Arthur's feeling for literature that he breaks down while translating in Greek class, "affected to tears by the most touching thing in Homer."[93]

5. *Bad heredity.* Arthur's father died of overwork and typhus, among the causes Krafft-Ebing's prominent Russian colleague Benjamin Tarnowski lists for congenital "passive pederasty" in the second generation.[94]

6. *"Effemination,"* which, Krafft-Ebing explains, often manifests itself in childhood as a pleasure in feminine things—witness Arthur's overidentification with his mother and sisters—and as an attempt to become the perfect Angel woman.[95]

The discrepancy between the two profiles is that Krafft-Ebing's subjects are liable to exhibit precocious sexuality—while Hughes intends us to view Arthur as above animal urges even in adulthood. (This intent may explain why Tom's friend makes no physical appearance in *Tom Brown at Oxford*: a postpubescent Arthur would be impossible). But while Arthur's purity would have struck most mid-Victorians as praiseworthy, Krafft-Ebing's alerted readers would more likely have found it a dangerously naive blunder on Hughes's part. For late-nineteenth-century sexology there was no such thing as the perfectly pure boy—and if there were, there probably should not be. And in majority opinion "manliness" underwent its transformation: while its mid-Victorian exemplar sublimates sex in same-gender friendships, his Edwardian counterpart must sublimate same-gender friendships in "normal" sex.

And so at least as an ideal for boys, the Angel in the House turns into the Degenerate in the Closet. By the end of the century celibacy becomes suspect, and passionate male friendships become "morally undesirable."[96] To approximate femininity is no longer fashionable, in large part because of homophobia; for example, in 1884 the headmaster of Haileybury advised parents to warn their sons against "talk, example or impure solicitations" while he simultaneously discouraged female nicknames among the boys and forbade students to play female roles in school entertainments.[97]

At the same time, however, turn-of-the-century commentators were often just as concerned as their predecessors that women retain their womanliness—now viewed as very much the opposite of manliness. Darwinian theory, Nancy Armstrong observes, supported the idea of the fundamental opposition of maleness and femaleness; while men were "supposed" to compete for women, women were "supposed" passively to watch, so that Nature itself upheld the doctrine of separate spheres.[98] The androgyny of the New Woman therefore disturbed eugenicists such as R. Murray Leslie, who worried in a 1911 article that women were rendering themselves unfit for motherhood by taking up masculine intellectual pursuits instead of developing their talent for "sympathy and tenderness." That way lay sterility and the race's doom; women needed rather to remember that true patriotism involves "self-sacrifice," not "self-gratification, even should this take the form of self-culture."[99] Likewise, Ellis descries a link—still apparent to some of our own contemporaries— between women's emancipation and lesbianism.[100] In the post-Darwinian era, not only is unselfishness inextricably linked to biology rather than to spirituality, but biology's successful operation necessitates two widely disparate sexes. If boys must not act like girls, neither must women act like men.[101]

It would be specious to argue that the overtly androgynous ideal of manliness vanished utterly from boys' fiction; as we shall see in Chapter Three, one can still find the model (together with passionate schoolboy friendships) in many best-selling Edwardian school stories, for example. Nor can one claim that masculine manliness has no place in children's books before Darwin, just as not all late-century writing espouses Darwinian ideals and not all early-century writing is tinctured with evangelicalism. But it is nonetheless clear that fashions in writing for boys changed drastically over sixty years and that a crucial distinction lies in the way the majority at any given point thought about manliness—which may in turn have had great effect not only on Victorian opinions of *womanliness*, but on our own.

For while many turn-of-the-century feminists tried to connect "normalcy" and "purity" to maintain woman's moral advantage, arguing like Frances Swiney in *The Bar of Isis; or, The Law of the Mother* (1907) that "deep down in the heart of humanity has ever been a rebellion against the abnormal and fostered sensuality of the human male,"[102] men whose sensuality had been newly validated could now expose the corruption at the heart of antisexual women. As Nancy Armstrong puts it, "The creation of analytic discourse marks the return of Mr. B [of Samuel Richardson's *Pamela*] and revaluates his undisplaced sexuality as liberation rather than libertinism";[103] and the woman's duty was to be liberated whether she liked it or not. The "man-hater" was soon as suspect as the "natural bachelor," and the contributions of the sexologists, Lillian Faderman comments, "'explained' why some women had such a grave craving for independence from men,"[104] such a need to define their difference as superiority. The "explanation" put the incipient feminist in a potentially damnable position. Hence, for feminism to be acceptable from the beginning of this century onward, it had to play safe by approving the very sexual freedom and masculinist bias that mid-Victorian femininism had disapproved. Bonds between women slowly became as suspect as bonds between boys. And whereas evangelical Victorianism defined woman's power as unique and at least potentially triumphant, a phenomenon closely related to the redefinition of manliness was the post-Victorian assertion that woman's power could only be located in its resemblance to man's.

• THREE •

The Angel in the School

The British boys'-school story flickered into fitful life in the early nineteenth century, with such titles as Sir Richard Phillips's *First Going to School, or, the Story of Tom Brown and His Sisters* (1809) inaugurating a genre that seemed unlikely ever to become first in the hearts of its countrymen. Nor, in the days before Thomas Arnold and his contemporaries began to reform British education, was there any reason why tales of school life should have had much appeal, except perhaps to the prurient mind. While Victorian public schools seem repellent enough to twentieth-century Americans, their predecessors were ghastly even by contemporary standards. The uncontrolled freedom allowed to the boys after class (subsequently to be checked by the prefect system) gave rise to every possible abuse, from the great school rebellions to murder; anarchic and violent, Britain's schools were—as Lady Caroline Lamb wrote of Lord Byron—"mad, bad, and dangerous to know." Jonathan Gathorne-Hardy reports a story nicely illustrating the reputation of one Eton dormitory for turning boys into survivors: "A Dr. Oakes was applying to an insurance company in 1826 and mentioned in passing that 'he had slept in Long Chamber for eight years.' At that the chairman of the board interrupted: 'We needn't ask Dr. Oakes any more questions.'"[1]

In the beginning, then, the school story had little chance to become popular because it could not exploit alumni nostalgia, and it is significant that the first boys'-school story of major importance, Harriet Martineau's *The Crofton Boys* (1841), sprang from a woman's pen; lacking personal memories of the horrors of school life, Martineau could present a reasonable, ordered world where violence and mutilation resulted from accident rather than malice.

With the evangelical attempts to reform the public schools, however, it became possible for middle-class Britain to believe that most boys were essentially good—or at any rate could be forced to behave as if they were. Once God had officially entered the educational system, the school novel could pretend to realism without shocking even those readers who had never experienced Rugby or Harrow. (Even so, Fitzjames Stephen's remarks on *Tom Brown* in an 1858 *Edinburgh Review* both emphasized that Hughes discussed only "the bright side of a Rugby boy's experiences" and regretted the passing of the old disorder, so useful for dispelling illusions about human nature; Stephen wondered whether Hughes, like Arnold, didn't overdo his moralizing.)[2] Paradoxically, the Victorian school story for boys, set in a world largely devoid of family ties and indeed of women, developed into the male analogue of the Victorian domestic novel for girls; both forms typically discovered in the humdrum safety of everyday life moral questions of crucial import for the developing soul. In the school story as in the domestic novel, it is not what people do but why they do it that begs our attention: because "realism" demands that the list of possible events be both limited and unsensational, character, not plot, is all.

It is worth asking, then, whether the values espoused by the twin genres are also parallel. In reading stories set on the cricket field or in the study, do we glimpse the same devotion to duty and the "higher good," the same taboo against self-aggrandizement and individual preference, the same belief that love is better than success, that are so apparent in the works of Charlotte Yonge? If so, exactly where do the two forms part—and why do we seem instinctively unwilling to admit that they were ever joined in the first place?

To answer the last question first, the apparent antidomesticity of the school novel must result at least in part from the attitude of its typical protagonist, who sees a sharp demarcation between the home where he is a child and the school where he is potentially powerful. The eponymous hero of Frederic Farrar's *Eric; or, Little by Little* (1858), for instance, begins his career by shouting "Hurrah! hurrah! hurrah!" over "the commencement of schoolboy dignity," which fills him with "immense importance."[3] However loving and nurturing the child's home life might be, the neophyte schoolboy is almost invariably eager to move into a world that promises him the chance to be captain of the cricket eleven or head of the sixth form. Moving out of the feminine sphere of the Angel, school-story heroes rejoice in the thought that they have left the "soft" feminine values behind as well.

But it is a central part of the message of the school story that this belief is naive, since (at least within the realm of school fiction for boys) to live in a feminine world is no way to absorb the feminine virtues. Apparently no family can consist wholly of selfless members, and in both the school story and the domestic novel it is the pre-school boy who tends to be the most selfish and spoiled, the farthest from the Angelic ideal. Essential to the classic novel of public-school life, therefore, is the early, shocking feeling of utter powerlessness that is part of entering any unaccustomed environment and, more particularly, the neophyte's discovery that his old self doesn't fit his new surroundings. In the hierarchical world of the Victorian public school, the hero begins at the bottom. Despite the fantasies he may have had about instantly becoming what the young George Osborne in *Vanity Fair* calls the "Cock of the School," he learns willy-nilly what any Yonge heroine could have told him—that character and influence come only through hard work and suppressing the ego.

And while the obvious power structures of the school run vertically, from first-former to headmaster, equally crucial are the horizontal, leveling bonds. Chief among the latter are friendship and the knowledge that boy and master alike are held to the same abstract standards of honor before God and Country. Not only a quasi-military mess of conflicting statuses, a school strives also to be a brotherhood. It is these antihierarchical values that instill honor, which is independent of power and indeed potentially antithetical to it. Except in the cases of the bully and the "fast" blade (who exemplify the school's failures), the acquisition of character precedes the acquisition of status—because if one is to avoid power's corruption, one must know through experience that it is virtue rather than glory that matters. And like evangelical writers dreaming of the Christian family, authors of school stories (and indeed actual headmasters of actual schools) shared a highly specific ideal of a highly artificial end product; the individual ego must die that the public-school boy might be born.

Hence the moral assumptions governing the school story are in many ways identical to those that govern the Angel. Having already given some thought to the novel that stands for most of us as the archetypical novel of school life, *Tom Brown's Schooldays*, in this chapter I shall begin by examining its near contemporary and doppelgänger, *Eric; or, Little by Little*. The school-story genre hit its peak in quantity (though perhaps not in quality) only after the beginning of the redefinition of "manliness" and the restructuring of sexuality, and inevitably these changes affected fictional ideals and patterns. Nevertheless, the original school-story model set by *Tom Brown* and

Eric, coupling selflessness with passionate homoemotionalism, remained dominant throughout the period under examination, although occasionally the conventional forms outlived their original functions—athleticism, for instance, often comes to be not a character-building means to an end but an end in itself.

But toward the latter years of the century a new type of school story arose. Its chief formal characteristic was its willingness to criticize the mainstream tradition on grounds of hypocrisy, unreality, or unforgivable naivete, while its chief stylistic trait was its use of a humorous tone to puncture the pretensions to earnestness of its rival and particularly to correct the tradition's version of friendship between boys. It was in part the accusations leveled by this radical wing that induced the more conservative school stories—in the most radical restructuring of all—to shift their emphasis from character to plot, so that the post–World War I juvenile school story often found its interest in science masters who doubled as German spies or football captains who detected murders between matches. We might take the demise of the traditional interest in *being* rather than *doing* as a sign that the antitraditional school story repudiated the ideals of the Angel as old-fashioned or false. But in fact, what seems to lie at the root of the criticism is the feeling that the conventional stories do not sincerely believe their own preachings: it was not that the Angel had betrayed the classic schoolboy hero, but that he had betrayed her. Beneath the sophisticated veneer of antitraditional novels from *Stalky & Co.* to *Mike and Psmith* to *The Loom of Youth* are buried many of the same ideals that lie on the surface of Farrar's *Eric*.

Terence Wright argues that from *Eric* onward, the school story exhibits two separate and opposite traditions: the extrovert tradition typified by *Tom Brown* and the introvert line demonstrated in *Eric*.[4] For Wright, *Tom Brown* is about authority and learning to fit into society; *Eric* is about the individual conscience and learning to fit oneself for the hereafter. And most critics concur that the two novels have almost nothing in common. Robert Lee Wolff suggests that *Eric*'s real genre is less the school story than the frightening juvenile tract of the *You Are Not Too Young to Die* variety, while Jeffrey Richards finds that Farrar's novel "looked back to the past and the dominance of the Evangelicals; Hughes's to the future of a school system geared to athleticism and imperialism."[5] But as Richards observes, Hughes and Farrar were not so dissimilar that they could not be friends[6]—and their fictional creations, while different in style, also share much more than is immediately apparent.

Like Tom Brown, Eric Williams is proud, high-spirited, and impatient of authority, "the type of a thoroughly boyish nature."[7] Brought up by a spinster cousin while his parents are in India, Eric at twelve is pure and innocent but lacks discipline; again like Tom, he has no sense of his own faults. Accordingly, he is sent to Roslyn School, where sound early training gets him off to a superlative start with the masters and the best boys; but his immature inability to recognize the dangers of arrogance sows the seeds of his destruction. As John Rowe Townsend aptly describes the novel in his introduction to the 1971 reissue, Eric is a "moral cliffhanger."[8]

Its plot concerns a Manichaean tug-of-war for Eric's soul, in which the loving influences of home and noble friends struggle against the forces of the world while Eric's egotism leads him into temptation: anger, carelessness, profanity, disobedience, drunkenness, sexual oversophistication, and finally near-dishonesty. So difficult does Eric find the squashing of self that even the affecting deathbeds of his feminized best friend (an invalid) and his own younger brother have no lasting influence for good. Finally, it is not enough for the boy to have Angels around him—he must become one himself. Shamed into running away from school, he ships as cabin boy under a brute who flogs him into Christlike pain, submission, and ultimate inspiring death. The physical powerlessness and humiliation that save the souls of so many protagonists of girls' fiction work their magic also for Eric: "Eric had bowed his head, and had listened to the messages of God, and learned his will; and now, in humble resignation, in touching penitence, with solemn self-devotion, he had cast himself at the feet of Jesus." The pitfalls of masculinity have been avoided at the eleventh hour, as Eric has finally become the ideal Angelic androgyne; in his shattered state, "all was gentleness, love, and dependence, in the once bright, impetuous, self-willed boy."[9] So his friends and masters give thanks over the grave.

Certainly Farrar expresses himself very differently from Hughes; the former's prose is rooted in sermons and is intended, far more than Hughes's, to serve "not only as description or communication, but as education, interpretation, even exorcism, when he is describing evil."[10] There is nothing in Tom Brown similar in style to Farrar's often-quoted exhortation to Eric:

Now, Eric, now or never! Life and death, ruin and salvation, corruption and purity, are perhaps in the balance together, and the scale of your destiny may hang on a single word of yours. Speak out, boy! Tell these fellows that unseemly words wound your conscience; tell them that they are ruinous, sinful, damnable; speak out and save yourself and the rest. Virtue is strong and beautiful, Eric, and vice is downcast in her awful presence. Lose your purity of heart, Eric, and you have lost a jewel which the whole world, if it were 'one entire and perfect chrysolite,' cannot replace.[11]

Nevertheless, Farrar's sentiments would strike a responsive chord in Hughes. The major moral issues of *Tom Brown*—Tom's initial fear of prayer, the question of cribbing, Tom's and East's defiance of the masters, the need to examine one's motives and to eradicate whatever in them seems discordant with the will of God—all have their counterparts in *Eric*. Farrar and Hughes are at one on the "unmanliness" of drinking, the horrors of what Hughes calls the "small friend system" and Farrar knows as "taking up," the value of making friends—even passionate friends—across economic and class boundaries, even the necessity of a fistfight if one knows one is in the right. Ultimately, those critics who see the novels as representative of contrasting trends within the genre are creating differences where only distinctions exist.

Thus what Terence Wright finds peculiarly characteristic of *Tom Brown* is equally true of *Eric*, which like Hughes's novel is about authority and respecting the social order: Eric's moral decline is signaled by his delight in the "open casting off . . . of all authority" afforded by profanity, for instance,[12] and the boys who survive at the end are each assigned to an appropriate role in society—the good making or enforcing the law, the bad breaking it. Similarly, Wright's observation that *Eric* deals with preparing the soul for heaven is certainly also the case with *Tom Brown,* although admittedly in the latter work heaven can wait. Both novels propose the creation of the selfless self, upon which introspection has bestowed control, and look forward to a world governed by the earnest and virtuous rather than by the ambitious or merely attractive.

To be sure, it is not *Tom Brown*'s moralizing that we usually remember after closing the novel, but its general jolliness and love of fun—good clean fun, of course, but fun nonetheless. Herein lies the major distinction between the two works: not what Hughes and Farrar have to say, but how they say it. The difference is not one of didactic purpose so much as of authorial personality; Hughes seems simply to have been more cheerful than Farrar. Tom Brown's creator can focus on the role of team sports in building character and unselfishness, for instance, so that in the words of one of Tom's teachers, the individual "doesn't play that he may win, but that his side may." The author of *Eric,* conversely, finds that his hero's role as captain of the eleven "made him giddy; favour of man led to forgetfulness of God."[13] Both authors agree on the ideal—but Hughes looks on the positive, Farrar on the negative side of the means proposed. Unsurprisingly, Hughes implies in *Tom Brown* that one effort to reform can suffice (although in fact *Tom Brown at Oxford* demonstrates that in Tom's case more will be necessary). Contrastingly, Farrar finds that the struggle to be good—under the combined handicaps of such ego-feeding qualities as good looks, strength, intelligence, and popularity—must be incessant and desperate. Farrar's humiliations as a master at Harrow, where his pupils treated him as "a freak and a joke," left him with a lower opinion of the natural goodness of boys than he might otherwise have had.[14] Thus while Hughes is enthusiastic about Rugby's worth as a training-ground for morality, Farrar sees Roslyn, if not as an embarkation point for perdition, at least as a spiritual obstacle course in which the hidden mines are fatal. But the differences between optimist and pessimist hardly set the two authors at odds.

Like Farrar, Thomas Arnold seems to have believed that the only good boy is a grown-up boy; indeed, modern critics commonly assert that Farrar's general outlook is a more faithful reflection of Arnold's than is Hughes's.[15] Nevertheless, it seems not to have been Arnold's middle-class heirs who established *Eric*'s popularity but readers who might never see even the outside of a public school; conditioned to emotionalism and spiritual melodrama by their other reading, the lower middle class understood *Eric* as evangelical literature and found nothing disturbing in its worries about sin in high places.[16]

Middle-class commentators often caviled at Farrar's Arnoldian pessimism, his suggestion that middle-class boys were morally in desperate straits requiring desperate and even fatal remedies. Yonge, whose novels for girls recommend quite as much soul-searching and earnest moral effort as does *Eric,* complained in 1869 that "that morbid dismal tale, 'Eric's School-days' [*sic*]," couldn't hold a candle to "the unapproachable Tom Brown";[17] the lugubriousness of Farrar's novel made virtue seem downright dangerous. In an 1886 *Fortnightly Review* Edward G. Salmon judged *Tom Brown* "the best boys' book ever written" because it eschews sensationalism and lets the moral unfold gradually instead of shoving it down the reader's throat.[18] Salmon ignored *Eric* altogether.

In one sense it is thus entirely correct to assert with Richards and Newsome that Hughes's novel looks forward, Farrar's backward; already by the early 1860s reviewers were finding Farrar's mode of expression too extreme to be appropriate to a story for boys. Writing in *Blackwood's* in 1861, W. Lucas Collins called *Eric* an "utter failure" whose popularity "has probably lain most with mammas and sisters." Collins complained that Farrar's novels "are decidedly of the weaker sex" in their overdemonstrativeness and sentimentality: "*Tom Brown*, whether at Rugby or at Oxford, is the masculine, and *Eric* and *Julian Home* the feminine, of school and college life."[19] Note, however, that the complaint is not about the message itself so much as about the way in which it is conveyed. It is quite all right for a mid-century boys' book to espouse the values of the Angel—so long as it sets them in a suitably boyish context. Thus reviewers singled out the most emotional, most morally intense parts of *Tom Brown*, the Tom-Arthur passionate friendship and Tom's grief at Arnold's death, for special praise as the most truly "manly" sections (in the presexual sense of the word), because Hughes made clear that he appreciated the essential purity and decency of the child and of childish pursuits.

Farrar's tone, which accounts for the contemporary complaints that *Eric* was morbid and dismal, seems to result from his initial inability to agree with the prevailing belief that good children were, well, good. While Farrar's second boys' novel, *St. Winifred's; or, The World of School* (1862), more conventionally recounts the progress of its hero from original sin to eventual virtue, his first novel reaped criticism for its "lachrimosity" even from its own author. Eric disturbs us because, with his "pure young heart,"[20] he is a natural hero—yet school can uncover in him tendencies toward profanity, drunkenness, bullying, dishonesty, and sexuality, so that we fear that childhood may not really be a time of innocence but merely a latency period before overt sin begins.

Fictional schools of the postreform era are not supposed to resemble the cynic's reality so closely. The traditional school story usually contains its complement of villains—the bully, the cheat, the debauché. But authors make clear that these disreputable boys are but a tiny fraction of the population of the school, and if the bad boy is a stock figure in this literature, he seems to be so not only by plot-driven necessity but by didactic design. For the school, an artificial home far outside "real life," is a closed community, almost an anti-society. If the worst elements of the adult world occasionally worm their way (dressed not as violence or dishonesty or sensuality but as ordinary schoolboys) into this childish Eden, that we can so easily penetrate their disguises to establish that these boys differ from their peers merely underscores the essential innocence of the rest of the idyll. Ideal schools, like ideal homes, are in the world but not of it (right down to the curricula, which make it a point of gentlemanly honor to have as little practical value as possible); and even the worst schoolboys generally turn out to be themselves the tools of disreputable local publicans.

The classic fictional school (and one might add the real-life school as seen by rhapsodic Victorian observers; fact and fantasy, equally colored by nostalgia or the utopian impulse, are often inextricably intertwined in writings on education) bears a striking resemblance to the Christian community postulated by tract writers. Hierarchies are based not on birth or financial status but—at least purportedly—on personal achievement and character. Before the godlike headmaster all new boys, from country clergyman's son to duke, are equal; all students work toward a common goal. Each seeks not to gratify his own ambition but to do his duty to parents and school. Heroism is not then a matter of sensational rescues and publicly bestowed credit; the best heroes are unsung, giving up their chances for glory on the football field to secure the advancement of a misjudged enemy, or enduring the unjust calumny of all the school rather than getting a friend into trouble. Self-sacrifice, purity, devotion to duty, comradely love, unobtrusive influence rather than aggressive "jaws" about how others should behave—all the qualities of the Angel—are essential to the schoolboy code.

Nor do authors approve of those boys who try to substitute for these ideals the ideals of the marketplace. Hughes's Flashman, buying popularity "by dint of his command of money,"[21] or the villain of Talbot Baines Reed's *The Fifth Form at St. Dominic's* (1882), who hopes to win a scholarship not through hard work but through insider trading (an illicit look at the exam paper), are contemptible rather than clever; while they may fool their naive fellow pupils for a time, they never gull the omniscient reader. Invariably, morality wins out over shrewdness. Dominic Hibberd's comment that in *Tom Brown* "school society parallels society at large" misses the point; rather, in fiction, as in Arnold's vision of real life, school society offers a model of what the larger society might be but is not, by attempting to establish a community built on the "values of home and family."[22]

As in the world of tract literature, that all souls are equal does not preclude a stratified power structure. Ian Watson (who disapprovingly reads the communitarianism of Hughes's Rugby as "an exercise in class solidarity, the definition of the political and cultural/ideological affinities of an élite") reads the school's motto as "Even those who rule must learn to obey."[23] But obedience has other uses than the political, and the prefect system coincided with the religious revival. Prereform anarchy placed little stress on conduct; outside school hours masters made no attempt to discipline the pupils. The theory was that boys best learned to conquer evil by experiencing it, and most boys seem to have done their wholehearted best during their school careers to experience as much as possible. It was Arnold who introduced one of the key means of extracurricular discipline, fagging, in an effort to protect the persons of the smaller boys and the souls of the larger ones. Intended to teach sixth-formers to appreciate and champion the defenselessness of their juniors, the fagging system was originated not to augment the hegemony of the strongest but to encourage a chivalric alliance between strength and weakness.[24]

The effect of fagging was to create a gendered hierarchy within a single-sex society. Real women were almost entirely absent from the schools; the youngest boys, Isabel Quigly observes, took their place: "How else can the fagging system appear?—the way in which the youngest and freshest did chores (wholly domestic chores, considered totally 'feminine' in a period when no male would ever, in other circumstances, make toast and tea or lay and light a fire) for the . . . most powerful."[25] Contemporary commentators using fiction and nonfiction alike found this enforced femininity of inestimable value, since humility was an essential prerequisite of virtue. Edmund Routledge's *Every Boy's Annual* editorialized in 1863 over "the incalculable amount of good that has been done to many a lord by his having been put under the authority of those inferior to him by birth."[26] And writers of the classic school stories make much of the powerless, "feminine" stage. It is commonly as a new boy and a fag that the hero—"depersonalised, lost in a common identity"[27]—forms his passionate and immortal loves, recognizes the threats to his innocence, understands his own insignificance, and in short, becomes socialized into the community while simultaneously providing an essential element in its artificial domesticity. The enforced obedience of fagging makes possible the school story's equivalent to tract literature's conversion scenes.

Nor does enforced femininity yet suggest enforced inversion in the midcentury years; quite the opposite. With reference to *Eric,* for instance, there has long been debate as to the exact nature of the "unseemly words" Eric hears in the dormitory: Do they tempt Eric to homosexuality, to masturbation, or simply to sexual knowledge? But in 1858 the precise form sensuality may take has little interest for

Farrar, whose concern is rather to save boys from masculine excess by enjoining them to feminine "purity of heart." The passionate loves of the fag are therefore officially innocent because of, not despite, the fag's feminine role; only when the fag attaches himself romantically to an older boy, whose position more closely approximates the masculine, do authors begin to worry.

The other major instrument of obedience and social stratification in the post-Arnoldian school world was organized games. Athleticism was not an Arnoldian reform. Like Farrar, Arnold worried that success in sport—as in any other worldly triviality—distracted the mind from the quest for moral self-improvement; and the general view of early-Victorian Britain was rather against games than for them. Thomas Tegg reminded apprentices in 1848 that in general "good players are but miserable and useless persons"; one sign of Eric's moral deterioration is that he devotes himself overmuch to sport; and as late as 1882 Frederic Harrison could complain, "The extravagant value set on games today is a national disease. It degrades our whole standard of manly excellence. It has brutalised our manners and ruined our tastes and habits."[28] Nevertheless, when Arnold's former pupil G.E.L. Cotton became headmaster of Marlborough, he found in athleticism the ideal stratagem not only for controlling the boys' leisure hours, but for ensuring that those leisure hours "reflected religious goodness."[29] And that "religious goodness" is in turn reflected in the classic fictional depictions of organized games.

Discussing nineteenth-century "natural pathology," Bruce Haley argues that its theoretical side draws on an essentially Christian enthusiasm, demonstrating "a truly religious commitment to the ways of nature which almost exactly parallels the evangelical commitment to the ways of the Lord."[30] Athleticism eventually developed all the religious fervor that should have animated boys' attitudes toward Arnoldian Christianity. While Arnold would have found the idea of sport as a sacrament both irreligious and ludicrous, however, later school administrators generally considered games mania something to encourage, since athleticism "promoted manliness and chivalry" in all the best Arnoldian senses.[31]

In part, adult approval of juvenile sport was based on its symbolic qualities. Harrow's C. J. Vaughan, for instance, professed to see in games' merging of the individual in the team an analogue of the soul's membership in the body of Christ.[32] Over and over in fiction and nonfiction alike, this selflessness is emphasized; theorists were wont, like Tom Brown, to arrange pastimes according to merit, so that activities stressing individual success were at the bottom of the moral hierarchy, those stressing team success at the top. Even at the end of the century, with the stories published in *The Captain* magazine, P. G. Wodehouse made clear that cups for boxing or fives might be won *by* individuals, but they were won *for* the house.[33] As late as 1916, John Astley Cooper could argue that the point of organized games was "not only to produce . . . physical and mental qualities" of practical value, "but to encourage unselfishness."[34]

There was another major reason why school administrators gradually decided with regard to games that (as a prospectus for Bedford School put it in 1899) "all those who like to participate may participate, and all others *must.*"[35] This concern had to do with sex. In the 1850s, when the playing fields of Eton first began to take precedence over its classrooms, some theorists had proposed that weaklings were more likely to fall prey to sexual desire (conversely, giving in to desire sapped the vitality). On the appearance of *Tom Brown,* for instance, one reviewer commented that "sensualism, both at school and in the world, is found to lie among the quieter natures."[36] While initially few authorities believed that Arthur-like frailty might be a sign of impurity, as time went on their numbers grew—and the "sensualism" in question was increasingly homosexual. In other words, the Victorian privileging of gentlemanliness over macho manliness and reinscription of sexual woman as asexual Angel often sustained attacks from the older, opposite ideals they had supplanted, which indeed were eventually to dominate.[37] Femininity was thus simultaneously safe because it was innocent and suspect because it had been oversexed; while early-Victorian schoolmasters institutionalized girlish behaviors in order to raise moral tone, their late-Victorian successors took the opposite path to the same goal. The games revolution was attractive not only because it instilled womanly virtues such as unselfishness, but because it did so in a uniquely manly way.

So as the ideal of asexuality gave way over the last quarter of the nineteenth century to that of heterosexuality, the role of games increasingly became to encourage normalcy—because in a boys' school, any sex is necessarily of the "abnormal" variety. Even religious organizations recognized the necessity of exercising the body if the soul was to be saved. When the Religious Tract Society founded the *Boy's Own Paper* in 1879, the paper signaled a new current of thought: the assumption that "healthy" boys' literature describes healthy boys. While earlier evangelicals had held that the strongest souls generally occupied the weakest frames, many *Boy's Own Paper* writers suggested instead that the strongest souls belonged to boys who rose at five for a cold bath and a brisk run—in W. Gordon Stables's columns, the usual specifics prescribed against masturbation, since "the stronger the body the greater the strength of will to resist temptations."[38] But it would be a grave mistake to assume that this new emphasis on the body meant that traditional school stories no longer treated the same moral issues that mark the work of Farrar and Hughes. While the genre inevitably made use of the peculiar institutions of stereotypical schoolboy life, from fagging to cricket, its factual dimensions never entirely escaped from the spiritual context dictated by the Angel.

It surprises J. S. Bratton that the *Boy's Own Paper* should have serialized not only "the latter-day evangelical boys' writers like Gordon Stables, but also the remarkably un-Christian Talbot Baines Reed school stories."[39] Perhaps evangelicalism is in the eye of the beholder. Jack Cox, a twentieth-century editor of the paper, comments that "Reed regarded his work for *B.O.P.* as personal service to the cause of Christian literature and the Society. . . . His *B.O.P.* work was done for the sheer love of the task, and his copyrights in the *B.O.P.* stories were transferred to the Society for little more than token payments."[40] This unwillingness to contaminate his charity with profit represented a considerable financial sacrifice, since by the late 1880s the magazine was printing 500,000 copies a week (owing to boys sharing copies, actual readership was probably two or three times that),[41] and Reed's stories were among the most popular offerings. His first *Boy's Own Paper* serial, *The Adventures of a Three-Guinea Watch*, began in October of 1880, the periodical's third year; and although Quigly reports that "Reed disliked directly didactic stories, thought Farrar knew nothing about boys and considered *Eric* 'a religious tract thinly disguised as a school story,'"[42] the evangelical heritage of *Watch* is strongly marked.

The unconscious model for Reed's novel may well have been another Religious Tract Society serial, George E. Sergent's influential *The Story of a Pocket Bible*, published in the *Sunday at Home* magazine in 1855 and continued in 1856. In this episodic narrative, the bible goes from owner to owner, each new character exemplifying a different stage on the spiritual path and all of them pointing up the need for humility and selflessness. We share in the improving death of an obscure but saintly mill girl, in the conversion through scripture of a working-class man who consequently becomes sufficiently gentle to convert his wife, and (in the story's continuation) in the hopeful friendship, à la Hogarth, of a Good and a Bad Apprentice; conscientious Albert exchanges bibles with sinful James in order that friendship may reinforce piety and save James's soul. After half a century and much hard use, the title character finds itself again in the hands of its original purchaser.

Not only formal elements but specific plot twists in Sergent's novel have their counterparts in Reed's, which traces the peregrinations of a silver watch from its original schoolboy owner, Charlie Newcome, through a series of such other masters as a pawnshop proprietor, a thief, and an Irish army recruit, until finally Charlie recovers it. Along the way the watch observes the comforts of religion, the value of male friendship, and the horrors of the dissolute life. And while the watch itself is not particularly Christian (having a tendency toward envy, pride, love of glitter, and—especially when under the influence of the pawnshop environment—vulgar backtalk), the story certainly is.

Charlie is the classic schoolboy hero in the George Arthur tradition. Innocently chatting to a fellow passenger in the train before he arrives at Randlebury, he promises to befriend her son, Tom Drift (most of the names in this saga are allegorical), and holds to the promise even after he discovers that Tom is a wastrel who gambles and reads "yellow-backed" novels. Charlie's own virtue is above suspicion; like Arthur's, his public prayers set a dormitory trend, while like Montagu in *Eric* (and like Tom Brown), he himself fights only in just causes. From the first he has risen above the ego, being able to forgive his enemies even unto seventy times seven. Tom is not so lucky, and we find that "his vanity rendered him as pliant as wax to the hand of the flatterer." If the prose style at dramatic moments is reminiscent of both Sergent and Farrar, so is the plot: as with Eric, it is only illness that can wean Tom from his "vicious" and "unwholesome-looking" friends, who form the usual amalgam of sensuality and unmanly masculinity. Charlie's devoted attendance at his enemy's sickbed creates a lasting friendship, in which "no longer was Tom the vain, hectoring patron, but the docile penitent, over whose spirit Charlie's character began from that time to exercise an influence which, if in the time to come it could always have worked as it did now, would have gone far to save Tom Drift from many a bitter fall and experience."[43]

Three years later Charlie is simultaneously "the hero of the cricket-field" and a perfect example of the Angel in the School, having "by his quiet influence . . . given Tom's life a new direction towards honour and usefulness." When Tom leaves school to study medicine in London, Charlie also gives him the watch ("Somehow," Tom says tearfully, "I feel as if I can't go wrong as long as I have it"), but a mere souvenir can't exert Charlie's own influence. Tom again falls in with his evil friends, who skillfully rouse his sleeping vanity to lure him to billiard-rooms, music halls, and perhaps worse. Like Eric's, Tom's morals deteriorate: "His will had been the first to suffer, his conscience next. Then with a rush had gone honour, temperance, and purity"—all within three weeks.[44] Tom also loses Charlie, the watch, and his place in medical school.

The watch makes its way to Cambridge in the company of George Reader, "a modest, quiet scholar . . . not presuming on his talents to scorn his humble origin," and discovers in a touch reminiscent of *Tom Brown at Oxford* that of the university students only George seems to be "in earnest." Games could work no moral improvement in this hero, but unfortunately through neglecting muscles for mind he brings on his own death from exhaustion. (The same fate befalls Sergent's Albert Norton.) George leaves the watch to his friend Jim, by a curious coincidence Charlie's best friend from Randlebury, a "manly, open-hearted young clergyman" who selflessly spends his time visiting prisons. Among the prisoners is Tom, doing six months for drunken assault; Jim effects Tom's conversion—a lasting one this time—by leaving Charlie's watch in the cell overnight for Tom to ponder. When at length, in another Sergentian twist, Charlie, now a soldier, recovers the watch just before the Indian Mutiny, it saves his life by deflecting a bullet, and the attending doctor is (of course) Tom. We may be confused about who is succoring whom, however, as we hear how Tom "knelt there and sobbed; and Charlie, as he lay, took his hand into his own, and held it."[45] Tom's worthy mother could make no headway with him; it is her emissary Charlie who most successfully embodies the qualities and the potency of the Angel.

Watch, like other Reed serials, has a high opinion of athleticism, which in Charlie's words can't be valued too highly "for the moral training it gives a man . . . for the pluck, manliness, and endurance it puts into him."[46] As should be evident, however, athleticism here is not a replacement for the Angelic code but an addition to it, just as friendship doesn't substitute for Sergentian piety but bolsters it. Moral strength, not physical strength, is the real issue; selfless virtue and pure-hearted schoolboy devotion are more important than scoring a century in cricket.

Other *Boy's Own Paper* stories of the early 1880s even take the Arnoldian line that success in sport, and indeed in all activities tend-

3. *The Struggle for Influence.* Charlie's letter is part of a heavenly light as good and evil wrestle for Tom's soul. Illustration by Gordon Browne to the *Boy's Own Paper* serialization of T. B. Reed's *The Adventures of a Three-Guinea Watch* (3, no. 100 [11 December 1880]).

ing to boyhood popularity, may form a doubtful adjunct to the code. The anonymous author of "Mazeppa" (November 1880) uses as hero not the charismatic Orator Brown but the solitary Bob Henderson, generally regarded in the school as "rather a muff." (For one thing, Bob "did not, as a rule, care for cricket or football very much.") Orator leads a mock war in the swamp and, when the school gets in trouble over the escapade, a real rebellion against the kindly head-master Dr. Preston. And while the author recognizes the fun of both episodes, we are not to approve the boys' lighthearted irresponsibility, punctuated as it is by the unjust suspicion that it was Bob who "peached" to the Doctor about the war. Orator suggests punishing Bob by tying him in a punt and sending him over the dam, a treatment our hero accepts in the calm dignity of innocence. When he is nearly killed, the balance of moral power in the school finally rights itself: the Doctor reveals that far from peaching, Bob "had been spending that beautiful half-holiday by the bedside of his invalid friend, whom I afterwards found he had cheered and greatly benefited, and who loves him most heartily for his gentleness and unfailing kindness."[47] Henceforth Orator's influence is nothing to Bob's.

Similarly, "Toby" (August–September 1881), the creation of another popular *Boy's Own Paper* writer, Ascott R. Hope (A. R. Hope-Moncrieff) takes as its hero the captain of the second eleven, who is also good at footraces, the high jump, and rugby. But Toby's successes in the field are outweighed by his failures in keeping his temper and in respecting those whose worldly status is ambiguous; he can keep from impertinence to those masters who are themselves public-school men and cricketers, but not to Mr. Brooks, the English teacher, "a neat, prim, formal little old man" of neither athletic nor sociointellectual attainments.[48] After a series of rudenesses (which Mr. Brooks endures with Angelic forbearance), the master who narrates the story calls Toby in for a heart-to-heart chat about the value of patience, submission, and obedience in any community; he tells him with evangelical sympathy that "we have all our own faults to fight against" but that sad experience has taught him

> what comes of giving way to the evil passions of our nature. It is not because I am your master that I urge you thus, but because I . . . see with sorrow how often I did wrong and foolishly, and think how grateful I should be now to any man who had persuaded me against my errors in time to save me from their consequences.[49]

But words cannot prevail with Toby; only the sudden loss of physical strength, when he breaks his leg impulsively saving Mr. Brooks from a runaway lawn roller, can work a lasting change. As with Eric, through illness, "Toby's proud, angry humour had all vanished like a burst soap-bubble. . . . He was surprisingly quiet and patient when once the fever left him; he showed himself in quite a new light under this affliction, as if the roller had crushed the cantankerousness right out of him."[50] Cantankerousness, fever, and headstrong masculinity appear to be one and the same; their opposites are patience, physical weakness, and femininity.

"Toby" is slightly atypical of the school story in that the instrument of the hero's conversion is female: the matron, Mrs. Mayfield, an "oasis" of "gentle tendance and kindly words . . . in the desert of tasks and jeers and scoldings and strugglings," substitutes for the mother Toby never knew. She reads the Bible to him ("Charity suffereth long and is kind; charity envieth not; charity vaunteth not itself, is not puffed up") and wins from him a more complete obedience than even the most athletic masters could. Hence the narrator reminds himself that "'when pain and sickness wring the brow,' a woman is the ministering angel who can best bring home the lesson of affliction. . . . [Toby's suffering might] prove a real blessing in disguise." Where athleticism failed, pain and "influence" succeed. After Toby's leg heals, he finds that the best way to control his temper is to remind himself of the lessons of injury, applying blistering ointment to his body to mortify the flesh. The narrator is dubious about this expedient, for like strength, self-control should be moral rather than merely physical. But that Toby understands that humiliation, not power, is the source of virtue is certainly cause for hope, and thus "Mr. Brooks declared that he was quite a different boy since the accident. . . . Toby was tamed."[51]

The comparatively rare boys'-school story written by a woman is also, as we might expect, part of this tradition. In Ethel C. Kenyon's *Jack's Heroism: A Story of School Boy Life* (1883), sin is pride and heroism self-sacrifice—the "feminine courage" we have seen *Girl's Own Paper* writers laud is clearly appropriate also for boys. Jack dies rescuing the headmaster's daughter from a fire, after having demonstrated his Angelic charity by succoring starving children. Mrs. G. Forsyth Grant's assortment of school titles in the 1890s and early 1900s were, as we shall see, redolent of sentiment and androgyny. In the same line, the *Boy's Own Paper* also published the occasional woman-authored boys' domestic novel. Mrs. Eiloart's *The Ill-Used Boy; or, Lawrence Hartley's Grievances* (*Boy's Own Paper*, 1881–1882) has a moral message essentially identical to that of "Toby," with the proud, selfish, uncharitable, and reckless Lawrence only able to redeem himself through experiencing powerlessness and humiliation, as he wanders destitute through Germany. The latter genre, however, never fully established itself even in the pages of the *Boy's Own Paper,* perhaps because the magazine was aimed primarily at the middle class. Since by the 1880s it was assumed that the privileged boy would be educated at school, not at home, the school novel generally took the place of the domestic novel for boys.

Until the 1880s, then, the school story is more or less a monolith, its predominantly male authors preaching to a predominantly male audience an ideal essentially femininist and domestic. Toward the end of the century, however, the atmosphere begins to change. In the schools themselves we find the rising fear of the feminine and the "abnormal" creating an intensely rigid environment. Hence a Wellington boy trying to decorate his room with flowers was prevented from doing so by his dormitory captain, who destroyed the blooms with the admonition, "There is no room for this rotten effeminate stuff here."[52] Similarly, J. R. de S. Honey comments on the frequent late-Victorian attitude that schoolboys should be kept safe from "the molly-coddling influence of women"; so suspect had androgyny become that one headmaster asserted that music "'rotted the moral fibre.'" Whereas only a few years previously schoolmasters' celibacy was a matter of course, by 1905 Eton's Edward Lyttelton sent around a memorandum to the bachelor teachers recommending that they find wives.[53] Whether it masked homosexuality, irregular relationships with women, or indeed purity, the sexual abnormality implicit in the unmarried state was cause for concern.

Possibly because school stories were usually written by authors whose own public-school days, if they had existed at all, were at least a decade or two in the past, the classic tradition could linger on in fiction even while reality was becoming increasingly hostile to the ideals that tradition espoused. In the schools, as J. A. Mangan reports, social Darwinism was gradually strangling Christian gentility, so that while the ideal was Christian, the reality was not; despite the early endorsement of organized games by organized religion, the result of athleticism was to set a seal of approval on the doctrine of the survival of the fittest.[54] But in the traditional school story, the ideal schoolboy still reigned supreme and unchanged—and to some extent feminine.

In J.E.C. Welldon's *Gerald Eversley's Friendship: A Study in Real Life*

(1895), for instance, the love Gerald Eversley feels for his more masculine classmate Harry Venniker is identical to that Harry's sister, Ethel, feels for Gerald. Both passions are hero-worshiping, sexless, and essentially religious. What draws Gerald to Harry at thirteen is the set of qualities Harry shares with his Angelic mother and sister; what saves Gerald from suicide after Ethel's death just before the wedding is Harry's sympathy. The two possibilities for life, as we see when the two fathers bid their sons farewell on the first day of school, are the market and the temple. Harry's father is a feudal aristocrat confident that at least within the Venniker domains and the Venniker church, he outranks God; he gives his son a large sum of pocket money and tells him not to swear or cheat. Gerald's father is a clergyman whose real marriage is not his formal tie to his bigoted second wife but his sexless bond with Gerald; he advises his boy to behave like Christ. Honor in the marketplace is attractive but secular and ultimately egotistical, while Christian love is poverty-stricken and "peculiar"—but ideal.

The novel is long and complicated but stresses all the usual themes: Gerald's boyish piety and unworldliness; Harry's critical illness, which, much more than his athletic prowess, raises the moral tone of the house; the enforced femininity of being a new boy ("the nearest parallel to [choosing the fags] may be said to have been the sale of slave girls in the market at Constantinople"). The central issue is androgyny. Not only is Gerald one of "those shy, delicate, sensitive creatures who do not understand the rough give-and-take of life," but Welldon suggests that the distinction between Harry and Ethel is largely artificial. Mr. Eversley's church, which serves as a metaphor for school and for the larger world, has a custom the wise minister dislikes: the male communicants sit on one side of the aisle, the female on the other, and the congregation will tolerate no mixing. But the reader knows that the boys' masculine qualities (Harry's strength, Gerald's intellectualism and ambition) are unimportant or even dangerous, as when Gerald's reading creates religious doubts until Ethel cures him. What Welldon wants us to emulate are rather their feminine virtues: Harry's modesty and sympathy for the underdog, Gerald's talent for love. Harry and Ethel are two halves of one whole, and if Ethel's feminine fragility causes her death, Harry's continued presence can assure Gerald that she is not really lost. Gerald finally amalgamates both sets of qualities, Harry's popularity and energy and Ethel's charity and influence, into one Angelic and sexless being: "He was a man beloved and honoured. . . . Wherever any social good was to be done, labour to be provided, thrift to be fostered, temperance to be promoted, sorrow to be relieved, he was found there. He was never married."⁵⁵

Welldon's novel dramatizes the sermons he preached in the mid-1880s, at the beginning of his tenure as headmaster of Harrow.⁵⁶ A cursory examination of these homilies reveals the traditional themes: games exist to teach unselfishness; men should embrace feminine standards of purity; prayer is the most effective form of action; true manliness is often demonstrated through lack of worldly success (and Christ is most impressive because "although He was so great, He became so humble"); schoolboy friendships are morally invaluable, teaching selflessness in the wish to give up everything for the beloved; and the boy who is likely later to shed "the richest lustre on his School" is he who "cannot excel in games . . . is shy, sensitive, delicate . . . called a 'muff.'" Welldon's approval of "the really delicate, sensitive boy, who cannot bear roughness" is odd, considering that in Chapter Two we saw him castigating just this sort of boy as "troublesome" to the schoolmaster. Apparently when other adults brought up issues relating to homosexuality, Welldon saw fit to criticize effeminacy; when the context was one of character molding, however, he praised the trait. Thus in order to do its duty as a nursery for morality, every school should aim to stamp out the masculine ego in its pupils, for "selfishness and vanity . . . are the twin roots of every wickedness on earth."⁵⁷ Social Darwinism, as Mangan describes it, had undoubtedly made it to Harrow by the time of *Gerald Eversley*, but it had no place in chapel or in novel, although it didn't take long for Welldon's tale to become passé on account of its overemotionalism.⁵⁸

Another 1895 tale, Grant's *The Hero of Crampton School*, similarly exhibits no hesitation in making use of conventions that were coming to seem outmoded or even dangerous. The passionate friendship between the manly but tender Hercules and the feminine Trevor ("slightly made, not very robust, with a pale, refined face; a shy, sensitive boy, of a reserved temperament—reserved certainly to others, but never to Hercules. . . . Trevor adored Hercules") strikes author and characters alike as praiseworthy, "one of those marvellously unselfish, boyish friendships which, if well chosen, help so much to elevate the character of boys." The chief good in Grant's world is depth of feeling. Success at cricket is valuable—Trevor even prays for runs: "For Jesus Christ's sake. Amen."⁵⁹ But this is more because athletics, in a Hughesian touch, offer a vehicle for unselfish fervor (Hercules uses his skill to benefit the school, not himself) than because they have any intrinsic worth. Likewise, Grant approves Trevor's unselfishness in deliberately missing an important examination question so that Hercules may come out ahead; love is more valuable than academic honesty.

In exalting spirit above all else, *Crampton School* may strike the modern reader as deliberately anti-Darwinian, especially when it hearkens back to the midcentury cult of the invalid, patching up a rift between the heroes by feminizing Hercules with a paralyzing accident. "Henceforward his life would be full of pain and weakness," Hercules knows, but his spirit gains "an indefinable something, a something deeper"; he becomes "wonderfully unselfish," a greater influence for good than ever before.[60] While Hercules is miraculously cured after ten months of sainthood, we are left with the firm impression that interrelated invalidism, femininity, virtue, and true feeling are far superior to the cheerful animal vitality characterizing lesser boys.

The last important school story to carry on in this lush fashion most of the assumptions of *Tom Brown* and *Eric* is probably H. A. Vachell's *The Hill: A Romance of Friendship* (1905), which enjoyed twenty-one printings in its first eight years, nine of these issues occurring in 1905 alone. The subtitle of this homoemotional if not homoerotic work gives the reader an idea of what the book will be about—a love triangle involving the popular but pure Harry Desmond (AKA Caesar), the "sexless"-voiced John Verney, and the precociously masculine and worldly Scaife. But so firmly does Vachell draw the line between purity and impurity that the novel seems to have raised no hackles (even in 1913 the *Boy's Own Paper* uses *The Hill*, along with *Tom Brown*, as a sound example of a novel about "ideal friendship" and offers a prize for the essay best explaining the attractiveness of such a relationship).[61] We can tell at a glance—as Vachell intends that we should—that John, whose influence brings Desmond to religion and stops him smoking, is good; that Esmé Kinloch may be known as Fluff and have a "delicately-tinted face . . . small, regular, girlish features . . . red, quivering mouth" but that his hero-worship for John has no sensual component; that Desmond's "exquisite refinement . . . magnificent upbringing . . . youth unspotted—white" must inevitably draw him toward John and unselfishness, away from temptation.[62]

Conversely, we instantly know what Beaumont-Greene, "pulpy, pimply, gross in mind and body," wants in trying to force Fluff to be his "friend," just as we know that for all Scaife's physical attractiveness, there is something morally repellent about him. Competitive, anticommunitarian, and reckless, Scaife is keen only about athletics, disdains the idea that masters should be the boys' friends, drinks, gambles, and plays on the democratic ideals of the school: his comrades are afraid to cross him because they don't want to appear to be prejudiced against a hod-carrier's rich grandson. Heredity dooms him nonetheless, since his forebears, who "were earning their bread before they were sixteen," have bequeathed him an unfortunate precocity.[63] Thus, as Quigly has commented, the tensions of *The Hill* derive from the contrast between Scaife's "masculinity" and "the good boys' manliness,"[64] between Darwinian virility and Angelic sexlessness. Appropriately, Scaife gets the body, in that Desmond's liking for this "personification of evil" leads him to join the other's regiment in the Boer War; but John gets the soul: in the letter Desmond writes John on the eve of his own death in battle, he comments that John is "the only one I love as much as my own brother—*and even more.*"[65] Influence, purity, and unselfishness have the moral victory, and as the headmaster reminds the surviving scholars, it is better to sacrifice one's body while still pure than to live to fall into sin. As so often in Angel-influenced stories, dying young is the best revenge.

The denouement of *The Hill* is a good example of what has happened, over the course of the classic school story, to the noble death. While originally Hughes's Arthur, Farrar's Russell, and Reed's Charlie sustain fatal or near-fatal illnesses to set others on the right moral track (or, like Farrar's Eric and Hope's Toby, to save their own souls), by the end of the century self-sacrifice has become less religious than patriotic. Indeed, it often seems that with the decline of evangelicalism the religious impulse has been transmuted into love of nation, especially as manifested through love of friends. Even the athletic mechanism becomes primarily a means of strengthening the boy's relationship with Country rather than with God; thus Harold Avery writes in his preface to *An Old Boy's Yarns* (1895) that "in a hard fight to save his goal, we see in those grey eyes the first kindling of that light which will some day be burning brightly in them as he stands face to face with danger, and perhaps with death,"[66] and the subsequent stories give their sentimentality and didacticism a comradely rather than a religious direction.

The rhetoric of public-schoolboy patriotism grew directly out of the rhetoric of public-schoolboy evangelicalism, taking over the latter's urgings to self-immolation on the altar of community responsibility, and making its preachments with tractlike fervor. Speaking to the pupils at his old prep school just after the battle of Mafeking,

R.S.S. Baden-Powell explained that patriotism is the proper way to express religious devotion:

> If you can get into the way of thinking only of doing your duty while you are still boys at school it will come quite naturally to you when you grow up, to continue to do it for your Sovereign and your country, and you will never dream of trying to save your own life if your duty requires you to risk it.
>
> And in thus doing your duty whether it be to the Captain of your team, to your masters, or to your Queen—remember that at the same time you are carrying out a higher work because you are doing your duty to God.[67]

The implication of many of these exhortations was that the boy who failed to give his life for his country should feel guilty not to have made the supreme sacrifice. Hero after hero of fiction, essay, and verse embraces death unflinchingly and even joyfully; like Rupert Brooke, they owe their auras of purity and nobility to the fact that once having ridden gallantly off into the sunrise, they do not return. By the end of the century, then, the acid test of self-abnegation had become not whether moral good was accomplished, but whether lives were lost—a twist most evangelicals would have found startling, but which surely helped after the Great War, and indeed helps today, to discredit mid-Victorian moral earnestness as unforgivably wasteful.[68]

It was not, however, the twentieth-century consciousness that dying for Britain might be neither *dulce* nor *decorum* that sparked what I have termed the antitraditional school story in the 1880s. Rather, we may credit this subgenre to its authors' feeling that the classic hero was a prig whose exploits bore no relation to the behavior of boys in real life. Far from being the demiparadises of traditional school fiction, schools were in fact red in tooth and claw; masters were not sympathetic spiritual comforters but uncomprehending tyrants or buffoons; and should the model hero arrive and start doing his stuff, he would influence his peers to stunned laughter instead of to moral improvement. When the classic tradition claimed realism, the new writers asserted, it lied. The true patterns of schoolboy virtue worked otherwise, and the antitraditional stories played tricks with convention to show as much. Appropriately, they commonly replace the earnest tones of their forebears (which they implicitly condemn as sententious) with irreverent humor.

Vice Versa (1882), by F. Anstey (Thomas Anstey Guthrie), is an anomaly among these fictions only in that it uses a magical "Garudâ Stone" to undermine its own claims to veracity. Anstey plays on the antiegotism theme with deconstructive wit: while most new boys find that they must relinquish their old selves in order to conform to the schoolboy model, Paul Bultitude has given up not his ego but his body, having inadvertently traded places with his son Dick. At the mercy of a headmaster as pompous and unfeeling as himself, Paul can make no one understand his plight; adults find him deficient in proper respect, while boys find him cowardly, dishonest, and lacking in class solidarity. What the erstwhile Mr. Bultitude called "the innocent games and delights of boyhood" turn out to consist of poor food, physical pain, and boredom in the classroom and on the playing fields; and the school is marked by all the snobbery, sycophancy, and dog-eat-dog desperation that could possibly exist in the marketplace. The boy who exerts the greatest "influence" is the worst boy at Crichton House; his androgyny lies in "feminine spitefulness," and he uses his much-vaunted and wholly spurious scruples only to get other boys into trouble. And the only master who might have helped Paul is too distressed to dig deeper after discovering that the change in the soi-disant Dick does not, after all, result from an evangelical conversion; Mr. Blinkhorn "was an ardent believer in the Good Boy of a certain order of school tales" and "was always waiting for some such boy to come to him with his confession of moral worthlessness and vows of unnatural perfection," being "too simple and earnest and good himself to realise that such states of the youthful mind are not unfrequently merely morbid and hysterical, and too often degenerate into Pharisaism, or worse still, hypocrisy."[69]

In the Blinkhorn episode we see the reason for Anstey's criticism of the traditional school stories: it is not goodness he objects to, but artificial goodness. (The same distinction exists even in Grant's traditional *Crampton School,* wherein among the crippled Hercules's torments is the bombastic and judgmental piety of the tactless master Mr. Martin. Martin's insincere religiosity is condemned; the headmaster's true feeling, expressed in "much the same words as Mr. Martin's," is consoling and praiseworthy.)[70] For while *Vice Versa* undercuts the clichéd expression of the Angelic ideal, it upholds the ideal itself. Women provide all the comfort and tenderness in the story; the problem with the Bultitude home is explicitly that Mrs. Bultitude has died three years previously, and the headmaster's wife and daughter are warm and sympathetic where the headmaster and his son are cold and superior. Paul's spiritual problems arise from having assimilated too well the ideals of the marketplace: "He had not a grain of chivalry in his disposition—chivalry being an eminently unpractical virtue." And ironically, it is precisely his temporary powerlessness and humiliation that lead, just as they ought, to his spiritual betterment by teaching him finally to appreciate home and family. Dick's usurpation of his father's position may be a commercial disaster, but his boyish warmth of heart is just what the unhappy house requires in its master. After the transformation is reversed, we find that Paul will never again "consider his family as a set of troublesome and thankless incumbrances; thanks to Dick's offices during the interregnum, they would henceforth throw off their reserve and constraint in their father's presence," so that the family is at last united.[71]

In his 1882 review of the novel, Andrew Lang remarks, "We are afraid that with the other sex it will not find equal favour, but that is to be expected from the nature of the work." Although Lang singles out for special praise "the quite natural pathos of the last pages,"[72] the implication, as with other late-century male commentary on the school story, is that women cannot appreciate rollicking fun, preferring *Eric*-like lugubriousness. Nonetheless, if women disapproved of *Vice Versa,* they would probably not have done so because they felt that Anstey denigrated Angelic ideals, but because they resented the novel's suggestion that—to their discredit—schools and fathers might be less affected by Angelic influence than they professed. For what Anstey is really doing is revealing the hypocrisy in Dr. Grimstone's pretensions to being a caring headmaster (though he plays football with the boys, tries to keep them "pure" by segregating them from girls, and worries about their spiritual welfare) and Mr. Bultitude's to being a doting father. The problems of the adult male, perhaps, are only to be cured by magic.

Like *Vice Versa,* Rudyard Kipling's *Stalky & Co.* (1899) rejects not so much the ideals behind the pious model schoolboy as the conventions that have come to mark him. Masters and prefects alike at the United Services College have taken too literally the preachings of Farrar and the *Boy's Own Paper,* so that Stalky and his "Co."—M'Turk and Beetle—who shun sports, mock the honor of the house, smoke, and consistently flout authority in all its forms, appear to be manifestations of evil rather like Scaife in *The Hill*—dishonest, dissipated, probably sexually precocious, and certainly liable to corrupt the "pure-minded" boys of the masters' fancy. And it is true that the precise moral recommendations of the Hughes/Farrar tradition (prayer, self-examination, studiousness, respect for masters "in loco

parentis") are consistently and deliberately undercut here. But Kipling attacks the clichéd letter of the law in order that the spirit might
live.

The College has not been united by moral earnestness into an
ideal community, but it is the adult rather than the boyish ego that is
to blame. As the chaplain, the headmaster, and the Co. well know, a
schoolteacher's is "a dwarfing life—a belittling life, my brethren."
Locked forever into the world of boyhood, King and Macrae and
most of the other staff members have become tyrants whose worst
offense is their pettiness, and as the Head points out, "It isn't the
boys that make trouble; it's the masters." Stalky and his cohorts, passionately idealistic in a way that only the Head has sufficient perception to understand, find themselves faced with an authority structure
built on hypocrisy: the masters claim to be the boys' moral superiors,
but in fact rule purely by physical power, pretending all the while
that their strength is as the strength of ten because their hearts are
pure rather than because increased maturity brings increased mus-
culature. Worse, the goal of this unjust hierarchy is to force pupils,
too, to give up the gold for the tinsel, so that the Co. will surrender
its carefully worked-out system for determining what moral qualities
deserve respect and learn instead to say "'Yes, sir,' an' 'No, sir,' an'
'Oh, sir,' an' 'Please, sir,' like a lot o' filthy fa-ags."[73]

The Co. finds ostentatious earnestness to be simply a weapon with
which to beat the self-righteous at their own game ("Didn't I 'Eric'
'em splendidly?" gloats Beetle on one occasion). The self-sacrifice
that draws no attention to itself, however, is still grounds for hero-
worship. The crowning glory of the Head's career is when, at the
risk of his own, he saves the life of a boy dying of diphtheria and
tries his best to keep the exploit secret. The example of the alumni
who make little of wounds sustained in the service of their country is
better able than any master's harangue to exert influence upon the
boys as "an object-lesson, for moral effect and so forth."[74] Conversely, the slick jingoism of the "jelly-bellied flag-flapper" who ad-
dresses the school, to the disgust equally of the boys and the Head,
so repels Stalky that the boys disband their cadet corps lest their own
sincerer patriotism may be likewise too openly displayed.

The lessons of schoolboy life carry over into adulthood. Practically
speaking this means that guerrilla warfare against masters becomes
guerrilla warfare against Pathans and Sikhs—but also that those
graduates of the College who had learned in their time to form
"company" bonds with their peers and to operate as a group instead
of as individuals will be best able to serve their queen. (And, for that

matter, to feel dependent filial love for their old headmaster, who *is* "in loco parentis," all the more because he has never made a point of being so.) The chaplain doesn't talk to the boys "about ethics and moral codes, because I don't believe that the young of the human animal realizes what they mean for some years to come"; still, the moral codes are unconsciously formed and assimilated, and involve many of the same issues of comradely love and invisible self-sacrifice that they always have. Schools still mold character, but in Kipling's world they are not permitted to advertise the fact—so that in *Stalky*'s counterpart to the scene in *Tom Brown* when Tom suddenly realizes the Doctor's authorial influence on his soul, Beetle discovers that the Head has secretly arranged a career for him. "The Head says he'd been breaking me in for this for ever so long, and I never knew—I never knew," Beetle exclaims; but "breaking in," the reader knows if Beetle does not, has involved more than job training.[75] As Steven Marcus adeptly observes, *Stalky* is "both anti–*Tom Brown* and *Tom Brown* revived": iconoclastic in its revelations that in the masters, Victorian idealism has become corrupt, Hughes-like because "the boys are not opposed to these ideals in themselves. . . . Their rebelliousness is in fact intuitively directed by their feeling for them." Just as in its less emotionally complex predecessors, the overriding value in *Stalky* is "disregard of self."[76]

And the boys' all-for-one, one-for-all camaraderie, which has given them their position of "moral influence" in the school despite their lack of standing in the corrupt prefect-master power structures, ensures (as the adult Beetle points out) that Stalky and true morality will triumph—even if more conventional soldiers may have a hard time recognizing that Stalky is morality's agent. Stalky's incompatibility with the bureaucratic hierarchy in adulthood, as in boyhood, is at once a sign of virtue and a source of strength.

Robert F. Moss has written of another unassimilated Kipling hero, Mowgli: "The boy's alienation from his own society accounts for both his unhappiness and his spectacular success";[77] a similar point might be made about Stalky, who can intuit that the ordinary officer's rigidity is not a military virtue but a sign of the erosion of that virtue—just as in school, the masters' earnestness and sincerity have become, in Marcus's phrase, "their own corrupt opposites."[78] It is of course this corruption that accounts for the bitterness of *Stalky*'s tone. Good and evil, once so easily distinguishable, now masquerade as each other, to the disgruntlement of the good. Flexible enough to scorn custom, Stalky is paradoxically the greatest upholder of the Law—which in its ideal manifestation is less a chain of command than a cooperative comradeship; Kipling's dicta have much more in common with Hughes's than is immediately apparent. The primary difference between Stalky and Tom, and the reason that Stalky is cynical while Tom is "merry," is that Kipling's hero cannot expect society's approval for obeying the Law; only a few like-minded souls will have the moral perception to interpret his actions correctly.

While *Stalky*'s lessons may not always be immediately evident, Kipling admitted to a didactic intent.[79] It is improbable that Wodehouse would have made such a claim for his own school stories (of which the best, *Mike and Psmith,* appeared in 1908); yet while Wodehouse disliked the self-conscious religiosity of *Eric* and *Gerald Eversley* and rejected the idea of ostentatious self-sacrifice, it was the ostentation rather than the self-sacrifice that offended him. Thus, "while outdated conventions are scorned, Wodehouse's stories are profoundly supportive of the public school code and spirit."[80] Like the other antitraditionalist authors in this genre, he attacks the model for its insincerity, self-importance, and misreading of the boyish character—while endowing his heroes with updated and witty versions of precisely those virtues the model seeks to inculcate in readers.

Much of the humor of *Mike and Psmith* arises from Wodehouse's deft use of school-story conventions. Psmith arrives at Sedleigh aware that tradition requires him to acquire a new identity and communitarian ethics; accordingly he changes the spelling (though not the pronunciation) of his name and announces that his sudden conversion to communism justifies his "redistribution of the wealth" to ensure that he and Mike may have a study. Psmith is similarly in control of the sentimental rhetoric of the genre's classic wing: "'Your sisters froze on to your knees like little octopuses (or octopi), and screamed, "Don't go, Edwin!" And so,' said Psmith, deeply affected by his recital, 'you stayed on till the later train; and, on arrival, you find strange faces in the familiar room, a people that know not Spiller.'" Finally, he knows his plots. "Are you the Bully, the Pride of the School, or the Boy who is Led Astray and takes to Drink in Chapter Sixteen?" he asks Mike, while clearly casting himself as the Androgyne who must fight against Masculine Habits; his exquisite clothes and affectation of effeminacy mask a dreadful secret: "Imagine my feelings when I found that I was degenerating, little by little [the echo of *Eric* must be intentional], into a slow left-hand bowler with a swerve. I fought against it, but it was useless, and after a time I gave up the struggle."[81]

For all this gentle mockery, however, Psmith and Mike are hardly immune to the lure of the ideal. Mike has his moment of insight into his own failings, realizing that his unwillingness to forget his loyalty to his former school has been an unattractive blend of sullenness and egotism; he must learn to sacrifice his personal preferences and contribute his cricketing genius to the glory of Sedleigh. Psmith, meanwhile, has developed such a comradely (in the nonpolitical sense of the word) love for Mike that he will confess to wrongdoing not his own in order to get his innocent friend out of trouble. He objects, however, to the impropriety of having his sacrifice correctly interpreted: "'What really made you tell Downing you'd done it? . . . I believe it was simply to get me out of a jolly tight corner.' Psmith's expression was one of pain. 'My dear Comrade Jackson,' said he, 'you wrong me. You make me writhe. I'm surprised at you. I never thought to hear those words from Michael Jackson.'"[82] The new convention of the stiff upper lip, deriving from the shift in male sexual mores, has reclassified forthright statements of male affection as obscenity; only in novels such as *The Hill*, which represent the old guard against which Wodehouse is fighting, may two boys confess mutual fondness. But as long as it is conducted tacitly, the passionate friendship is as much an ideal in the turn-of-the-century antitraditional school story as it had ever been.

Ultimately, then, it was not the school story that betrayed the evangelical Arnoldian pattern; it was the school itself. The shock value of Alec Waugh's *The Loom of Youth* (1917) did not lie in Waugh's revelation that boys were prone to irreligion, homosexuality, cribbing, and all the other schoolboy sins, for *Eric* had said the same sixty years earlier. Rather the novel caused a furor because its realism could not be denied (Waugh had been a schoolboy a scant two years before publishing his roman à clef) and because readers therefore had to consider seriously its accusation that in investing all in athleticism, the modern school system inevitably creates precisely the opposite of the stated ideal.[83]

Unlike Farrar, Waugh finds that the fault lies not in ourselves but in our schools. His prep school has reared Gordon Caruthers to be an English schoolboy of the Angelic type, to whom swearing, lying, cheating, and sexuality are all anathema; his public school, Fernhurst, teaches him rather that it is the surface and not the substance that counts. Football both forms the surface and rots the substance; Gordon begins to crib so that he can have time to discuss games and learns that as long as one is games-minded no one minds anything else. As a minor character, Jeffries, complains on being expelled for homosexuality: "Who made me what I am but Fernhurst?

. . . Fernhurst made me worship games, and think that they alone mattered, and everything else could go to the deuce. I heard men say about bloods whose lives were an open scandal, 'Oh, it's all right, they can play football.' I thought it was all right too. Fernhurst made me think it was." The model English schoolboy, whose athleticism supposedly demonstrates his normalcy and team spirit, is in fact impure, ambitious, dishonest, ill-educated, irreligious, and shallow. "The one object of the Public School is to produce not great men, but a satisfactory type," avows Waugh, and the type produced is satisfactory only in the most superficial way. Leaving a school that has attempted via athleticism to subvert all his impulses toward truth and beauty, Gordon concludes that, after all, Fernhurst has prepared him well enough for adulthood; he "felt himself well equipped and fortified 'for the long littleness of life.'"[84] It is a double-edged tribute, both to the school and to adult society. England, it would seem, needs to replace real (evangelical?) men with cardboard cutouts of muscle-bound old boys because England itself is too shallow to tolerate maturity.

Like its predecessors, *The Loom* recapitulates *Eric;* unlike them, in doing so it condemns not the individual but his environment. Eric—and most of his heirs—had free will to make moral choices; a pawn in the hands of the public-school system, Gordon has none. And with the loss of moral power comes the loss of the ideal. By World War I, the evangelical hopes for the schoolboy as Angel have crumbled. Not the soul but the body rules, so that every pure-minded young Gordon Caruthers (or Alec Waugh) must resocialize himself to conform to the law of the jungle rather than to the law of heaven—and will very likely, like Waugh himself, be asked to leave for homosexuality. As late as Kipling we can hope that a good boy will become a good man, his need for character answered by the British schools. The disillusioned of the early twentieth century fear that "English character" is only a euphemism for all the adult sins the evangelicals had been trying for a hundred years to root out. As Waugh and many of his contemporaries suggested, it was possible to make a boy conform; it was not possible to make him combine conformity and virtue. The evangelicals, it would seem, had been right all along: at least in adolescence, goodness and normalcy are incompatible. Perhaps one reason for the demise of the Angelic ideal in fiction, then, was that beside it reality seemed too disheartening.

· FOUR ·

Character and Action
in Historical Tales

While school stories early accepted the ideals of androgynous manliness and abandoned them only with reluctance, the boys' historical novel in the period under discussion offers a muddier case. The school story's relatively smooth movement from the overtly to the covertly feminine is complicated in the historical novel by the tension between competing forms of didacticism within the genre. Perhaps because the children's historical novel precipitated out of the adult historical novel, its authors frequently disagree about whether they should teach history, character, patriotism, or nothing at all. Hence the prose style, focus, and ethical content of the historical novel may have little in common with contemporaneous examples of the school story; while most school stories of a particular era bear an astonishing family resemblance to each other, the checkered past of the historical novel permits great variation. Nevertheless, generalization is possible: over the half-century we are examining, the form wavers between two contradictory beliefs about the human relationship to history and about individuals' abilities to shape their own destiny. One group of authors primarily cares about historical truth, the other—more subversively—about "poetic truth." The first describes action, the second character. And while these two schools exist simultaneously throughout most of our period, by Edwardian times it was the interest in exterior rather than interior struggle that had achieved dominance, as the Angel gave way to the soldier.

Historical fiction in Britain took its impetus from Walter Scott, whose appeal for the Victorians was not merely the charm of costume drama but the fascination of sociological insight. Because

Scott's real interest is not in the individual but in the representative of a historical movement, his "real protagonists . . . not the leading characters but the states of society out of which they grow,"[1] the British historical novel was born with a tendency to view the hero as helpless in the grip of political destiny. Thus while such early novelists as Samuel Richardson had used the domestic form for moral didacticism by concentrating on character as grace under pressure, Scott used history to emphasize the pressures themselves, not as personal actions but as components of human progress. Character was not the point.

An unfortunate byproduct of Scott's phenomenal success was that less talented writers often concluded that since the genre's real protagonist was not an individual so much as an age or a social class, characterization was superfluous. The emphasis of the historical novel thus fell more often on what people did than on what people were like, leading to a tedium of early-Victorian novels in one of two categories. One was the historical romance, which James C. Simmons characterizes as "intrigue, costume, and history mixed together with little imagination and less art"; the other was the academic fiction, designed to teach historical facts rather than eternal truths.[2] The first was flavor without substance, the second substance without flavor, and neither satisfied the critics.

In the second half of the century, although critical disdain had almost put an end to the historical novel as a reputable form, nearly every Victorian author of note wrote an exercise in the genre—but few wrote more than one. For all the nineteenth-century fascination with the past, the historical novel never quite lost the hybrid status its qualifying adjective suggested. As a vehicle for escapism, education, or religious propaganda (Kingsley, Wiseman, and Newman all tried their hands at it in the 1850s), the historical novel could succeed. As art, critics increasingly suspected, it could not. Denigrated critically while enjoyed popularly, by the end of the century the historical novel had become a forum for hacks. Although more historical tales appeared between 1870 and 1914 than between 1820 and 1870, few of them were intended as high art, and most were aimed at children.[3]

The form that children inherited was thus traditionally biased against concentrating on character. But since forming character is the central concern of Victorian children's literature overall, a tension arose between impulse and medium. It is to this tension that we may trace the split within nineteenth-century historical novels for boys, wherein one branch shows history acting on the hero to reveal the "spirit of the hero," and the other places the hero within history to dramatize what Victorians called the "spirit of the age." The "hero" novel chiefly cares about personality, the "age" novel about plot. And while the first tends to support androgynous manliness as an ideal and especially to value asexual love, the second typically upholds physical manliness and sees its heroes as emotionally isolated.

One element that often indicates which emphasis will dominate any given novel is historical setting. Most historiographers hold that the nineteenth century was the first to experience a general sense that the past might differ significantly from the present. John Clive comments that "the idea of comparing one's own age with former ones, or with one's notion of those ages yet to come, had never before been as dominant,"[4] and in drawing these comparisons Victorian historians were primarily interested in discovering which ages had a particular bearing on their own. "The spirit of the age" was a popular concept, and finding kindred spirits a popular activity. Properly used, history could illuminate the present, if only one could discover which historical period was especially relevant to the concerns of the nineteenth century.

Originally this comparative method had developed out of the eighteenth-century assumption that history worked by means of never-changing laws, so that a thorough knowledge of classical battles would help one to defeat Napoleon. By the 1850s, however, Augustan generality was giving way to German particularity, and in the second half of the century, the tendency was to compare past to present in order to criticize one or the other. If all pasts were not alike, the particular past in which a particular writer was interested naturally suggested something about that writer's conception of the present. Hence authors with an evangelical bias were wont to set their tales during the Reformation or among the persecuted Lollards or Huguenots; self-criticism being a constant concern for this group, their novels often suggested that the vanished age was superior in enthusiasm, comradely love, or religiosity. Authors whose main concern was imperial, on the other hand, tended to concentrate on secular warfare. Their tales show less interest in androgynous manliness than in the qualities that make good soldiers and may leave readers with the impression that the nineteenth century represents civilization's apogee because Victorians wage more sophisticated wars than their predecessors. The didacticism of the two strains is different as well: the one mainly seeks to teach morals, the other to teach facts.

The Carlylean view of history as the story of great men seemed particularly suited to history for children, whom example might inspire to greatness on their own account. To most Victorian writers, true greatness was moral rather than worldly; in her study of school history textbooks from 1800 to 1914, Valerie Chancellor finds that before the end of the century character, not cleverness, decided lesson-books' attitudes toward any given ruler, and that text authors generally viewed history as a mine of moral good examples and awful warnings.[5] Such ideas obviously animate the first group of historical works we shall consider. What greatness consisted of in the "great man" novel (as opposed to its "great battle" counterpart) may become apparent from a discussion of J. G. Edgar's *The Boy Crusaders* (1865). In *Crusaders* we have a typical work by a prolific author for whom history was primarily an opportunity for didacticism, as we see from the subtitles of such of his nonfiction works as *The Boyhood of Great Men; Intended as an Example to Youth* (1853).

The tale's preface immediately orders the tale's priorities—to disseminate historical knowledge by giving "as faithful a picture as possible of the events which Joinville has recorded," but more importantly, "to convey, at the same time, as clear an idea as my limits would permit, of the renowned French monarch who, in peril and perplexity, in captivity and chains, so eminently signalised his valour and his piety." That Edgar depicts Louis IX in chains instead of armor immediately establishes the novel's definition of greatness; distinguished neither as statesman nor as soldier, Louis has mastered all the feminine virtues, and "his saintliness, his patience in affliction, his respect for justice and the rights of his neighbours, entitle him to a high place among the men of the age which could boast of so many royal heroes" of a more masculine stamp.[6]

Throughout the novel Edgar points up the contrast between the merely glamorous heroism of popular chivalry and the deeper, inconspicuous heroism of sainthood. Louis defines this distinction as that between *preuhomme* and *preudhomme*: "By preuhomme I mean a man who is valiant and bold in person, whereas by preudhomme I signify one who is prudent, discreet, and who fears God, and has a good conscience."[7] The task of the preudhomme, apparently, is to endure in womanly fashion the trouble the preuhommes bring upon humanity, and in the novel we see flashy masculinity lead again and again to disaster. The Crusaders' arrogance after having taken Damietta ultimately destroys the expedition, as English successes spark French jealousy and endanger the alliance's solidarity. Likewise, the count of Artois's physical courage is a liability, since it causes but can't control the count's disastrous impetuosity.

Louis's spiritual courage, on the other hand, is at its best when his fortunes are at their worst: "In chains and captivity [a recurring phrase] he exhibited the dignity of a king and the resignation of a Christian, and his jailers could not refrain from expressing their astonishment at the serene patience with which he bore adversity." Unlike the count, the king is a man for all seasons; androgyny is reliable because it is whole. Appropriately, the monarch never loses his instinctive respect for femininity, telling his captors that he cannot pay his ransom without his queen's approval. When the Saracen ambassador expresses surprise that Louis should consult someone "who is but a woman," the preudhomme is quick to teach: " 'She is my lady and companion,' answered Louis, even at that moment mindful of the principles of chivalry; 'and it is only reasonable that her consent should be obtained.' "[8]

Although he is the hero of the novel, Louis is not the protagonist. To the extent that there is a main character, he is Walter Espec, who joins the Crusade to seek his brother, a monk who disappeared during the Children's Crusade. But the author treats Walter's quest, attainment of position, and inevitable good marriage with obvious lack of interest; the boy's personality is largely a blank into which readers may project themselves, the better to pay their respects to Louis. Thus the stock romantic hero, young, handsome, burdened with a secret sorrow, and trying to win his spurs through glorious adventure, really doesn't count. Walter's brand of heroism just isn't as good as Louis's, and again and again the author drives the point home.

One problem facing the researcher into mid-Victorian historical tales for children is assessing the stories' intended audience. Edgar's novel, with a masculine title and an author whose *Crecy and Poictiers* had been the first serial in Samuel Beeton's *Boy's Own Volume* (Midsummer 1863), presumably aimed at a predominantly male group. Other cases are less clear-cut. Charlotte M. Yonge, for instance, wrote her domestic novels largely for girls and women. Her historical novels, however, often have male protagonists and titles redolent of knightly adventure; nineteenth-century editions unearthed in secondhand bookstores are as likely to have a boy's name on the flyleaf as a girl's. While she recognized that most fictional genres appeal to one gender or the other, Yonge seems to have considered historical tales unisex; in *What Books to Lend and What to Give* (1887) she explains that such novels "are of considerable value [to children in general], not only as serving as 'sugared history' and conveying facts, but sometimes as supplying the element of romance which is almost essential to a wholesome development." It is this "element of romance" that strikes her as the key to providing boys with models that will prove at once wholesome and popular: "Boys especially should . . . have heroism and nobleness kept before their eyes; and learn to despise all that is untruthful or cowardly and to respect womanhood. True manhood needs, above all earthly qualities, to be impressed upon them, and books of example (not precept) with heroes, whose sentiments they admire, may always raise their tone."[9]

What Yonge means by "true manhood" is, as we might expect, highly androgynous and thoroughly Christian. In *The Caged Lion* (1870) the protagonist and most of the supporting characters are male, but few of them are "true men"; the action takes the fifteenth-century Scottish hero, Malcolm Stewart, through a variety of types of manliness until he is at last advanced enough to meet the heroine on a plane of genderless and sexless equality. When we first meet Malcolm he is markedly girlish, "a boy of about seventeen, with soft pensive dark eyes and a sickly complexion,"[10] and his enemies are trying to shame him into a monastery on the grounds that he will never become a real man. In fact, Yonge suggests, Malcolm's eagerness to enter the pleasant life of cloistered meditation, leaving his sister and the outside world to take care of themselves, lends some weight to these criticisms; so Malcolm is lucky to become attached to the train of the captive Scottish king, James I. Immediately attracted to his young cousin's gentleness and sensitivity, James introduces the boy to society, hoping to bestow on him physical strength through warlike exercise and worldly power through a marriage to the wealthy Esclairmonde.

Finding physical and sexual manhood, however, may lose Malcolm his soul. As he gains muscle he gains egotism, and "those tokens of superiority to the faults of his time and country which had caused the King to seek him for a companion seemed to have vanished with his feebleness and timidity." While the charitable Esclairmonde tries to excuse him by noting that he has grown "more manly" in his year at the wars, her friend Alice perceives that "his boyhood was better than such manhood." Malcolm commits the cardinal sin of disrespect, setting himself against Henry V of England (James's friend and jailer—in Yonge's world the two roles are compatible) and, even worse, sacrilegiously planning the sexual humbling of Esclairmonde, who is destined to be not his bride but Christ's. To some extent Malcolm's sexual pretensions to the heroine are James's fault; not entirely sound himself on true manliness, James thinks that the boy's femininity and the woman's strength signal a perfect match and asserts, "Love is the way to make a man of him." Only Henry's inspiring death (a common trope also in Yonge's domestic fiction) forces Malcolm to recognize the danger into which his ego has led him, and the last third of the novel explains how "the expense of all possible earthly projects for his own happiness or ambition—was such as to bring out that higher side of his nature that had well-nigh collapsed." After his own near-fatal illness, Malcolm rises "from his bed notably advanced in manliness," having regained all the "elevation, tenderness, and refinement" he had demonstrated in his younger days.[11] At last he finds his mission: he joins the priesthood to roam Scotland as a pauper, teaching the people. Only in joint celibacy and renunciation of egocentric aristocratic goals can Malcolm be united to Esclairmonde, and he places their betrothal ring on the altar at Jerusalem.

For Yonge sexless love is at the heart of both true manliness and true womanliness. Virtue in *The Caged Lion* is inextricable from continence, so that Henry's early unrequited love "had a beneficial effect. Next after his deep sense of religion, it kept his life pure and chivalrous." Similarly, Esclairmonde's refusal to marry a man who, unlike Malcolm, attracts her physically fills her with the ecstasy of renunciation; at last she has "a *real* sacrifice to offer." The long, hard "spiritualizing" of Malcolm's feeling for his ladylove is necessary before she can offer him true inspiration, while his early dreams of her "more as the woman, less as the saint" indicate that strength of body has overpowered strength of soul. Likewise, the passionate friendship of Malcolm and James may spring from "something in . . . Malcolm, that makes a man turn to [him] for fellow-feeling, even as to a wife," as James says, and their embraces may provide "a strange bliss,"[12] but homoeroticism here is blessing rather than bane; since to a mid-Victorian their love must be pure, it must also be elevating. *The Caged Lion* shows surprising frankness about the sexual drive, possibly because Yonge is writing for a mixed audience, and the message is always the same: real men, like real women, sink the flesh in the spirit.

Just as Yonge contrasts asexual androgynous manliness with the merely macho, so too she contrasts the true nobleness of fifteenth-century England with the barbarism of a Scotland that is more chivalric than Christian. Scotland is lawless, violent, and ignorant;

4. *The Androgynous Pilgrimage*. Similarly costumed, featured, and posed, Malcolm and his sister flee a threatening world. An 1880 illustration by W. J. Hennessy to Charlotte Yonge's *The Caged Lion*.

brought up in this backward land, Malcolm's cousin Patrick may do credit to "his training in the highest school of chivalry" but is too masculine to be genuinely civilized. Pursuing the Scottish nobles who have abducted his sister, Malcolm loathes the contrast between gentle England and its northern neighbor, for "the horrible scurrility and savagery that greeted him on all sides made his heart faint at the thought of his Lily in this cage of foul animals"—yet what revolts him is in fact "all the state that Scottish majesty was capable of."[13] In the absence of true religion, the Scottish Middle Ages are dark indeed, and Malcolm's effort to gentle them, as by offering Christian consolation to his adored James's murderers, is the keystone of his life's work.

Considering the nineteenth century's fascination with the Middle Ages, Yonge's rejection of chivalry may seem odd. Prince Albert, for instance, perennially tried to link the code of the Victorian gentleman with that of the medieval knight; Albert sat for an 1844 portrait in full armor. Through the middle of the century, image-makers supplied a chivalric gloss to everyday life, and a special feature of Victorian knightliness from the 1850s onward was the equation of chivalry and purity.[14] From Tennyson and the Pre-Raphaelites to reenactments of tournaments and an explosion of novels with medieval settings, a fascination with the Middle Ages was crucial to the Victorian imagining of the past. Alice Chandler argues that this obsession signaled a rejection of the fragmentation and hurry of the industrialized world in favor of an era putatively superior in piety, order, and general human happiness. The medieval stood for an emotional approach to life instead of a soulless utilitarianism and symbolized for many Victorians a golden age in which society had been able to control a human mass perennially "fallible, selfish . . . and prone to weakness, error, and greed."[15] If medievalist criticisms of modern life so closely resemble Yonge's own, and moreover emanate from people as influential as Carlyle and Ruskin (to name but two), why doesn't she join the crowd?

One reason may be that she shares Thomas Arnold's feelings on the subject. Mark Girouard reports that Arnold opposed the chivalric fashion on the grounds that it "set personal allegiances before God, and the concept of honour before that of justice."[16] Similarly, Scott (an early hero of Yonge's) had also portrayed chivalry as insufficient,[17] although for all Scott's influence on Victorian views of history, this was one of his views that generally failed to persuade. But more important, perhaps, is that Yonge's portrait of the medieval age is plainly intended also as a portrait of her own, just as her dicta on true manliness don't apply only to boys dead for four centuries. In exposing medieval chivalry as much show but little heart, she can comment obliquely on the Victorian chivalry that paid women elaborate courtesies but little real heed. Despite their Angelic pretensions, both codes merely provide men excuses for self-aggrandizement and hinder self-improvement. The unreformed Malcolm never offends against chivalry with regard to Esclairmonde, since knights are supposed to woo ladies; nevertheless, his suit is wrong because it is egotistical. Similarly, chivalry encourages such perversions of love as dueling for a woman's favor, and so favors the physical over the spiritual. As Yonge demonstrates, the code grows out of lust, violence, and money, none of which can compete morally with the asexual Christian sisterhood that is the basis of the novel and of any ideal society. In rejecting the fashion of both ages, Yonge's novel goes outside time to preference feminine worlds above masculine worlds. Like Charles Reade's *The Cloister and the Hearth*, it "turns the historical setting itself into the hero's antagonist. The novel becomes the story of the hero *against* his age."[18]

Paradoxically, then, Yonge's novel, hymning renunciation and passivity, pits the hero against the dominant values of his society to give that hero extraordinary ultimate power. Like the heroines of nineteenth-century tracts, Malcolm has apparently inspired a real improvement in his contemporaries; he has done something to influence the "spirit of the age." Thus the character-centered or femininist branch of the genre may offer androgynous manliness as the solution to a helplessness that in action-centered historical novels appears inescapable. Harry E. Shaw argues that one of historical fiction's ground rules is that character illuminates events and ages but does not cause them[19]—a generalization that rings false for Yonge and her ilk, but that does aptly describe "masculinist" historical fiction. In the latter school of novels, the hero may go "with Wolfe in Canada" or "with Kitchener to Khartoum," but for all the swashbuckling activity inherent in such adventures, he is essentially an observer. To the character-centered historical novelist, this "realism" is anathema; since by Christian doctrine every human soul is "involved in mankind," the most obscure person in worldly terms must still affect society for good or ill.

By the twentieth century, as the masculinist form was coming to dominate the genre, Yonge often struck critics as annoyingly ahistorical. Eveline C. Godley wrote in the *National Review* in May 1906: "Much of her later work is hopelessly disfigured . . . not only by archaic mannerisms, but also by a habit of making all her favourite characters, of whatever nation or period, talk and act on sound Church of England principles."[20] In fact, such criticism is irrelevant to the aims of the femininist historical novel, which cares less for reproducing the past than for offering a model for the present.

John Henry Raleigh suggests that some of Scott's appeal for nineteenth-century readers lay in the wealth of homely detail he included in his novels: "He made the great familiar, and he made the past believable."[21] His audience felt that they were glimpsing not only the smooth surface of official history but also the ragged underside, the everyday lives of the little and forgotten. We might suppose that this delight in viewing history through the worm's eye would ally Scott with the femininist writers who succeeded him. On the contrary, Scott seems to have adopted this concentration on the Rosencrantzes and Guildensterns of the historical tableau because it gave him an excuse to make character secondary. His protagonists, as Culler argues, are usually more acted upon than acting, and "because Scott is interested in society and does not wish to embody a 'great man' theory of history, his hero has a kind of passivity, or 'negative capability,' which enables him to register the forces directed upon him but not himself to constitute a force."[22] To Scott, moral growth matters little.

While they inherited many of the conventions Scott established, however, the writers of femininist, character-oriented historical tales nonetheless manage to combine a focus on the supposedly unimportant with their own brand of "great man theory." They imply that while worldly power comes and goes, real action—which changes not status but hearts—lasts forever. Indeed, because worldly power tends to enlarge the ego and shrink the communicative faculties, it is usually incompatible with true greatness. Thus while femininist historical novelists would agree with Carlyle that history is the story of great men (or women), most of them would add a footnote to the effect that the history of the truly great is seldom known. We only hear about the notorious.

To some extent, then, character-centered historical novels serve as a rejection of traditional history, which is biased toward the flashy, just as nineteenth-century philistines chased commercial glitter instead of heavenly gold. Because of these novels' implicit stance that our sense of history is inside out, historical accuracy can be a low priority. Thus another popular femininist effort, *The Carved Cartoon* (1874), by Austin Clare (Wilhelmina Martha James), not only shares with Yonge's work the occasional authorial remark that poetic truth demands a loose attitude toward fact but even gets the title cheerfully wrong; Clare's contemporaries gleefully noted her mistake in calling a wooden plaque of Tintoretto's *Crucifixion* a "carved cartoon." But Clare aims to give her readers (again presumably boys, given the pseudonym of the author and the gender of nearly all the characters) more than mere details of art and history: her object is to explain the nature of true greatness.

Set in Restoration London, *The Carved Cartoon* offers glimpses of all manner of famous men, from Charles II to Paganini. The Yongean emphasis, however, is on those "unlike the great kings, statesmen, and warriors, whose actions [took] immediate and powerful effect" on their environment—those who, "by the more unobtrusive character of their lives and occupations, have left but little trace of their presence" but whose greater merits may become clear to more discerning generations.[23] The central character is Grinling Gibbons, the obscurity of whose biography is for Clare at once a convenience and a major thematic point. For the story deals primarily with the young Gibbons's gradual coming to terms with powerlessness and his simultaneous achievement of an androgynous influence outlasting and exceeding Charles's male power.

When first we meet him Gibbons has all the basic heroic virtues but has yet to attain the finishing touches of spiritual refinement. He is honest, hardworking, modest about his talent, and kind to the needy. He saves Silvio, a young Italian violinist, from an anti-Catholic mob and spends his money on a new violin for the other boy instead of on the new carving tools he needs himself. This first unselfish act makes possible all Gibbons's later spiritual successes, for in the passionate friendship that springs up between the two boys, both can give free rein to the noble, emotional, feminine traits that are the wellsprings of their talents. Although Gibbons initially has "all an English boy's dislike to seeing anyone cry," within a few minutes of their first meeting this masculine prejudice crumbles when "his own eyes [become] suspiciously wet" from Silvio's gratitude. Similarly, Silvio's altruism takes a feminine context, as he repays his debt by nursing his benefactor through the Great Plague. Illness and tenderness have their usual effect upon the English boy; he revels in the way Silvio "took the sick lad's hand and fondled it after the caressing fashion that Gibbons had grown to love," and the invalid's "deep blue eyes . . . seemed daily to grow larger and more spiritual, fixed upon the old print of the great example of patient suffering [the Tintoretto print from which he gets the inspiration for his masterpiece]."[24]

Physical helplessness and moral courage as exemplified by both nursing and suffering are the basis of a manliness that Clare sees as equivalent to unselfishness, and which the novel's heroine (a "Christian Jewess" who exists chiefly as a marriageable surrogate for Silvio) is also achieving offstage. As Gibbons undergoes more and more tribulations with greater and greater patience, his art improves proportionately. He learns that art should glorify not its creator but *the* Creator. Christopher Wren appears in the novel in order to present its moral: "It is the fate of most men in this weary world of ours to be overlooked and misunderstood; to have their projects slighted and laid aside, even though they be designed for the glory of God. It *is* hard, my lad, and yet— . . . It is best so, perhaps; if these projects *are* really for His glory, they will be carried out in due time." The London Fire parallels the metaphorical flames of the persecutions heaped on Gibbons by a jealous inferior and by his future wife's money-loving father, and both city and boy emerge more beautiful for the experience. After years of patient work spent in obscure domesticity with Silvio, "the thought of personal fame no longer held the prominent, all-absorbing part it had once done. Frequent disappointment, frequent checks, and, perhaps still more, the uneventful quiet of the last four years, had done much to subdue the too eager spirit of the young carver." Gibbons has finally learned "to seek the glory of God rather than his own advancement."[25]

In his willingness to abandon personal ambition, Gibbons has taken the only route to real power. His talents approach a perfection impossible to artists ruled by petty ego and gain him not only worldly success as official carver to Charles II (actually to George I, as Clare observes in a footnote—again, accuracy is secondary), but also eternal success as one of the great artists who in praising God teach humankind. The awe we feel in St. Paul's, Clare suggests, improves our characters even though we may not know Wren's name, just as the inspiration Gibbons gets from the long-dead Tintoretto outweighs the encouragement he gets from the living and "powerful" king. We must therefore accept the fiction that Silvio becomes Paganini's successor; history may not note his existence, but the equivalency of genuine greatness and androgynous humility means that official history will often fail to chronicle the happenings that really matter. As femininist historical novels typically suggest, we can't believe what we read in the history books.

The rewriting of history characteristic of this branch of historical novels may extend to a rewriting of sociology as well. In W.H.G. Kingston's *Exiled for the Faith*, originally published as *Villegagnon* (ca. 1870s), the emphasis is on the souls of religious groups rather than individuals. Kingston's aim is to prove the superiority of Protestant-ism over Roman Catholicism by suggesting that the former is the truly feminine creed, the latter only spuriously so. Thus of Catholics he comments that "when in the minority, they are humble and meek, plausible and silver-tongued; and when there are none to op-pose them, haughty, indolent, sensual, and self-indulgent." In other words, they cover their masculine faults, when expedient, with a cloak of feminine virtue. Not so the Huguenots, who are innately good and innately nonviolent, because "it becomes us not to fight with carnal weapons; such is Dr. Calvin's advice."[26]

The false femininity of Kingston's Catholic priests suggests a greater insincerity: the author argues that they disbelieve their own religion and support it only from a wish for power; as his priests explain, "We cannot allow a doctrine which so greatly supports our authority to be called in question." Conversely, his Huguenots are spotlessly honest, refusing, for example, to be rescued from their Catholic captors unless the rescue can be accomplished in a "mild, gentle, and forgiving" spirit. Such is the obvious superiority of Prot-estantism in Kingston's mind that when the two groups reach South America, his Indians immediately recognize that Catholicism is so like their own religion in "worshiping images" that it must be idol-atrous, whereas Calvinism rings true because it is so alien to every-thing the Indians have believed hitherto.[27] In Kingston's improbable version of local history, the native South Americans become Protes-tant, underscoring their conversion to the feminine ideal by giving their final allegiance to a woman chief. Sly Catholicism gives way to humble Protestantism, violence and trickery to peace, morality, and Christian missions. And while the Catholics seek world domination, the hero and heroine want only to reach England, a country offering less wealth but more personal freedom than Romanist France.

The religious historical novel forms an enormous subcategory within the nineteenth-century historical novel for children (and for adults), given the commonness of the inclination to use the form for propaganda. Nevertheless, the rejection of the social criteria that confer greatness on seekers of glory instead of on seekers of good need not be overtly Christian. An intriguingly secular example of a historical novel that finally comes out against the deeds that make history is Robert Louis Stevenson's *The Black Arrow* (1888), written by a man who early grieved his father by professing unbelief—but nonetheless concerning itself with many of the same issues of an-drogyny and passive virtue that typify the novels of Yonge, Clare, and Kingston.

Stevenson's romance of the Roses has left most critics cold; they follow the pattern Stevenson himself set when he called it "a poor thing," "a whole tale of tushery. And every tusher tushes me so free, that may I be tushed if the whole thing is worth a tush."[28] True, the implication that the novel's dialect is artificial is irrefutable; still, the saga of Richard Shelton and Richard Plantagenet is far superior to most nineteenth-century juvenile historical novels and well worth examining for its relationship to other Stevenson works and to antisociety, character-oriented tales of the past. In *The Black Arrow* we witness what Leslie Fiedler terms the typically Stevensonian romance of "the Boy and the Scoundrel"; but that theme dwindles beside the rival and (for Stevenson) atypical romance of a virtue that succeeds through its androgyny in becoming attractively rebellious, escaping that other Stevensonian trope, "the unloveliness of good."[29]

Richard Shelton is one of Stevenson's more stupid boy heroes, taking several chapters more than the average reader to figure out that his foster father is a villain, his milksop sidekick a girl, and—most importantly and most subtly—his own derring-do a disaster. Reared by his father's murderer, Sir Daniel, to believe that manhood consists solely of physical valor, Dick has no opinion of women and only a cursory interest in the news that he is engaged to the heiress Joanna Sedley, whom he has never seen. Over the first part of the novel, Stevenson discredits Sir Daniel, showing that "his dash, his proved courage" mean little next to his indefatigable money grubbing and his belief that might is right. Unconcerned with personal honor, Sir Daniel finds political decision making easy: "This old Harry the Sixt has had the undermost. Wash we, then, our hands of him." Understandably, Dick's upbringing has left him a social Darwinist; he believes that "the better man throweth the worse, and the worse is well served."[30] He thus desperately needs Joanna to supplant Sir Daniel as his moral tutor.

When Dick first meets her, she is disguised as a boy and fleeing Sir Daniel. Dick offers assistance somewhat against his will; the soidisant Matcham impresses him as effeminate and tearful, though possessing certain manly skills (such as swimming) that Dick envies. Joanna's belief that right matters more than power strikes Dick as peculiar, and still more, subversive: such a reordering of priorities, he senses, will turn society upside down. While he thinks her a boy, then, they spend most of their time squabbling; despite his realization that her version of manliness might be superior to his own, he is loath to embrace it. On discovering that she is female, however, he leaps to embrace *her*, believing a boyish girl infinitely preferable to a girlish boy. "Y' are the best maid and the bravest under heaven," he decides on knowing her gender, although a minute earlier they had been at one another's throat, "and, if only I could live, I would marry you blithely; and, live or die, I love you."[31] Dick's reaction to the revealed Joanna is encouraging, in that it replaces the commercial motivation for their marriage with an emotional one, but it is still inadequate, since he has yet to accept that not her boyishness but her ideals make her valuable. The courage he applauds is all very well, but Joanna's code has more to offer than courage.

The second half of the novel thus concentrates on Dick's quest to regain Joanna and overcome Sir Daniel. The boy acquires new foster fathers, new bonds based on loyalties rather than money. Even these ties are inadequate, however, because they hinge on arms instead of love. Slowly Dick recognizes warfare's heavy component of luck— "How easily the battle had gone otherwise," he marvels on one occasion—and so learns that justice differs from strength. He sees too that one can't depend on strength to obtain justice for oneself but only to condemn innocent people to suffering when one makes the attempt. True manliness is antithetical to arrogant masculine force, as it is to the irresponsible masculine sensuality of Dick's attractive but aptly named new comrade Lawless: " 'Beast!' he hissed—'beast and no man! It is worse than treachery to be so witless.' "[32] These discoveries, and Dick's growing capacity for guilt when his thoughtless instinct for action ruins the livelihoods of bystanders, represent an important innovation in the pattern of fifteenth-century society, which Stevenson suggests was predicated on the assumption that those who lack power also lack human feelings.

By the end of the story, therefore, Dick finds himself at odds with the spirit of the age into which he had previously fit so well. While at first he thought only of personal advancement, under Joanna's influence he begins to wish himself out of society entirely. For a time, for example, he fights under the banner of the future Richard III (a footnote reminds us that the historical Richard was only a child at the time—another instance of a character-oriented novel preferring moral to fact). Richard Plantagenet is macho manliness gone wild, a great warrior and commander whose misshapen body mirrors his misshapen soul. Embittered by the thought that his deformity puts feminine love and tenderness forever beyond his grasp, Plantagenet suggests the Victorian invalid child turned inside out, so that when a battle pits "the tall, splendid, and famous warrior against the deformed and sickly boy," it is in the physical arena, not the spiritual, that the latter conquers.[33] There is something of a Jekyll-and-Hyde aspect to the relationship of the two Richards (that they share a name is underlined throughout), but in this version Jekyll may escape his alter ego; though Plantagenet offers Shelton worldly advancement, adventure, and martial manliness, Dick accepts Joanna's influence by "wasting" his chance in begging the life of a Lancastrian sailor he had earlier injured. The boy has learned that might and right are separate, even contradictory, and discovers as well that even sacrifice won't always atone for force.

Renunciation intoxicates the reformed Dick, who even considers giving up Joanna when he worries that he has wronged another young woman and may owe restitution. Fortunately, however, the second girl (one of Joanna's friends) understands the situation better: Dick should sacrifice glory but has no right to sacrifice virtue and love. After Dick has proved his worthiness by abandoning his vengeance against his father's murderer, thus turning from masculinity's teachings and endorsing instead the morality of Joanna and the Church, the marriage can finally take place. It puts the pair outside history, and the last we know of hero and heroine is that "the dust and blood of that unruly epoch passed them by."[34]

In its suggestion that both happiness and morality dwell in feminine obscurity instead of in masculine history making, *The Black Arrow* offers a new twist to the Stevensonian obsession with evil. For once, good appears more attractive and complex than its opposite, which in the final analysis only offers blood, sweat, and tears. That its author played down the novel's importance may relate to its entire acceptance of the ideals of androgynous manliness and feminine virtue, a paradigm that by 1888 was already becoming old-fashioned. These values, after all, had more to do with Stevenson's childhood than with his adulthood; Paul Binding reports that the young Stevenson was teased for his androgyny (town boys would greet him with cries of "Hauf a laddie, hauf a lassie, hauf a yellow yike") and for the pacifism that got him "called 'daftie' and 'softie.'" In Binding's view, Stevenson's coming of age entailed the arduous realization 8that there are many other ways of being good than those of the tract child in the Puritanical Sabbath story."[35] Thus *The Black Arrow's* attempt to tie the tract child's feminine virtue to Stevenson's fascination with heroic rebellion may well have struck its author as an unsuccessful bastardization.

Andrew Noble comments that one of Stevenson's favorite themes is that of the destruction of the young man unable to extricate himself from corrupt authority.[36] In *The Black Arrow* the young man does succeed in divorcing himself from the social hierarchy, but paradoxically, he can only do so by joining a literary tradition that Stevenson may have associated with his own immaturity—and to be immature is to be under authority. In one sense, then, the conventions Dick escapes are the conventions of Stevenson himself. We should perhaps not wonder that the Scottish writer's other important historical novel of this period, *Kidnapped* (1886), is usually considered more "mature"; the sage of David Balfour and Alan Breck Stewart generally follows the same boyish ethic, slowly beginning to dominate fashion in this period, that the story of Dick Shelton rejects as inadequate.

But in harking back to midcentury androgyny, *The Black Arrow* is no anomaly among late-Victorian historical romances. Arthur Conan Doyle's *The White Company* (1891), which Doyle himself, at least, much preferred to his detective stories, likewise shares many of the concerns of Yonge's historical novels—not least the feminine hero. Set in 1366, the novel follows the adventures of the monastery-educated Alleyne. Since Doyle is writing in a time when true manliness must be patently heterosexual, his protagonist causes him a few problems: with his "gentle, monk-bred ways," artistic and musical talent, "not a hair to [his] face, and a skin like a girl," "eyes of a bashful maid, and hair like a three years' babe," Alleyne obviously deserves his coarse brother's taunt, "Art neither man nor woman, young shaveling." Faced with the task of demonstrating to incredulous readers the "native firmness and strength" that "relieved him of any trace of effeminacy,"[37] Doyle follows Stevenson's late-Victorian lead by equating Alleyne's spiritual growth with his discovery of heterosexual love.

Although "a woman, in monkish precepts, had been the embodiment and concentration of what was dangerous and evil," Alleyne soon discovers "that in [women's] presence he was conscious of a quick sympathy, a pleasant ease, a ready response to all that was most gentle and best in himself, which filled his soul with a vague and new-found joy."[38] Romance thus frees Alleyne to become more androgynous, to explore love instead of power, and to escape the wrongheaded manliness of the cloister, where the dearth of femininity had transformed the celibates' spiritual strivings into petty bickering and underhand ambition. Because neither the brotherhood of the monks nor the brotherhood of blood kin is possible for Alleyne, he joins the military brotherhood of the White Company; that this is the right choice is immediately apparent when we notice the androgyny of its commander, Sir Nigel Loring, a feminine man married to a masculine woman. The military, it seems, offers men their best chance to get to know women—and in some wise to become them.

Sir Nigel's daughter, Maude, is Alleyne's destined wife, and here again the bride may be more naturally masculine than the groom: like *The Black Arrow*, *The White Company* telescopes same-sex passionate friendships and heterosexual love into a single relationship by bending genders. But Maude's advantage in being biologically female apparently makes her sounder than her beloved on moral doctrine. It is she who explains to him the selfishness of the clergy and the comparative nobility of men like Sir Nigel; monks, praying in their cloister for their own salvation, have none of the advanced feminine virtues of the White Company's leader, who, according to Maude, "when he rides into the press of fight . . . is not thinking ever of the saving of his own poor body. . . . I would have them [ecclesiastics] live as others, and do men's work in the world, preaching by their lives rather than their words." "Men's work," in other words, is the same as women's: unobtrusive and selfless influence. Under Maude's sway Alleyne concedes that "the men with whom he was thrown in contact, rough-tongued, fierce and quarrelsome as they were, were yet of deeper nature and of more service in the world than the ox-eyed brethren who rose and ate and slept from year's end to year's end in their own narrow stagnant circle of existence."[39] But most manly of all are those who combine unselfish usefulness with feminine refinement; Sir Nigel is the gentlest as well as the bravest of the group—and, saving only Alleyne, the most firmly in love with his chosen lady. Writing after celibacy had become suspect, Doyle must approach androgyny through "normal" heterosexuality.

Not territorial conquest but spiritual conquest animates the militarist ethos of the *The White Company*, permitting the equation of battle with androgynous selflessness. Although Doyle clearly has empire in mind (for instance, he dedicates his tale to "the hope of the future, the Reunion of the English-Speaking Races"), all the imperial spadework the White Company is accomplishing will go for nought when Britain abandons its claim to France. The company's bloody sacrifices do nothing lasting for British finances—but do eternal good to the British spirit. Economics are not the point; Sir Nigel has to purge from the troop fourteen men who care more for "a well-lined purse" than patriotic poverty. More important than profit are the spiritual gains that come from sacrificing comfort, showing mercy, and generally becoming worthy of a good woman. Military strength alone confers neither virtue nor brotherhood, as we find when

Alleyne's horrible brother falls at the hands of his own men while attempting to carry off Maude for her money. Nor is war an end in itself, since nothing can substitute for androgynous married bliss; Alleyne returns at last, "a long seam upon his brow and a scar upon his temple [giving] a manly grace to his refined and delicate countenance," to save Maude from the cloister in his turn.[40] Sex and selflessness win.

We now turn to the rival school within the boys' historical novel—to those narratives that center on plot instead of character, care more about historical truth than about moral truth, and prefer denouements that place the hero within society to those that oppose him to his era. Their authors suggest that worldly success, not heavenly rest, is true happiness, and they stress such values as physical strength and courage, industry, common sense, and even good luck. In short, they preach the secular manliness that was slowly replacing androgynous manliness during the latter half of the nineteenth century. From its beginnings the historical form had lent itself to a nonfemininist depiction of protagonists with little interior life and less influence; nevertheless, it took the arrival of G. A. Henty on the literary scene—as the most influential boys' writer of the late nineteenth century[41]—to enthrone macho manliness as the genre's dominant ethic.

Like most Victorian historical novelists, Henty writes about the past in order to comment on the present; whether set one year or a thousand before the publication date, his subject is always in some sense current events, just as he always views current events as part of history. His focus is almost exclusively political—the international balance of power, the duty of subject to monarch, the need for a strong navy, the role of empire in the future of Britain and of the world. Thus an early Henty effort, *The Young Franc-Tireurs* (1871), was chiefly intended to warn his young readers against the German menace; not individual character but national character was at issue.[42] It is in an 1881 preface to this same work that Henty describes his overall goal in writing: less to inculcate morality or improve society than to teach military history by "giving under the guise of historical tales full and accurate accounts of all the leading events of great wars."[43] For Henty life was a matter of physical rather than moral struggle; indeed, the difference between him and his rivals of the androgynous school is perhaps best illustrated by the story that he once recommended Stevenson to "have less psychology and more claymores."[44]

Henty's preference for action over thought complicates his didactic urge. Because he cares so much about how events happened, accuracy edges out morality in his novels. As editor of the short-lived boys' magazine the *Union Jack,* perhaps his chief concern was that "lads [might] rely upon the information conveyed in [the magazine fiction] to be trustworthy and genuine."[45] Accordingly, André Rault explains, while after 1870 adult historical fiction was moving away from facts and toward the free play of imagination, Henty led his followers in the opposite direction; "moins littéraires que péda-gogiques" ("less literary than pedagogical"), their works are teaching tools meant to illustrate the glories of the British constitution or the role of the British navy in establishing the empire.[46] By reading about what English boys have done in the past to make England great, modern English boys will learn how to act in the future to keep her so. A knowledge of the glorious past is essential to a glorious present.

Naturally the sturdy virtues of the British yeomanry are also crucial to greatness, and another of Henty's aims is to inculcate his own brand of character and manliness in his readers. To do so he created the Henty boy-hero. Middling in intelligence, birth, and native ability, the Henty hero represents Henty's idea of what the average British schoolboy could be if he tried. The model never varies; Rault aptly terms it the " 'portrait-robot' . . . qui . . . est un peu toujours le même" ("who . . . is a little monotonous").[47] The idea behind having such an accessible and predictable hero is plainly to encourage the reader to project himself into the character and thereby to take a personal interest not only in the details of battles and campaigns but in the hero's ultimate success. Ideally, some sort of imprinting process will take place, and the manliness of the hero will become the manliness of the reader.

But the pitfall in this method of transmitting ideals is that Henty's formula is essentially anti-ideal. Henty heroes don't worry about becoming better people; within their limited type they are born perfect. While over the course of the story sturdy, broad-shouldered boys may develop into tall, well-muscled men, mentally and morally Henty's heroes spring full-grown from the head of their creator, producing what J. S. Bratton calls the "implication . . . that the boy—the idealised self of the reader—is the highest form of life."[48] None of Tom Brown's introspection and humbling here; Henty's boys are concerned not with what they feel but with what they do. If virtue lies within the reach of any public schoolboy with his fair share of health and shrewdness, the reward of virtue is money and its result an unevangelical complacency. Jeffrey Richards, for instance, sees Henty's work as a recasting of Samuel Smiles's *Self-Help*, and the early critics who castigated Smiles for promoting "ruthless self-interest"[49] might justifiably have tackled Henty as well. Henty's glorification of the factual world of purely physical struggle undercuts his efforts to provide a spiritual dimension for his heroes.

The confusion inherent in Henty's approach to character building is especially evident in his attitude toward money. On the one hand, a wealthy nation is decadent; according to Hamilcar in *The Young Carthaginian* (1887), lamenting Carthage's inability to keep its empire, "It seems to be the fate of all nations, that as they grow in wealth so they lose their manly virtues. With wealth comes corruption, indolence, a reluctance to make sacrifices, and a weakening of the feeling of patriotism. Power falls into the hands of the ignorant many."[50] Thus some critics see Henty as anticapitalist.[51] On the other hand, for all his disdain for a society fixated on gold, Henty found it necessary to integrate his heroes into the English middle class by rewarding them with money so they could join the power structure. So as Guy Arnold has observed, for Henty good character is inextricable from worldly success.[52] Manliness for Henty is the ability to make one's way in the world; thus, while money doesn't confer manliness, manliness does confer money. Suspecting that money ultimately saps manliness, Henty finds himself in a double bind, trying to sweep the problem under the rug by manipulating improbable plots so that "personal advancement is made to coincide exactly with the demands of duty."[53]

If manliness is wedded to worldly success, androgynous manliness becomes impossible, not only because one achieves androgynous manliness through humility and self-sacrifice but because one achieves masculine manliness through activities forbidden to the middle-class girl. Predictably, gender divisions are far wider in Henty than in Hughes or Yonge, and he reinforces them constantly, for example by separating his heroes from feminine influences as quickly as possible. Feminine boys and feminine girls alike are regrettable; "there is nothing jolly" about women.[54] Incompatible with the politics of empire, domesticity is incompatible with the Henty myth, and nowhere does his fiction suggest that women or androgynous men have contributed much to English greatness.

Patrick Dunae observes that one of Henty's conscious goals was to combat the mass-market shockers known as penny dreadfuls, with their low morals and high excitement.[55] While a more religion-oriented writer would have attacked this problem by focusing on the soul's individual quest for perfection, Henty prefers to focus on Britain's collective quest for power; thus the hero (identical in any case to all other Henty heroes) seems a twig in the torrent of English destiny. The focus on the group—the single mass of hero and reader and British yeomanry—makes general patriotism outweigh even individual pluck, and Henty's plan to provide "bright personal examples of morality" inevitably takes a back seat to his determination to "teach patriotism" and "to inspire faith in the divinely ordered mission of the country and the race."[56] Despite this flouting of the character-centered moral conventions of femininist fiction, Henty's work could nevertheless seem ethically acceptable because he recast egotism as a morally admirable chauvinism. Henty had inherited from Scott an interest in flat characters who could represent whole classes; he takes the myth of the plucky boy who is the backbone of English greatness and makes decent the reader's pleasure in identifying with this hero by making the identification seem patriotic. Unlike the authors of penny dreadfuls, he exalts not a single ego but what Martin Green (who finds this trope also in Scott) calls "the aristomilitary caste."[57] A product of a post-Darwinian world who believed that heredity was martial destiny—Nature "instills the love of a military career in continental nations because these plains afford such a magnificent ground for great battles"[58]—Henty finds a species more significant than an individual.

Appropriately enough in these circumstances, any one of Henty's novels is very like any other. We may then focus on a Henty novel published in the same year as *The Black Arrow* in order to illustrate the contrast between the two schools. *Bonnie Prince Charlie* deals in an un-Stevensonian way with a Stevensonian subject, the Jacobite rising of 1745. The questions of moral growth that dominate character-centered historical novels are not at issue here; the brief discussion of the hero's childhood recapitulates only his mastery of practical skills (such as swordsmanship) he needs for his worldly advancement. Ronald Leslie, son of a French countess and a Jacobite colonel exiled after 1715, is lucky enough to lack resident parents and so to escape the powerless role of child; from the boy's infancy, colonel and countess have languished in jail on account of their illegal marriage. Instead, Ronald lives with a pair of middle-class Scots in dull domesticity, and while Ronald owes them gratitude he and Henty are agreed that he need not espouse nor even obey their orderly principles. That Ronald's nominal task in the novel is to secure his parents' release is misleading: he does not seek to re-create the family circle so much as to serve justice and win his spurs.

After he does free the elder Leslies, he immediately packs them off to an obscure chateau so that he may fight for the Stuart prince unhindered.

The fear of ego that characterizes so many children's books in the first half of the century is wholly lacking here. Ronald well knows at eighteen that he is the best swordsman in France, one of Charles's best tacticians, and more competent than either of his parents. Henty need not worry about feeding his audience's egos—the thrill of vicarious pride that we feel at Ronald's perfections serves as a foretaste of the joys of masculine manliness, motivating us to go and do likewise. Nor do the plotting techniques of the androgynous school have any place here; Ronald's injury in battle, which earlier writers would have used to refine and spiritualize their protagonists, affects him only as a temporary nuisance.

Similarly, while a Henty hero must marry to signal his absorption into the biological and social web, Henty never suggests that men and women have anything in common or might find each other interesting. The entire description of Ronald's courtship and husband-hood reads as follows: "He had before this married the daughter of a neighboring gentleman."[59] Ronald doesn't marry an individual but a piece of Scotland, and we never even discover the lucky woman's name. In the words of Henty's contemporary biographer, G. Manville Fenn, "There was nothing namby-pamby in Henty's writings, for his adolescent characters were not so much boys as men, saving in this, that he kept them to boy life, and never made his works sickly by the introduction of what an effeminate writer would term the tender passion." By virtue of their immunity to the namby-pamby, sickly snares of effeminate domesticity, Henty's boys are more manly than his men can be. While Doyle, for instance, thinks of marriage as completing the male, bringing him to full androgynous flower through his union with the feminine, in Henty it suggests rather a diminishing of masculinity—necessary if the hero is to achieve full worldly success, but a pity nonetheless. Thus Fenn's biography, which re-creates in its subject one of Henty's own one-dimensional heroes, "an ideal comrade—a brave man, amiable, happy in temper, straightforward . . . ready at a pinch to dare danger to the very death,"[60] feels it necessary to downplay Henty's emotional life as much as possible. Fenn reports minute details of Henty's travels with various armies, but omits the names of Henty's four children and two wives, the second of whom—formerly Henty's house-keeper—appears for the first time on the book's last page. Although domesticity did play its part in Henty's life, Fenn clearly feels that it shouldn't have.

But for all that Henty's works would seem a complete rejection of the ideals of androgynous manliness, we can yet discern undercurrents of the opposite position in their author. Like Stevenson, Henty had been a perfect example of the Victorian invalid child, "a puny, sickly boy who was looked on by his relatives as one who could never by any possibility attain to man's estate," scorned by his fellow scholars at Westminster for his botanizing and versifying. Reading Fenn's description of Henty as a man who hated "milksops" and "had a horror of a lad who displayed any weak emotion and shrank from shedding blood, or winced at any encounter,"[61] it is startling to remember that Henty had been just such a frail boy himself.

It is still more startling to read Henty's musings on the nature of "True Heroism" in an article by that name published in the *Home Messenger* in March 1903. "Good health and physique" are irrelevant to character, he explains with evangelical orthodoxy; "boys are apt to make heroes of those who are strongest and most skilful in games, and to despise those who are unable from ill health or constitutional weakness to bear their full share in any sports. They do not reflect . . . that the shrinking, delicate boy may be as true a hero as the captain of their football or cricket team." Real heroism, we find, consists of the very unselfishness that is so strikingly absent from the unselfconsciously upwardly mobile hero of Henty's fiction. We see it best in "patient, brave women, who hide their troubles from the world, make the best of things, and carry a cheerful face even when their hearts are breaking. . . . No comparison can be made between these heroines of private life and the men who [merely] perform heroic deeds in battle." Soldiers are prisoners of their sex; inheriting their aggressive tendencies through the male line, they fight because "they have in them . . . the remnants of a time when all men fought for their lives, when their position was little beyond that of the beasts of the field." Women have none of this beastliness, and "the truest heroes lie among those who do and suffer quietly, without hope of praise, without a thought that the work that they are doing is noble, without a thought of the opinion of others—this is the highest and noblest class of heroism."[62] Pure Charlotte Yonge, this, and yet the only Henty work in which it seems to surface is the long short story "White-Faced Dick," an American Western in which a frail and timid boy dies saving a benefactor from a flood. Whether submerged because of Henty's conception of what historical novels should teach or because of the teasing he endured in boyhood, androgynous ideals nonetheless lurked within his consciousness.

The tension between the two varieties of manliness has unfortunate results in the work of some of Henty's imitators, who like Henty must juggle contradictory balls of plot and character but who fail to control either realm. The Henty trick of putting the reader into the hero's shoes degenerates into blatant flattery. Thus Dick Granville, hero of Captain F. S. Brereton's *In the King's Service* (1900), manages to be at once well born, a natural strategic genius, peerlessly brave, attractive to women, and—incredibly—modest. Throughout the novel his elders defer to him in awe, exclaiming, "Faith, ye seem to have more brains than all the rest of us put together" or "Dick, me boy . . . we always said ye had the heart of Cromwell, but for pluck and honest generosity of feeling ye beat him hollow." "Every bit a boy," Dick is not too young to rescue General Ireton and later Cromwell himself from assassination (Dick himself is a Royalist, of course, but a Royalist who plays fair), survive Drogheda, fortify a castle so well that his garrison of 250 nearly holds out against Cromwell's two thousand, save his future wife from Roundhead kidnappers, and finally recover his hereditary estates. Fortunately, "ever since he was a tiny child the folly of undue pride had been taught him," so that at the end of the novel and the beginning of a new life as a pacifist, Dick answers his uncle's praise with a self-deprecating "I think you overestimate the part I took in the matter."[63] The reader knows better.

Such lip service to antiegotistic evangelicalism, when simultaneous with the flat Hentyesque paragon hero, produces an unconvincing hybrid. Brereton cares little for historical accuracy, given his fictional hero's tremendous impact on the age; but neither does he care about tracing Dick's spiritual progress—since Dick is perfect from beginning to end. Nor does Brereton's work make any implied comment on late-Victorian society, except perhaps that the seventeenth century was more exciting. Pretending to adhere to the principles of both camps by creating a hero who is both selfless and a projection of the reader's ego, religiously solemn in possessing "a quietness and reserve which were remarkable" and extrovertedly masculine in being "ready to enter into any piece of fun,"[64] *In the King's Service* has no ideology of its own. The novel is pure escapism, displaying the combined flaws of both schools of juvenile historical fiction.

Not so *Marcus: The Young Centurion* (1904), by Henty's biographer G. Manville Fenn, which is innocent of any ideological impurity; it succeeds—incredibly—in simplifying Henty's tactics in the portrayal of manly character. Aware that his public-school readers would probably know more about Roman history than their own, Fenn feels no need to explain Caesar's military campaigns. Rather, his historical instincts display themselves in attempts to prove the homeyness of the classical era. We first see Marcus "snoring like an English lad of this year of grace," exclaiming "in fine, old, sonorous, classic Latin: 'Bother the flies!' " and wearing a "loose, woollen, open-fronted garment, not very much unlike a tweed Norfolk jacket without pockets or buttons, very short in the sleeves."[65] But the familiarity of ancient Rome to an audience of modern Britons is only one reason for Fenn's selection of this setting; he has also a point to make about the proper role of the manly boy in an empire—and a markedly pre-Christian empire at that.

Fenn's conception of the boyish ideal is easily interpretable: the manly boy is the exact opposite of the womanly girl. Marcus's father, Cracis, is a general who, discredited after a falling-out with Julius Caesar, has retired to the country disgusted with Roman military life. Marcus, he hopes, will be a scholar and a gentleman. But despite Roman emphasis on filial duty, Marcus's one idea is to disobey his father—and Fenn backs him up. Study is effeminate (the sedentary life is "right enough for women and girls"), obedience humiliating. When Cracis and Caesar reconcile and Cracis returns to war, Marcus rebels at receiving orders to stay home: "I only a poor, feeble boy to be left behind to mind the house, as if I were a girl!"[66]

The antidote to androgyny is armor, since the opposite of "female" is not "male" but "soldier": thus according to Marcus's servant and mentor, women may be fat because it "makes 'em look smooth and nice and pretty . . . but a soldier [not "a man"] wants bone and muscle." Donning warlike garb makes Marcus "feel ten years older" and infinitely braver; running away from home (together with his equally disobedient and martial servant) is manly if it involves fighting, for, says the servant after Marcus has saved him from robbers, "I won't call you boy no more, for I have made you a fighting man." And war is not only great fun, it liberates one from family ties. When Cracis expresses anger at Marcus's deliberate disobedience, Caesar overrules him, judging that Marcus has gained stature: "Since he [Cracis] left you, a simple scholar, you have become a soldier and bravely done your duty in your country's cause." Like Henty, Fenn finds that duty marches conveniently with glory. While the glamour may sometimes pall (Marcus twice notices that war is "horrible" before soldiering eagerly on), war, which equals manliness, underpins Rome's greatness. "Our country must rule the world," the old servant explains, and all understand that worlds never bow to women or scholars.[67] What Dunae writes of Henty describes Fenn still better: his books "not only point to a decline in religious enthusiasm; they reflect the secular ideals and the materialistic spirit which came to characterize late Victorian imperialism. . . . the popular press tended increasingly to equate empire with national pride, international prestige, and military power"[68]—none of which, naturally, played much part in a religiously based vision of androgynous manliness.

But although the worldly ethical code of masculine manliness took much of its impetus from imperialism, not all turn-of-the-century imperialism accepted this secular tone. From Baden-Powell to Buchan, commentators on British expansionism have emphasized the opportunities it provided for self-sacrifice, duty, and the merging of individual egos in the search for the larger good. Such a restatement of the practical politics of empire suggests practical politics' opposite: the evangelical message appears essentially unaltered within its worldly setting. The prophets of evangelical imperialism, like Douglas Haig in a letter of 1901, stressed the difference between unworthy ambition and altruistic duty; they introduced into school texts the concept of empire as a sacred trust and omitted all mention of financial profit.[69] Ideas of true and false imperialism succeeded those of true and false manliness, and the Boys' Empire League was founded in 1900 for the express purpose of fostering the true (selfless) variety and extirpating the false.[70] Historical novels concerned with empire could not be jingoistic.

Thus Rudyard Kipling's Puck stories, *Puck of Pook's Hill* (1906) and *Rewards and Fairies* (1910), concentrate on a Britain that is the product of centuries of conquest (and so by extension defend a Britain that conquers other nations in its turn) but focus on ethics instead of profit. The ethics in question are more militarist than Christian; nevertheless, because Kipling ignores glamour to stress such ideals as duty, artisanship, and comradely love, his ancient Rome has much in common with the modern Jerusalem. Martin Green points out that the Puck stories' implicit comparison of England to Rome is unusual for the British historical novel, since Rome's role as the center of Catholicism made it an inappropriate model for a Protestant nation.[71] But while novels like Fenn's *Marcus* can draw the Roman-British parallel unconcernedly because their imperialism has nothing to do with religion, Kipling's Roman stories startle by implying that religion has nothing to do with churches. Imperialism for Kipling is a setting for self-discovery, for the separation of right from wrong and the good people from the uncomprehending. Thus war can be religion's ally, the conquest of territory a metaphor for the conquest of self.

Like his more overtly religious predecessors, Kipling emphasizes that the paths of glory—and even of humility—lead but to the grave. His historical personages come out of an irrevocably completed past in order to make the modern children, Dan and Una (based on Kipling's own offspring), free of England's history. But that history is less a series of separable events than of variations on a theme: the complex of concepts surrounding "Cold Iron," which is both the guiding image of and the title of a key chapter in *Rewards and Fairies*. Iron represents at once slavery and comradeship, sacrifice and salvation, sword and plowshare;[72] as responsibility and drudgery and the human condition, it offers a Reward of which mere Fairies (to whom iron is anathema) can never conceive. Hence Kipling's tales, which never invoke God, nonetheless have a Puritan flavor. His history, stern daughter of the voice of Duty, evokes a religion of humanity.

That the Puck stories typically suggest that "the victory of order over disorder . . . must be purchased by pain and suffering,"[73] links them to their ethical predecessors, those novels that recommend evangelical androgyny. Like Yonge, Kipling suggests that the powerless—a dying girl in "Marklake Witches," a medieval Jew in "The Treasure and the Law"—may still be able to change society by influence or by action; would-be world conquerors lose all they sought to hold, while those who heed duty gain immeasurable spiritual wealth. Like the heroes of R. M. Ballantyne's adventure novel *The Gorilla Hunters*, Kipling's eponymous "Knights of the Joyous Venture" take arms against the humanoid apes that represent to both authors the bestial, wild, undutiful side of man's nature. Evangelical themes continually appear in a secular key, and in the best evangelical tradition, Kipling's heroes often end up mutilated, sorrowful, and underappreciated—but satisfied to have done their duty. Sacrifice is the price of virtue, and personal ambition the chief obstacle in virtue's path.

But despite the evangelical parallels, we cannot forget that the Puck stories don't derive from the religion of Christianity, but from the religion of Englishness. They therefore can't reject "real" history after the fashion of Stevenson or Kingston, because real history is central to the moral: each Briton must be ready to make the appointed sacrifice, however individually painful and unrewarding, in order that Britain itself may continue great. Likewise, Kipling isn't interested in playing off age against age in Victorian fashion to suggest that one is better (or more like the present) than another. Thus the major tension at work in Kipling is the counterpoint between the "spirit of the hero" and the "spirit of the age," which combine to achieve a composite and timeless "spirit of England." He is at once the heir to the androgynous antihistorical tradition that seeks to impart moral lessons and to Henty and the literature of patriotism. Kipling may therefore be the one writer of historical tales in the period under discussion who manages to combine the two traditions successfully. In his short stories we can see both the "great man" and the "great battle" views of history at work—because the battle, ultimately, is the human battle, fought by great and obscure alike, with England as the prize.

• FIVE •

Adventures, Empires, and Strange Gods

Victorian school novels, with their pseudodomestic setting, readily lent themselves to offering the Angel as a role model for boys. Historical tales, didactic and frequently aimed at a dual-gender audience, often took the same androgynous tack. The adventure story, however, the third major genre available to middle-class Victorian boys, may seem to reject this ambiguous treatment of gender—to have nothing but admiration for the extroverted boy who gets out and acts, and nothing but contempt for his introverted brother who stays home and thinks. The first protagonists in middle-class boys' fiction to distance themselves from the evangelical code of introspection and selflessness, heroes of adventures typically suggest that if a boy leads an exciting life, he needn't be obsessed with virtue; the genre's tacit motto often seems to read, "Be clever, sweet lad, and let who will be good." Manliness may collapse into Hentyesque patriotism and pluck. Eschewing civilization, the adventure story can also omit all but the most perfunctory religious observances—in extreme cases even gentlemanliness becomes optional. Thus to Harvey Darton the adventure novel is the first real "boy's book," presented without moral and without the reformer's fire.[1] With these generalizations in mind, we don't expect to find adventures with a guardian Angel.

But even Henty paid public homage to androgynous worth and feminine courage, and in fact the real boy's book still succumbs to the influence of the true woman. Evangelical concerns and epiphanies stud early examples of adventure tales; authors enjoin boys to patience, humility, piety, and resignation. What, then, happened to adventure fiction in the 1870s? Did it indeed reject its Angelic roots altogether, as Darton argues, replacing the goal of virtue with that of profit and disdaining the pious for the picaresque? Or might it have expelled femininism from one door only to admit it again at another? A closer examination of representative adventures reveals a complex mythology animating the genre, in which the desire to reject the feminine ethic combats the desire to embrace it. The adventure's relationship with the Angel is more vexed than that of any other boys' genre; it tries to come to terms with her in tortuous ways that include setting the authorial voice against the boyish actors, emphasizing the secret femininity of the alien landscape that threatens to overpower the heroes, replacing the feminine religion of Christ with the masculine religion of country, and finally attempting to substitute a mythology of perfect manhood for the mythology of perfect womanhood. Thus in the adventure novel the Angel may be defeated or she may lurk in the shadows, but she is never absent.

Martin Green argues that the adventure novel is especially likely to glorify the uncomplicated masculinity he terms "aristomilitary" because of its sense of itself as a low-status literature. Having come to dominate the novel form sometime in the eighteenth century, the courtship tale—or the domestic tale in general, including the school story and the character-centered historical novel—feels the responsibility to be morally serious. With earnestness goes the onus of subversion, and accepting an Angelic agenda, domestic authors are wont to write out of a quietly passionate effort to change society through influence, in what Green calls "a literature of largely silent resistance." The adventure novel, in contrast, did not resist, perhaps seeing itself as too trivial to effect changes.[2] Green's suggestion is provocative, but it fails to explain completely the dilemma of adventure novels' moral stance: since evangelical doctrine held that the most humble might be the most effective instrument of God's will, if the adventure tale indeed saw itself as too trivial to count, it must already have rejected that religion in which nothing, no matter how slight, is meaningless. Nor, on the other hand, is it safe to assert that the adventure novel has no protests to make on its own account; paradoxically, its most serious moral purpose often seems to be the rejection of serious moral purpose. Even antifemininist adventures, in short, don't simply ignore the Angel: they wrestle with her.

It may be that the ethics of adventures result not from the genre's form but from its content. Necessarily occurring in a context of imperial expansion, these stories profess a commitment to "realism" that often dictates heroes who are not rounded characters but concatenations of national stereotypes. Captain Mayne Reid's *The Boy*

Slaves (1865), for instance, stars a triumvirate of midshipmen: Harry Blount, Terence O'Connor, and Colin Macpherson are "representatives . . . of the Rose, Shamrock, and Thistle, and had the three kingdoms from which they came been searched throughout their whole extent, there could scarcely have been discovered purer representative types of each."[3] This Anglo-Saxon inclusiveness is popular; W.H.G. Kingston uses it in *The Three Midshipmen*, serialized in *Kingston's Magazine for Boys* in 1859, where the very similar heroes are called Jack Rogers, Paddy Adair, and Alick Murray. In a rewriting of Angelic doctrine, such generic heroes replace the selfless with the personalityless. And not only did they free mediocre writers from the necessity of characterizing, or boost sales by giving most British readers a figure for local chauvinism to identify with, they created a parable. The struggle between stereotypical hero and equally stereotypical villain becomes emblematic of Britain's noble quest to civilize non-Western societies. Like the boy hero, Britain is brave, hardworking, and only concerned with her duty toward those unpromising natives. In such a formula there is no room for subtlety, introspection, or self-criticism; no one will suggest that British civilization is anything but superior in every respect to the cultures it seeks to supplant.

The imperialist adventure thus lends itself to an ethical system that is Darwinian rather than evangelical, "proving" Britain's claim to hegemony by equating virtue with military strength. Patrick Dunae locates in the late 1880s the point at which the emphasis of the *Boy's Own Paper* shifted from spiritual to materialist imperialism, as missionaries went out and merchants came in,[4] but because of its religious stance the paper may have been late to change. For his part, Ian Bradley suggests that it was the Indian Mutiny of 1857 that convinced many Britons that contrary to evangelical doctrine, all souls were not equal before God. Correctly interpreting the Mutiny as a protest against Anglicization, "the Government realized that . . . the Indians were clearly beyond redemption." This discovery brought a new atmosphere to post-Mutiny Anglo-Indian relations, replacing the desire to convert with the desire to conquer. If, as Bradley states, it was the missionary zeal that had sparked imperialism in the first place,[5] in bureaucratic fact as well as in exotic fiction, the tail quickly began to wag the dog: the longing for evangelical brotherhood soon lost out to the pleasures of enforcing temporal hierarchy.

To be sure, even at the height of imperialism not all adventures have an imperial setting, and not all adventures with such a setting are imperialist. Sea stories and Crusoe-like epics may focus on their heroes' struggles against the elements, stressing humanity's puniness within the cosmos; romances of African exploration may be metaphors for the evangelical mastery of the self. Brian Street writes of the adventure story's need to create strangeness by "emphasizing . . . the gap between European and native"; in many cases, authors project the undesirable—and overly masculine—qualities the Victorians hoped to repress in themselves onto the alien.[6] While the outward form of the adventure may be Darwinian, then, the underlying symbolism may well be evangelical; androgyny has its place even in a genre that often eliminates character.

Reading the adventures available to readers in the early part of our period, indeed, few would guess that androgyny might have to go underground. Stories of the 1850s and 1860s frequently swashbuckle in title alone; narratives may stress the impropriety of seeking excitement at all, larding each danger-filled episode with homilies about the benefits of Christian meekness and passivity. These fictions are clearly still based on the pre-Mutiny imperialism that emphasized charity and Christian brotherhood and shut its eyes to profit; as Lynda Nead has observed, such imperialism works on the model of the "Christian family home," of which the Angel is the moral head.[7] In such a context the androgynous hero thrives, and the woman author is at no disadvantage despite her inability to make capital (like such writers as Mayne Reid, W. Gordon Stables, and R. M. Ballantyne) out of the claim that she has had similar adventures herself; only spiritual adventures, after all, are desirable. Anne Bowman's *The Boy Voyagers; or, The Pirates of the East* (1859) is a case in point.

Abused by his vulgar schoolfellows for being "a milksop, and a spooney, and a little sneak," the football-hating Walter Thornville persuades Frank Freeman to run away to Calcutta with him. The expedition, Bowman observes, is a mistake; but the friendship is a blessing, as without Walter's gentle affection Frank "might have become a hard character." Between the pair of them, as a perspicacious sailor early notes, Walter represents feminine good sense and Frank masculine courage—"head on one side and pluck on the other." Over the course of the action the boys gain one another's virtues, after the fashion of Tom Brown and Arthur, so that physical hardship makes Walter a "tall, sunburnt, healthy boy" and spiritual trial so improves Frank's character that Mr. Thornville adopts him. In addition, Walter's prayers in the face of danger apparently sow the seeds of conversion in the tough sailors who accompany them: "the simple petition of the gentle boy seemed to produce some impression on the reckless, scoffing young man; he was silent for some time, and, the boys hoped, thoughtful and repentant."[8] More important still, readers gain a sense of a future empire that will be based not on temporal power but on a shared religion.

For the boys' rash venture does not, of course, run smoothly. The ship they originally embark in turns out to be a slaver, bound not for India but for Africa and America, so that Walter and Frank and their sailor friends Tom and Mike must jump ship near Madagascar. Their subsequent wanderings permit Bowman to sort ethnic groups according to redemption potential. One of her categories is the British common sailor; when the band meets the missionary Sinclair, who has survived pirate ravages by hiding in the catacombs beneath his African island, Tom and Mike's conversion becomes complete. Sinclair proves a valuable addition to the cast, able to explain why even the happiest native needs Christianity: contentment without true religion is merely a delusion. He can also demonstrate to the boys that humans have nothing in common with orangutans, since, he promises, "reason and revelation assure us, that man is a distinct creation; formed in God's image, endowed with spiritual gifts, and separated from the brute by that impassable gulf, which lies between mere animal life and the glorious hope of immortality."[9]

Sinclair's explanations help arrange a non-Darwinian spiritual hierarchy running from orangutans to pirates to the delusively happy Mauritians to the Chinese (whom Bowman describes as a harmless but ugly people, whose women are downtrodden) to the Japanese (whose natural gentleness and order so impress Bowman that the country seems to her obviously destined to be Christian) to the British. But ethnic and ethical boundaries may diverge. The Japanese noble Madsimano helps the group to escape from Japan and at length secures an English commission and an English bride ("nor did her mother object to his country when she learnt he was noble, and beloved by all who knew him for the amiable qualities of his heart and mind"). Clearly Madsimano is the equal of many Britons and the superior of some—such as the Scotch skinflint Captain Mackay, who has no sense of brotherhood even toward his own compatriots. The moneygrubbing of those in the secular service contrasts sharply with the indifference to finance of good Mr. Sinclair. Likewise, the feminist aspirations of the officious English governess Miss Griffin look tawdry beside the longings of her charge, Minna, to "learn Hindustani, that I might talk to the poor natives in India."[10]

All Britons are not spiritually equal, or even spiritually superior to all pagans; individual decency transcends national heritage.

The arrogance of race and class, which many later adventures take for granted, is impossible here. Any quality that assists the brotherhood of humanity is good; any that encourages self-aggrandizement and individual secular power is bad. Hence the ambiguous placement of the boys in Bowman's spiritual ranking: unwilling to submit himself to "the petty, wholesome trials of school-boy life,"[11] Walter has obeyed the promptings of ego and has thus shown himself flawed. The value of the adventure has been the opportunity it affords Walter to recognize the Christian basis of *all* trials, petty or thrilling. At the story's end he can therefore reach his Father in a dual sense; but we must remember that the perfect androgynous hero would never have left home at all.

However imperfect, though, Walter is a cut above the protagonist of Charlotte M. Tucker's *The Light in the Robber's Cave* (1862). Writing under the name of A.L.O.E. (A Lady of England), Tucker's commitment to evangelicalism was sufficiently strong to induce her to spend her last years as a missionary in India. In this novel she demonstrates that Europeans need missionaries too. The focus is on the spiritual struggle of the Italian hero, Raphael, to convert his brother and comrades; the other major emphasis (suggested through Horace, the arrogant protagonist) is on the idea that even British gentlemen and scholars are not necessarily Christians.

Like Bowman, Tucker distrusts the complacency of race and power, which influence their possessors to value pedigree over piety. As a school leader in study and sport, "It was clear at a glance that Horace Cleveland regarded himself as one of the lords of creation, and, from national or family or personal pride, considered himself superior to all such of his fellow-creatures as he might meet in Calabria. His manner, even to his mother, was petulant and imperious." Horace's mistaken trust in the worth of upper-class masculinity naturally makes him averse to lower-class feminine men: "I hate to see a man play a guitar!" he exclaims on seeing Raphael for the first time.[12] The familiar end of the story, however, is Horace's gradual realization that the masculine virtues aren't enough for true manliness, whose real exemplar is the feminine Raphael.

Arrogance betrays Horace into the hands of robbers. As a hostage, the English boy quickly realizes that his only hope is Raphael, who lives with the robbers but who is really a nurse, musician, Protestant, and pacifist. Unfortunately from Horace's point of view, Raphael's very virtues make it impossible for him simply to free the captive.

Raphael has duties also to his brother, Enrico, who needs Raphael's gentle influence if he is ever to quit the robber band; to the villagers, who depend on him to visit their sick; and to the thieves themselves, whose excesses can only be checked by "his presence, like that of some being of higher and purer nature."[13] Because his life isn't his own, he can't jeopardize his mission by offending his outlaw hosts; as always, the strength of feminine manliness lies in covert influence, not in force majeure. The uncomprehending Horace chafes at what he considers Raphael's passivity and cowardice.

But enforced inaction saves Horace's soul. Once he learns to discern Raphael's patience, faith, and feminine courage, he learns to value them; he realizes too that his hackneyed idea of masculine courage can't compare with the bravery of "the devoted men—yea, and *women*—who in densely crowded cities lead the assault against the enemy's mightiest strongholds." Horace absorbs Raphael's evangelical message— "Not to do our own will, but God's will; to make His love our inspiring motive, His glory our end and aim—this is the object, the only object, worthy of an immortal soul"—and achieves a sense of sin ("The proud lad, who, exalted by conscious superiority over his companions, had feared comparison with no one, now felt mortified and even disgusted with himself"). For solace, Horace too turns to music, daily coming into closer sympathy with his mentor, who needs only four days to teach his disciple the principles of androgyny and influence. Soon Horace understands that "his first post of duty must be home,—the second, the circle of his school-companions; he felt that his pride and self-will, the sins which most easily beset him, must be resisted and overcome there. Obedience to his parent would be the test of his obedience to God." When Raphael finally does sacrifice himself to the robbers' anger for Horace's sake, his physical death doesn't matter, since immortality is ultimate influence. Once "the martyr-spirit had spread its pinions and soared upwards, leaving a track of light behind," we realize that for both Horace and Enrico "the death of Raphael Goldoni had effected more than his life."[14] Again, the evangelical adventure criticizes the active values of the secular thriller, in which heroes never die; it asserts instead that home is the proper sphere for male as for female, that the soul of the Italian peasant is brother to that of the English gentleman, and that true manliness is not masculinity.

Nor are such messages unique to woman-authored adventures. On the strength of *The Coral Island* (1857), a light-hearted boy Crusoe story whose missionary aspects we forget in concentrating on the heroes' fun battling sharks and pirates, many critics characterize

R. M. Ballantyne as a purveyor of pure entertainment who provides "excitement or romance instead of moral prattle."[15] J. S. Bratton, for instance, sees Ballantyne as "the last stage" in the degeneration of Arnoldian manliness into "a simple code of conformity glorifying physical power, simplicity of speech and mind, softness of feeling, and self-satisfaction with the state not of manliness, but of being forever a boy."[16] But Victorians might have found this assessment surprising. Writing in 1887, Charlotte Yonge approves the novels as evangelically correct: "Mr. Ballantyne's tales of adventures are perfectly safe from the moral point of view, and always have a religious tone."[17] She follows the lead of Edward G. Salmon, who in "What Boys Read" (1886) ranks Ballantyne high among those authors who are morally "bright and healthy," full of "sweetness and light";[18] neither commentator suggests that moral health requires the absence of morality. Likewise, Ballantyne's modern biographer Eric Quayle depicts his subject as a darkly religious man consumed by sexual guilt. Thus if Ballantyne customarily stresses childhood's innocence,[19] he surely isn't oblivious to moral flaws; rather, he shares the mid-Victorian hope that boys may retain a childlike purity even amid the slings and arrows of adulthood. This is not to preach complacency, but its opposite.

The typical Ballantyne novel differs from the works of Bowman and A.L.O.E. in that the adventure that separates the young heroes from the real world has value not only in its results but in itself: whatever children don't share with adults is good. The child-centered society, tiny and primitive, is free from adult delinquencies. The desert-island fantasy is a common Ballantyne preoccupation, offering as it does the opportunity for implicit criticism of the unsatisfactory real world that looms outside. Thus *The Island Queen* (1885), for instance, rewrites *The Coral Island* to create a utopia based on the principles of evangelical androgyny.

This time the three shipwrecked teenagers number two brothers and their sister, Pauline, who because she knows much of the Bible by heart is both their channel to God and their natural queen. This title means little until three hundred working-class emigrants are wrecked on the same shore, every tough castaway instantly succumbing to Pauline's womanly power: "As each man entered he stood stock still—dumb, petrified with astonishment—as he gazed, saucer-eyed, at Pauline." That the girl's younger brother reacts similarly to his first sight of John Marsh, the shipwrecked surgeon who plays the romantic lead, suggests the affinity between the roles of Angel and

Androgyne: "There was something peculiarly attractive in the manly, handsome face of this young disciple of Aesculapius, worn as it was by long sickness and suffering, and Otto fell in love with him at first sight." As with Pauline, Marsh's physical frailty creates his spiritual fascination, since "when this peculiar conformation and expression [natural charisma] is coupled with delicacy of health, and obvious suffering, the attractive influence becomes irresistible." The attraction between Marsh and Otto, we learn, is mutual, "for Dr. Marsh also fell in love with Otto at first sight," but it is eclipsed by the doctor's discovery of Pauline, whom he immediately diagnoses as an "Angelic creature." Hitherto immune to sex, Marsh, "regarded by his friends at home as hopelessly unimpressible—in short, an absolute woman-hater—had . . . fallen—nay, let us be just—had jumped over head and ears in love with Pauline Rigonda!"[20] Ballantyne's syntax mirrors his hero's breathless confusion. With the perfect self-control we expect of the androgyne, however, Marsh conceals his feelings.

A government becomes necessary, and most of the men propose to appoint their ruler on the basis of physical strength. This suggestion naturally sparks fighting, as the men struggle for dominance; Pauline's older brother, Dominick, wins a precarious control because of his public-school boxing. But such rule is unstable, and the mannish Mrs. Lynch nominates Pauline instead, saying, "It's not a king's business to fight. No, take my word for it; what ye want is a *queen*." Everyone recognizes the worth of this plan, and Pauline takes charge, to establish a utopia based on the rule: "Whatsoever ye would that men should do to you, do ye even so to them." Strife vanishes, gardens flourish, schools appear (Pauline intends to teach scripture and, despite her lack of personal experience, motherhood), and the secret of Eden stands revealed in Mrs. Lynch's words: good government consists of not giving men "too much o' their own way."[21]

To her brothers' surprise, Pauline agrees with Mrs. Lynch. While Dominick has envisioned Pauline as his puppet, she quietly appoints a better-qualified man as her prime minister, explaining, "I have been made queen to rule, and I *mean* to rule!" Indeed, the doctor's nobility derives in part from his reluctance to usurp feminine power; he prefers to exert gentle influence when appropriate. Playing an ostensibly subordinate, feminine role throughout the story, Marsh is not only Pauline's ideal subject but her ideal consort after the utopia's volcanic destruction. Unlike most men, including Pauline's brothers, Marsh has his passions and ambitions firmly reined in and thus deserves a woman of Pauline's intelligence, "self-forget-fulness . . . sympathy, active good-will to man and beast," and fun.[22] Hero and heroine form one feminine whole.

In novels such as *The Island Queen, The Boy Voyagers*, and *The Light in the Robber's Cave*, evangelical androgyny obviously runs strong. But in the other tradition informing Victorian adventure stories, that of the working-class penny dreadful, religion had little place. Made possible by the early-century advances in literacy and in printing technology, the penny dreadful provided sex, violence, sensation, and escapism to an audience that by the 1860s was increasingly youthful, as "serial fiction became regarded as 'children's stuff.'"[23] What Marjory Lang characterizes as "the precocious independence and potency of [the dreadfuls'] boy heroes" was deeply disturbing to mid-Victorian observers of children's reading.[24] A countermovement soon sprang up to provide healthier periodical fiction for boys; it is of course to this trend that we owe the *Boy's Own Paper* and its confreres.

As Dunae points out, however, in the battle between sensation and sensibility, it was evangelical morality that lost ground. He explains that in the last thirty years of the century, boys' reading changed less than people's attitudes toward it. Consequently, what struck one dec-ade's commentators as liable to warp young minds seemed to the next group of critics just the thing for instilling patriotism. The rot may have set in with E. J. Brett's *Boys of England* story paper. Barred in 1866 from reprinting the famous penny dreadful *The Wild Boys of London* by the combined pressures of Victorian mores and police in-tervention, Brett started a new paper, promising to mingle excite-ment with virtue. "Our aim is to enthrall you by wild and wonderful, but healthy fiction," an editorial proclaimed, claiming that "a moral and healthy tone may be maintained in conjunction with [even] the boldest fiction."[25] Shrewdly adding a half-pennyworth of morality to his intolerable deal of shock, Brett professed to offer a new model of manliness that would have all the advantages and none of the prig-gishness of the old. The paper caught on immediately, selling per-haps a million copies a month in the early 1870s and driving newsagents to fisticuffs in the competition to get enough copies from the publishers.[26] The serial hero chiefly responsible for Brett's suc-cess was Jack Harkaway, invented in 1871 by a man whose earlier writings had hardly been aimed at children: Bracebridge Hemyng, author of the section on prostitution in Henry Mayhew's *London La-bour and the London Poor* (1861–1862).

For all Brett's claims of virtue, Jack may well have been the inspiration for the Religious Tract Society's 1878 complaint that most juvenile papers were "eminently fitted to train up a race of reckless, dare-devil, lying, cruel, and generally contemptible characters."[27] Jack, whose saga extends from his private-school days to adventures of his grandson and includes visits to the South Seas, China, America, Greece, Australia, and South Africa (for the Boer War), is nothing if not independent and mobile—splendidly calculated, Louis James notes, to appeal to "the latent motor energies of colonialism."[28] But Jack's ability instantly to master the most dangerous situation derives not from pious passivity but from violent action; in *Jack Harkaway's Adventures Afloat and Ashore* (1873), for instance, Jack discards gentle remonstrance in dealing with an eavesdropper, preferring to nail the offending ear to the door—where, when the door slams shut in a gust of wind, it remains after its owner has left.[29]

Thus the "healthy" attitudes Brett promised readers were likely to appear not within the narratives' natural flows but as artificial additives—as authorial asides that often contradict the "overt morality" of the sensational plots.[30] Hemyng asks us to believe that Jack is a moral paragon but shows him making butts of his elders, disfiguring his enemies, ignoring the Queensberry rules, and publicly and passionately kissing his girlfriend. True, the other characters are worse. In *Afloat and Ashore* the comic schoolmaster is a bigamist; the "angelic" Emily is a flirt; Jack's faithful native servant, Monday, is a traitor, having abandoned his duty as king to follow Jack; and the teenage villains are kidnappers, pirates, murderers, and scorners of Britain. The moral universe here rests entirely on physical strength and male camaraderie; truthfulness and chivalry are secondary, and charity and kindness nonexistent.

With their emphasis on sex and violence, their interest in end over means, and their implication that conquest and not conversion is the heroic activity, the Harkaway stories devalue the feminine ethical system that more respectable works promote and replace it with Darwinian masculinity at its bloodiest. In doing so, however, they offered an undeniably heady brew to a schoolboy population with low literary standards and new spending power. Brett's rivals soon saw the profitable aspects of his formula. Alfred Harmsworth, for example, both discredited and emulated the model established by Brett and the dreadfuls, in an effort to win middle- and lower-class readers simultaneously by satisfying both watchful parents and action-loving offspring.[31] Beginning in the lower-middle-class boys' periodicals, then, and spreading upward into the more respectable novel, stories of adventure more and more frequently rejected androgynous Christian values. By the late 1880s even the *Boy's Own Paper* was coming slowly into line with a popular press more interested in power than salvation—which ethic defines adventure as physical rather than spiritual.[32] Antiandrogynous adventure novels rapidly became the rule.

In this developing context of psychologically simple, action-oriented thrillers, a tale such as *Treasure Island* (1883)—written by an author who usually employed his talents in unfolding emotional and moral complexities—becomes intensely interesting. What Lloyd Osbourne apparently wanted his stepfather to write was a blood-and-thunder tale with values that would be dramatic, not virtuous; surely this atmosphere lies behind Robert Louis Stevenson's letter to W. E. Henley reporting the boundaries of his new novel: "No women in the story, Lloyd's orders; and who so blythe to obey?"[33] And indeed, many critics do read the work as pure escapism. Characterizing it as amoral, John Rowe Townsend comments, "The total liberation from didacticism is one of *Treasure Island*'s outstanding features."[34] Paul Binding concurs, observing that Stevenson "freed the boys' story from the moralizing, muscular Christian elements which had weighed it down"; although good triumphs, so does Long John Silver.[35] Even a reviewer contemporary with Stevenson, writing in the Chicago *Dial* in May 1884, worries that "there is no appreciable good accomplished by the book. . . . It will be relished by adventure-loving boys, but whether it will be wholesome reading for them is more than doubtful."[36] But such interpretations are too simplistic. Certainly one may read the story on this level—Jim Hawkins, consistently neglecting prosaic duty for illicit excitement, apparently does so himself. But just as certainly, Stevenson allows his adult readers (who included W. E. Gladstone and Lord Rosebery) to filter the apparent naivete of the moral action through an ethical sophistication that most of the characters in the story lack.

David H. Jackson quotes Stevenson as wanting mature readers to "consciously play at being the [child] hero" in a world in which, Jackson notes, children are "incapable of higher moral thought."[37] This element of make-believe is essential to our understanding of the novel, wherein the simplicity of the values of most of the cast is consistently undercut by an ironic tone that acknowledges an adult world separate from but overshadowing the play world of the fiction. Through an implied comparison with the unseen but androgynous values of the sophisticated ideal reader, the aggression, greed, sophistry, and misplaced trust that characterize Stevenson's nominal adults expose them as inadequate.

In *Treasure Island* Stevenson goes out of his way to underscore the childishness of good and bad characters alike. The intimidating but cowardly Billy Bones, dissolute, companionable, and a poor hand at spelling and addition, is simply a school bully in fancy dress. By way of contrast Dr. Livesay is a new version of the head boy, assessing character solely in terms of manliness: "'That man Smollett,' he said once, 'is a better man than I am. And when I say that it means a deal, Jim.' Another time he . . . looked at me. 'Is this Ben Gunn a man?' he asked." The squire, endearingly simpleminded and indiscreet, has almost no adult traits. Accepting the doctor's ministrations, the villains take their medicine "with really laughable humility, more like charity school-children than blood-guilty mutineers and pirates," and with childish theology are equally ready to accept Silver's warning that a Bible missing a page is invalid and unlucky: "What fool's cut a Bible? . . . You'll all swing now, I reckon." Ben's autobiography echoes the religious chapbooks that presumably formed his early reading; as he explains, "I was a civil, pious boy, and could rattle off my catechism that fast, as you couldn't tell one word from another. And here's what it come to, Jim, and it begun with chuck-farthen on the blessed grave-stones! That's what it begun with, but it went further'n that; and so my mother told me, and predicked the whole, she did, the pious woman!" Even Jim's blood-curdling dodging of the knife-wielding Hands as they circle the mainmast resembles "a boy's game."[38] In such a context, consensus naturally holds that manhood has its basis in money, which can buy power, possessions, and good things to drink. But Stevenson himself finds this viewpoint naive.

There is but one adult aboard the *Hispaniola*. Captain Smollett has no interest in the treasure, no concern for anything but his duty, and no sympathy with boyhood: "You're a good boy in your line, Jim; but I don't think you and me'll go to sea again. You're too much of the born favourite for me." It is Smollett who makes the only trustworthy moral judgments of the novel, castigating the squire, the doctor, and Jim for boyishly deserting their posts to share the adventure, praising Joyce for adhering to nursery ethics: "'Did you hit your man?' asked the captain. 'No, sir,' replied Joyce. 'I believe not, sir.' 'Next best thing to tell the truth,' muttered Captain Smollett."[39] Smollett's very maturity makes him impenetrable in a world where everyone else is a child; Jim, through whose eyes we do our seeing, may abandon his hatred of the man for a grudging respect, but Jim's own immaturity renders difficult our sympathy for the captain. The spotlight is therefore never on Smollett but always on his moral opposite, Long John Silver.

Silver's fascination derives from his androgyny. If Smollett is *Treasure Island*'s forbidding father figure, Silver is its enticing mother. Still grieving over his displacement at his mother's inn by a "clumsy stranger" of a new apprentice, Jim immediately falls for the proprietor of the Spy-glass, which is less a tavern than a domestic triumph: "It was a bright enough little place of entertainment. The sign was newly painted; the windows had neat red curtains; the floor was cleanly sanded." Silver has enlisted in the ship's company in the feminine role of cook by stressing not his qualifications but his pathos; says the squire, "I was monstrously touched—so would you have been—and, out of pure pity, I engaged him on the spot." And the pirate plays mother for all he is worth, telling Jim, "When you want to go a bit of exploring, you just ask old John, and he'll put up a snack for you to take along."[40] Advertising his weakness and hiding his strength, Silver's chief weapon in what one early reviewer describes as the way he "seduces the crew" is Angelic influence.[41]

The danger, of course, is that for all his androgyny the man's secret agenda is far from selfless. Perhaps swayed by the knowledge of a fictional tradition that had not yet been established by the time *Treasure Island* putatively takes place, Jim naively assumes at first that Silver is as kindly as Marryat's Masterman Ready, the island as free from adult corruption as Marryat's uncontaminated Eden. But as Nancy Armstrong observes of *Oliver Twist*'s Fagin,[42] Silver's motherliness cloaks its mercenary opposite. He has his share of second-echelon evangelical virtues; alone among the pirates he values frugality, for instance, and since he has married a black woman he may have that sense of universal brotherhood that seems to the disapproving squire to be simple bad taste. Like Smollett, he is a keen judge of character, able to tell Nature's gentlemen from her louts at a glance (another faculty the squire lacks). But the chief use to which he puts his facility at reading others is not to improve them morally but to manipulate their egos to serve himself. His seduction of the piously reared Dick is typical: "Look here: you're young, you are, but you're as smart as paint. I see that when I set my eyes on you, and I'll talk to you like a man." When Jim overhears this dialogue, his shock is again that of the sibling displaced in the mother's affections; he observes to the reader, "You may imagine how I felt when I heard this abominable old rogue addressing another in the very same words of flattery as he had used to myself. I think, if I had been able, that I would have killed him through the barrel."[43]

Silver's callous manipulation of the concept of manhood—the most sacred word in Victorian boys' literature—is not only brilliant, it is disconcertingly akin to Stevenson's own technique in this novel. For like his creator, Silver well knows that those whose manliness he pretends to validate aren't men at all; true manliness can't be led around by the ego. (Silver himself is immune to the pressures of outside opinion, not because he hearkens instead to the word of God but because precisely the opposite is true: he has no respect for his fellows because he cares only for his own will.) Stevenson thus puts us in the peculiar position of having to accept the intellectual judgments of the antihero while remembering not to trust this character spiritually; the pirate's kind of maturity is more culpable than immaturity, since he shows his contempt for androgynous morality by exploiting it to benefit himself.

To juggle both awarenesses is beyond Jim, who is clearly uneasy with the over-masculine "adult" world of greed and guile in which he must learn to operate if he is to survive, but who lacks the experience to recognize that what he is dealing with has nothing to do with true manliness. The game behind this complex and somewhat cruel make-believe depends on the reader's ability to recognize that the universe of *Treasure Island* is *only* the universe of boyish entertainment (the penny dreadful, the public-school novel, the sea story), which has nothing to do with the universe of adult morality. Roger Lancelyn Green identifies the "startlingly new" aspect of this novel as its antididacticism—"it was not 'written down'" to its audience.[44] He is exactly wrong: the startling aspect of *Treasure Island* is that the didacticism aims only at adult readers, who must "read down" through the haze of a century's worth of boys' books. Stevenson's placement of the novel within an amoral tradition of pure adventure is the chief irony in a work in which irony reigns supreme.

The popularity of *Treasure Island* lent a new impetus to adventure writing. Among Stevenson's fledgling rivals was H. Rider Haggard, who, denigrating Stevenson's best-seller, was challenged by a brother to write "anything half as good."[45] The result, completed six weeks later, was *King Solomon's Mines* (1885), which made an instant hit; the British edition alone sold 31,000 copies in its first year. Morton Cohen attributes the novel's success to its straightforwardness: "It was a tale of adventure and heroic deeds, and its hero was a well-adjusted Englishman, competent, strong, sensible. . . . There was no heroine, nor should there have been. Penetrating Africa was a man's job. The adventure was the thing, and there was plenty of it."[46]

But subsequent critics have diagnosed a sea of troubles beneath the narrative's apparently flat surface. Far from being a stock novel of imperialist conquest, Norman Etherington holds, what we have here is "a trek from the known into the unconscious unknown self," in which finally "Haggard's characters have moved progressively through a symbolic landscape from physical tests to moral tests. The closer the adventurers come to the mines, the farther they are removed from the psychological and moral verities of their age."[47] Hartwig A. Vogelsberger concurs, reading the tale as a conscious rejection of the Darwinian values Haggard's villains espouse. The British explorers "are constantly being tested, both morally and physically. The closer they come to the legendary mines they set out to find, the more alienated they are from the moral truths of their Victorian age."[48] In these readings Haggard's novel is no paeon to white masculinist supremacy, but a subversive parable intended to undermine it.

The key to Haggard's romances is his mythologizing of sex. Writing after the Darwinism he so disliked had gone far to replace the God of the spirit with the god of the body, Haggard fights back by continually suggesting that sexuality is not the enemy of religion but the cornerstone of a new theology. His impatience with *Treasure Island* presumably had to do with its unconcern with the sexual dynamic; in placing himself in competition with Stevenson, Haggard breathed life into a previously unimportant tradition—that of the adventure novel whose main tension is interior because its power derives from sublimated sexuality. The best pre-Haggard example of such a work is Ballantyne's 1861 sequel to *The Coral Island*, *The Gorilla Hunters*.

Inspired by Paul du Chaillu's popular travelogue *Exploration in Equatorial Africa* (1861), *The Gorilla Hunters* exploits the Darwinist fascination with apes. But it does so in anti-Darwinian style: the slaughter of every humanoid ape in sight by Jack, Ralph, and Peterkin acts as a metaphor for the three men's silent struggle against their own animal passions. Having accepted that the line between human and beast is thin, Ballantyne primarily cares about how we may keep from crossing it, thus preserving our pre-Darwinian status as a separate creation. Christianity and civilization tame instinct; and the instinct most in need of taming is sexuality, for which the blood-lust of whites and natives alike is an effective sublimation. At twenty-five, twenty-two, and twenty-one, Jack, Ralph, and Peterkin, single men all, have nowhere but in the jungle to vent their passions. That they do have passions is evident. Peterkin's dreams link danger, desire, and bestiality as he imagines hunting elephants that wear wigs, crinolines, and wedding rings; Ralph consciously analyzes the semi-sexual joys of the chase, to conclude that while the intellectual pleasures of observing Nature may last longer, the average man will prefer "the gush of excitement and eagerness" attendant upon killing animals.[49]

This orgasmic release seems to be what civilization is designed to control; for example, Christianity has taught the young men's native guide one sort of restraint by instilling in him chivalry. Ralph complacently notes how much more volatile Africans are than Britons; at a moment's notice "the jovial, kindly, hearty fellows" may be "darting through the woods, besmeared with blood, and yelling like maniacs or demons." The irony is that given the chance, Ralph and his friends act as wildly as their bearers; the real point of Western culture seems to be how strictly it regulates the opportunities to let the barriers down. One hunts in Africa; one conforms in London. Escaping to the jungle by invoking scientific discovery, Englishmen can let themselves go, claim virtue for their efforts, and return home satiated. Tallying gorilla carcasses at the end of the expedition ("Thirty-six, if you count the babies in arms"), Ralph observes, "If it were not that we have killed all these creatures in the cause of science . . . I should be perfectly miserable." Context counts. But Peterkin is more clear sighted: "Humph! I suspect that a good deal of wickedness is perpetrated under the wing of science."[50]

The point of this orgy of slaughter is not simply killing, but killing gorillas, apparently because the apes symbolize bestial masculinity. The "old bachelor" gorilla, "very large, remarkably fierce, uncommonly ugly, desperately vindictive, and peculiarly courageous," is the gorilla—or the savage—of legend and their chief quarry. Peterkin and Jack have a running joke in which Peterkin is a monkey and Jack a gorilla; in a sense, they hunt themselves. And the only gorilla whose life Ralph spares is female, a gorilla equivalent of the Angel: "There was a certain air of tenderness about this mother, as she stroked and pawed her little one, that went straight to my heart." Fittingly, the novel ends when Ralph has passed the ultimate test of manhood by killing his gorilla in single combat; symbolically, he has vanquished his passions, and we suppose that he is now entitled to marry an Angel. The three are ready to return to civilization, although Peterkin, always the most volatile and impetuous, gets the final ambiguous word. Addressing his erstwhile victims "with a deep sigh," he remarks, "Fare you well, ye monstrous apes—gorillas, fare you well!"[51]

For Ballantyne real manhood means leaving the jungle, but for Haggard it means entering it. Haggard's predecessors seek to extirpate sexuality, while Haggard seeks to sanctify it. That there is more going on in *King Solomon's Mines* than meets the eye first becomes evident with the topography of Haggard's Africa, in which explorers wishing to reach the mines in the hidden valley must cross the mountains known as Sheba's Breasts and pass ruins carved with sacred phalluses. Although the putative quest in this tale is for male bonding (Sir Henry Curtis seeks reunion with his estranged brother), the action actually revolves around the discrediting of the withered witch Gagool and her puppet king, who together represent wrongful asexual authority, in favor of the nubile native girl Foulata and the virile rightful heir to the throne. Love and sacrifice achieve victory through a sexuality that may not be evangelical but is certainly religious; simultaneously, the Africans rightly reject the sterile possibility of British governance.

King Solomon's Mines offers a tentative draft of the Haggard ethos, interweaving love, death, and power but never seeming sure of what to say about them. For the full-dress performance of the themes rehearsed in Haggard's first adventure, we must move to his second six-week spectacular, *She* (1886). In many ways *She* recapitulates the earlier story: the blunt old hunter Allen Quatermain becomes the misogynistic scholar Horace Holly; the superb male animal Sir Henry Curtis becomes the superb male animal Leo Vincey; the women, Foulata and Gagool, who represent good and evil, sexual devotion and selfish intellect, become Ustane and Ayesha—or Ayesha alone. Omitting the red herrings of imperialism and buried treasure, *She* concentrates on expressing Haggard's tangled feelings on religion, sex, and the religion of sex.

In its most oversimplified form, the paradoxical message of *She* is that sex is both death and eternal life. Last descendant of a Graeco-Egyptian priest of Isis named Kallikrates (one might loosely translate the name as "beautiful male strength") and his lover Amenartas, Leo is a dull young Englishman remarkable only for his looks and for his hereditary duty to avenge himself on Ayesha, She-Who-Must-Be-Obeyed, who two millennia earlier killed his ancestor. As Leo and his adoptive father, Holly, find, She is still alive in an unknown corner of Africa, mourning Kallikrates and awaiting his reincarnation and return—as Leo. But She's agenda is different from Leo's in that it involves not death but the long-awaited consummation of love. In fact, both events take place. As bewitched as he is horrified by Ayesha's sexual magnetism and ruthlessness (this time She kills her rival Amenartas, reincarnated as Leo's native mistress/wife, Ustane), Leo agrees to marry her but fears to enter the eternal flame that will make him immortal. Ayesha steps into it a second time, both to prove its safety and to cleanse herself of thousands of years of jealousy and rage, but the process reverses itself; She shrivels and dies, bewailing her fate and promising a sequel.

She constantly stresses the link between sex and death. Ayesha's country occupies the site of a former civilization, whose mummified inhabitants still litter the ground and attract the sexual appreciation of the living; both the native Billali and the supposedly civilized Holly fall under the spell of a fragrantly embalmed foot. Billali's own society is ruled by women, he says, "because without them the world could not go on; they are the source of life. . . . We worship them . . . till at last they grow unbearable. . . . [Then] we rise, and kill the old ones as an example to the young ones, and to show them that we are the strongest." Ayesha's first appearance, seductive and deadly, reminds Holly "most forcibly of a corpse in its grave-clothes. And yet I do not know why it should have given me this idea, seeing that the wrappings were so thin that I could distinctly see the gleam of the pink flesh beneath them."[52] The combined power of mortality and eroticism excites Holly's worship; he falls in love with She, as the perfect expression of womanhood—an unrequitable love, since unlike Leo Holly does not image maleness.

As Billali's social commentary suggests, the ultimate woman is more than the junction of sex and death; She is Nature, engendering, harvesting, and engendering again. Time and again Ayesha insists to Holly that She is in no way magical, and indeed that "there is no magic. 'Tis only a force that thou dost not understand." Controlling evolution, She creates a mute race of servants over centuries of breeding. But Nature is also true religion, and before the birth of Christ She preached to the angry elders in Jerusalem that "there is but one thing worth living for, and that is Love in its highest sense."[53] Neither entirely sexual nor entirely self-sacrificing, Love requires the union of Aphrodite and Isis, Christian love and animal passion.

In the 1905 sequel, *Ayesha*, the message becomes yet more explicit when we discover that in one sense Ayesha and Isis are one—and perhaps one also with the evangelical Angel, who like Ayesha wishes to unite men, "direct their destinies, and cause wars, sickness, and poverty to cease," to "uphold the cause of the poor and the oppressed against the ravening lusts of Mammon." This time it is Leo who dies at Ayesha's kiss, teaching her at last that "in death is love's home, in death its strength." At this the Angel, Nature as Mother rather than as Lover, finally reaches her full power: "All pride and anger were departed from [her face]; it was grown soft, wistful, yet full of confidence and quietness. . . . Now it was like, indeed the counterpart almost, of the holy and majestic semblance of the statue of the Mother in the Sanctuary."[54] As Etherington suggests, Ayesha's redemption symbolizes the expulsion of Darwinian brutality from Nature[55]—which makes possible the inclusion of sexuality in Haggard's new Christianity.

In Haggard's myth there is little need for androgyny because there is little need for men. Ayesha's interest in Leo has baffled readers from Andrew Lang onwards; on reading the proofs of *She*, Lang commented that Leo was "not made a very interesting person. Probably he was only a fine animal. Anyhow that can't be helped now and never could perhaps. I dare say Kallikrates was no better."[56] Haggard's work thus strikes at the heart of late-Victorian trends that sought to celebrate the fine male animal over the deathless (yet perennially dying) female spirit. The tale's fascination depends on this opposition to the mores of its age; as Sandra Gilbert observes, its invocations of Egyptology, spiritualism, and the New Woman are all subversive of masculinist Victorian political, scientific, and economic structures.[57] In the profit-driven and unromantic world of nineteenth-century imperialism, then, in which pundits were forever invoking Haggard's pet hatreds of Darwinism and Podsnappian stuffiness to excuse everything he disliked about his own society, Ayesha—the "antithesis of practicality"[58]—is the feminine savior who can at once destroy and heal the civilization that rediscovers her. Wendy Katz writes of imperialist romances that the exotic settings "seemed to offer a source of wisdom," a way to "the essence of being" buried beneath a pile of stodgy fripperies.[59] In this sense, Ayesha *is* the empire—but an empire that will strike back.

Rider Haggard's imperial vision, and his vision of femininity, were to some extent uncharacteristic of boys' adventure stories; as the dedication of *King Solomon's Mines* "to all the big and little boys who read it" suggests, he intended to address himself to the widest possible male audience and complained because his nonrealistic approach to sexual questions had caused his most successful artistic efforts to be "spoken of with some contempt as 'boys' books.'"[60] In contrast, most turn-of-the-century adventure writers had no individual mythic agenda and no objection to being labeled boys' authors.

They were in the business of providing wholesome reading to manly boys, and to do so they played no new variations on the imperial dream. As a result, the heroes of Edwardian adventure, for all their respectability, bear a startling resemblance to Jack Harkaway. They lack his sexual uninhibitedness and his frank sadism, but they share his eternal resilience, his ability to master any situation, his conviction that properly harnessed physical strength is the essence of manliness. In such novels, femininity can be no more than an annoying intrusion. Nevertheless, some evangelical virtues remain: honesty, devotion to duty, unconcern for money, sexual restraint. But by the early twentieth century authors present these traits as the qualities of an ideal soldier, not in God's army but in the king's. What the qualities of an ideal woman may be, antifemininist narratives seem neither to know nor to care.

A typical example of the school of fiction that sought to sit down patriotism in religion's seat is Frank T. Bullen's *Frank Brown: Sea Apprentice* (1906). The echo of Thomas Hughes in the hero's name suggests a deliberate attempt to evoke an image not of an Arnoldian androgyne but of an English Everyboy, adventure-loving, extroverted, and good-hearted in a careless way—a Tom Brown who rejects the lure of androgynous conversion. Frank's initial desire to go to sea rather than to join his father in the countinghouse (accountants are notable for "the narrowness of their minds, the restriction of their intellectual boundaries") reflects the evangelical distrust of the marketplace. But Bullen depicts not a conscious moral decision but the instinctive male longing to escape a stultifying domesticity. Frank, a "perfectly healthy young animal, and free from vice because he had led a sheltered life . . . had suddenly felt the call of the wild. . . . The primal need held him."[61] Bullen thus rejects the control that lies at the heart of androgynous manliness, concentrating instead on freedom. Although at the start of his career, seasick and bullied, Frank longs for home and luxury, he and Bullen (and even Frank's tomboy sister, doomed to stay at home forever) know that shore life is tame, routine, and effeminate. Comfort and order have their place in a sailor's life, but comfort must be all-male and order seamanly if they are to satisfy real men.

In this deconstructive context Frank's fellow apprentice, the "delicate-looking" Harry Carter, is contemptible. The most junior in a hierarchy based on strength and seniority, Harry has no moral influence to reorder the priorities of his new world; so he falls apart. Having "no backbone," Harry "just degenerated into a little loafer who skulked out of everything he could, and made the only man who tried to befriend him . . . so disgusted with him that he gave up trying to teach him." His moral progress is a downward spiral, his only response to the glories of ocean life "the cunning of the weakling . . . , [and he] gave the second mate no end of trouble hunting him out of holes and corners where he would hide himself at night." The other boys force him to do their housekeeping, a demeaning task, but all that a girlish boy is fit for. When Harry finally jumps ship at Fiji, ruining his career prospects, breaking his parents' hearts, and proving "his utter inability to understand the meaning of life,"[62] we nod sagely. The Edwardian sea story is no place for femininity; its androgynes are no George Arthurs.

Frank, on the other hand, scores an unequivocal success. Eager to master his environment, he readily acquires new skills from the rough but good-hearted seamen. (His fellow apprentices, though, make "scurrilous remarks," apparently sexual in nature, about Frank and his tutor; male camaraderie, everyone knows, can go too far.) His strength increases, enabling him to quell bullying that would never respond to moral superiority. He readily sees his duty, and when he returns from his first voyage his parents rejoice that "the boy they had sent away with trembling hearts had stood the ordeal well, had come back clear-eyed and manly, nothing of the braggart, or sneak, or cad about him." His sexual attractiveness, though not his sexual interest, has grown correspondingly: "Of course all his girl friends promptly fell in love with him, much to his annoyance"[63]— annoyance because he has no desire to fall into the domestic trap.

To be sure, Bullen sees that difficulties are inescapable in an entirely masculine world. Frank's career frequently brings him into contact (and conflict) with bad officers—alcoholics, brutes, and martinets such as Captain Forrest, who "had wilfully and deliberately crushed out of himself all the finer feelings of humanity." Some of these his manly bearing can win over; the American second mate, Mr. Jacks, learns that Yankee mercilessness has no place on a British ship, and though he grumbles, "You so-and-so lime-juicers don't know what a man is," he recognizes that Frank's British brand of manliness has its own soundness. After Frank has proved his courage, "he was . . . treated by Mr. Jacks with a courtesy and consideration greater than that offered to any other man on board,"[64] and Jacks develops the intention (which his untimely death frustrates) to retire not to heartless America but to manly Britain. So manly influence is still possible.

Other officers, however, aren't always susceptible to conversion, and often Frank finds that he must simply endure as best he can.

Real men respect power sufficiently never to criticize their superiors, and by demonstrating this deference alongside his manly courage, skill, and luck, Frank early becomes an officer himself, acting as captain on one disaster-ridden crossing while still a teenager. His trials as well as his abilities have leached any feminine weakness out of him, so that "only his father of all the family now met him as an equal." No woman will have a chance to tie him down; having rejected the enervating domestic world, Frank is "in very truth . . . wedded to his ship."[65] For all the harshness of the male domain, men without women are real men.

Thus Bullen manipulates traditional evangelical ethics—selfless adherence to duty, passive resignation to injustice, the rejection of sexuality—to praise a manliness that claims to have nothing in common with evangelical androgyny. And like certain mid-Victorian adventure writers, he invokes realism as the opposite of feminine other-worldliness, emphasizing his own seafaring credentials and firsthand knowledge of the processes that build men. This tack is common among Edwardian adventure authors, who often stress the "truth" of their Spartan vision of manliness by linking their fictions to their own lives and implicitly offering themselves as role models for their readers. W. Gordon Stables, author of over a hundred adventure stories and historical novels for boys, advertised his manly work habits to W. W. Mayland in the *Captain* magazine for September 1900: "While hard at work in winter, it is his habit to rise at 4.30 A.M., have his cold tub, no matter how hard the frost may be, and get away down to his wigwam, where he works all day long at the open window, for this wiry Scot never goes near a fire."[66] Stables, who edited the medical correspondence column in the *Boy's Own Paper*, recommended his regimen to premanly boys, stressing the role of bracing air, cold water, and hot porridge in building character. A typical line in his column from October 1903 suggests Stables's convictions about the nature of true manliness: "REPENTANT (Bombay).—Yes; you can hope, if you abstain from evil thoughts and actions. Daily ablution of whole body; constant life in the fresh air. We seldom prescribe medicine, but Easton's syrup may be found useful, and Virol. This last is a food, and greatly sustains the body."[67] Convinced that androgyny meant effeminacy and vice, Stables insisted that his boys conform to a boylike pattern.

From Slum to Quarter-Deck (1908) is classic Stables. It also illuminates the changes in the religious publishing industry since the mid-nineteenth century; produced under the aegis of the Religious Tract Society, *Quarter-Deck*'s piety overtly rejects feminine values. The life

of its hero, Johnnie Reid, is as full of incident as that of the protagonist of any shilling shocker and almost as empty of introspection.
Before he reaches his teens, he has been shipwrecked and adopted
by a motherly alcoholic; saved two little girls from a tenement fire
("'Humph!' he said. 'Were they both girls, after all?' Just like Johnnie. But he was the hero of that crowd all the same");[68] run away to
sea in hopes that the shock would cure his "auntie-mother" of drinking (surely no previous moral tale had allowed its hero's influence to
work through absence rather than presence); foiled two separate
pairs of burglars in as many weeks; survived a mysterious poisoning
attempt; been adopted into the upper middle class; won a cadetship
in the Royal Navy; weathered robbers' attacks in Madagascar and
fire aboard ship; and been revealed as a long-lost American mil-
lionaire with an evil uncle and a wrongfully imprisoned mother. And
these are only the high points. This superabundance of plot suggests
that Stables, who as a respectable author would once have joined the
critics attacking improbable sensationalism, has instead joined the
Edwardian revolution against tameness. Sensation—and plenty of
it—has become an inevitable ingredient of "realistic" adventure
stories, which wage war against the interiorized values of androgynous manliness.

Accordingly, while evangelical piety does exist in the tale of Johnnie Reid, it is a piety curiously mixed with the qualities the evangelicals most disliked. Johnnie admires the district missionary, Mr. Bell,
not for his Christianity but for his ability to punch out the wicked:
"Knocked him out in the third round." The boy, eyes "now fairly
dancing with delight," observes that the missionary must be strong;
"Fairly strong," Bell responds; "I could put you up like a forty-
pound dumb-bell with my left hand." So attractive is this brand of
religion that Johnnie agrees to attend Sunday school, even though
there are girls there—if Bell will teach him to box. The muscularity
is obvious, the Christianity obscure: "Mr. Bell was never 'preachy.'
His object was to teach Johnnie to think for himself." Stables has no
desire to be preachy either, even under the Religious Tract Society
imprint, and when Johnnie and his mentor discuss scripture, they do
so offstage. Similarly, although both Stables and Johnnie concede
that strong emotion is part of being a strong man, Johnnie never
brings himself to indulge in potentially feminine behavior. Earnestly
praying before he runs away from home, "he felt that to cry might
have done him good, although it would have been very girl-like"—
but no tears come.[69]

This tension between male and female ethics animates the novel throughout. More of a benefactor to Johnnie even than Bell is Pizzie the pugilist, by far the most respectable occupant of the slum; good-hearted, generous, devoted to his family, he saves his money, keeps a cozy house, and does the detective work to uncover Johnnie's true identity. Kindness and physical strength go hand in hand. Johnnie himself, taking more prizes than any other boy in the history of the naval training program, "strangely enough" prides himself only on "a first for boxing, a first for swimming and a third, I think, for rowing." If academic awards are meaningless, it's because in the new manliness mental and spiritual qualities are only offshoots of bodily strength. As Stables observes, "A boy will not have the true courage . . . to do much good as a volunteer if he does not keep himself in perfect health."[70] And if virtue depends on keeping fit, a boy who does his boxing exercises religiously has no occasion for the sense of sin so crucial to pious mid-Victorians like A.L.O.E. Thus Johnnie can look back on his early years as the happiest of his life, for in them he touched moral perfection by using his body to master his environment.

By the twentieth century, the romance of masculine power colors even woman-authored adventure stories. In *The Lost Prince* (1915) the versatile Frances Hodgson Burnett recants *Fauntleroy*'s support of Angelic ideals and goes *The Secret Garden* one better not only by underscoring the moral virtue of physical strength but also by suggesting that this quality is unique to maleness. At twelve, Marco Loristan (secret heir to the throne of Samavia) "was a very big boy— tall for his years, and with a particularly strong frame. His shoulders were broad and his arms and legs were long and powerful." His size somehow demonstrates self-discipline as well as maturity; Marco takes after his father, Stefan, whose charisma arises from the way his "fine limbs and muscles and nerves obeyed" his will. Strength and self-control go together, permitting the father to treat his son as a full-fledged soldier in the fight for Samavia. As Stefan observes, "I know you are—a *man*, though you have lived but twelve years."[71]

Uncontrolled, ineffectual, and weak, femininity is the opposite of soldierhood. Appropriately, Marco's chief antagonist, Eugenia Karovna, shams Angelic qualities in an attempt to sap Marco's discipline, undo his father's training, and reduce the young soldier to the level of a child. They first meet when Eugenia pretends invalidism by claiming a sprained ankle. The classic Victorian equation of frailty and goodness excites Marco's admiration; he can interpret her "only as a gentle angel." Indeed, "He could not help liking her. She was so lovely and gracious and brave. He could not bear to see

the suffering in her face." Having disarmed him by this manipulation of convention, she tries to weaken him by insisting on the androgyny of boyhood and the pleasures of letting go: "'Has he taught
you to be calm too?' she said pathetically. 'You are only a boy. Boys
are not calm. Neither are women when their hearts are wrung. Oh,
my Samavia! Oh, my poor little country! My brave, tortured country!' and with a sudden sob she covered her face with her hands."
But since his father has ordered him to hide his connection with
Samavia, Marco keeps silence. Nor does he break down when the
spy locks him in a dark cellar, since he and his father contend that
"only harm could come from letting one's mind run wild. 'A mind is
either an engine with broken and flying gear, or a giant power under control,' was the thing they knew."[72] Feminine wiles can't dent
his control, and when Eugenia realizes her lack of power over him,
she shrugs and vanishes from the novel. Femininity is sly, enervating, and dangerous, but it cannot harm alert manhood.

Burnett suggests that even femininity can redeem itself by taking
on masculine characteristics. *The Lost Prince* has its androgynous boy
in The Rat, the cripple whose body bars him from a military career,
even while his storyteller's imagination makes him the leader of his
pseudomilitary gang. His frustration and humiliation have inspired
his nickname, since, he says, "I feel like one. Every one's my enemy.
I'm vermin. I can't fight or defend myself unless I bite"; and again,
"I want to go to war! . . . I want to fight! I want to lead a lot of men
into battle! And I haven't got any legs. Sometimes it takes the pluck
out of me." His problem is clearly that of the woman who longs to
play unfeminine roles, but The Rat has a recourse. Having "fixed
all his mental powers on one thing," he has made himself a military genius; having conceived "a kind of desperate adoration" for
Stefan,[73] he motivates himself to overcome his disability to some extent by learning to walk with crutches. Once he has won some degree of masculinity, The Rat can both plan and join the mission to
restore Samavia's rightful monarch.

Burnett notes that "the admiration The Rat had for [Stefan] was
an impassioned and curious feeling which possessed him entirely. It
seemed to Marco that it was beginning to be like a sort of religion."[74]
Exactly so. As Phyllis Bixler has observed, Samavian nationalism has
strong religious overtones,[75] in which national and personal hopes
center on Stefan's return and Samavia's consequent acquisition of
perfect masculine strength and disciplined power. Stefan himself has
learned to pray "to the Power—to the Strength-place—to the
Thought that does things," and so much a part of him is this wor-

ship that there is more than a suggestion that Stefan is a God and Marco, of course, his Son. One notes chapter titles such as "How Shall We Find Him?" ("Him" refers to the Lost Prince, who is at once Stefan and Samavia's legendary savior) and bits of dialogue such as "I am the son of Stefan Loristan, and I have given the Sign to all. . . . The Lamp is lighted." To the Samavians "Marco was not a mere boy . . . he was the son of Stefan Loristan," and they almost go mad with worship on seeing him. Their priest has a better sense of the proper rituals of the religion of manliness, telling the frenzied mob, "Madness is not the homage you must bring to the son of Stefan Loristan. Obey! Obey!"[76] When Stefan finally gains his throne, and Marco and The Rat their military uniforms, the religion of masculinity has toppled the false Angel.

The dominating of adventure stories by the masculine concerns that resonate in the titles of Stables's and Burnett's novels is what David Daniell characterizes as the shift from "empire" literature to a more aggressive "imperialist" literature. The latter "leaves the christian family ambience and becomes all-male and public school: military values invade and take over the stories; religion is subordinated to fighting; weakness is at best discounted and at worst punished." It is the prevalance of this imperialist strain in boys' fiction that accounts for the changes editors imposed on John Buchan's only true juvenile thriller, *Prester John* (1910), when it ran serially as *The Black General* in *The Captain* magazine. Lacking the previous generation's tolerance for ambiguity, the editors eliminated the biblical cadences of Buchan's prose, the narrator's sensitivity to beauty and his occasional confessions of weakness or fright, and all passages—"as perhaps too dangerous"—that encourage us to admire the black antihero.[77] Even in its unmutilated version, however, *Prester John* has none of the emphasis on androgyny, the girlish heroes and boyish heroines so typical of Buchan's thrillers for adults. Rather, this twentieth-century reply to Stevenson and Haggard is a meditation on magnificent masculinity, a male counterpart to *She*.

John Laputa, the African priest-conqueror, has much in common with Haggard's heroine. The spiritual heir or perhaps the reincarnation of the legendary Prester John, he has the potential, according to a reluctant white admirer, to be "a second Napoleon. He is a born leader of men, and as brave as a lion. There is no villainy he would not do if necessary, and yet I should hesitate to call him a blackguard." John shares Ayesha's charisma, her ability to enchant even her antagonists; the narrator, John's enemy David Crawfurd, continually finds himself swept off his feet by John's oratory and sheer

5. *Accepting the Quest.* Manhood and war are equated as Marco's father explains the Samavian troubles. Illustration by Maurice L. Bower to *St. Nicholas*'s serialization of F. H. Burnett's *The Lost Prince* (November 1914).

physical presence. Arrogantly beautiful, with "a hawk nose like an Arab, dark flashing eyes, and a cruel and resolute mouth,"[78] the leader's bodily glories are only apparent when he is dressed (or undressed) as a savage. But he can also operate with considerable success in the white world, preaching in Scottish pulpits and dying with a quotation from Shakespeare on his lips.

By contrast, David is insubstantial, lacking John's magnetism and confidence. That civilization can prevail against John, containing the savage masculinity he arouses in his African warriors, seems doubtful, especially since John's attractiveness is such that neither we nor David are entirely sure that this noble force deserves thwarting. To John the priceless collar of Prester John is a holy relic to ensure freedom and African self-determination; to David it can only be treasure trove. White civilization, it may seem, has little to offer beyond a morally ambiguous domesticity.

Given Buchan's love for John Bunyan, we may read the novel as a

6. *Completing the Quest*. Marco, now nearly man's height, finally sees his father's true resplendency. Illustration by Maurice L. Bower to *The Lost Prince* in *St. Nicholas* (October 1915).

parable of the mythic clash between gorgeous instinct and dry self-discipline, in which both sides suffer from greed, dishonesty, and bigotry. Civilization ultimately wins because the white man has "the gift of responsibility," the sense that he must be "well content to find his reward in the fulfillment of his task"; but in order to turn from "a rash boy into a serious man," David must cultivate and harness his resemblance to John by sympathizing with the despised natives and acting as the dead king's mouthpiece.[79] Britain can win the contest for Africa only by Africanizing itself. Piety indeed has its place in this example of "empire literature," but not merely as an artifact of civilization; its primary role is to channel and discipline the spiritual power that riots too free in John's anticivilized brand of men. For Buchan empire is holy because in it order can gain the power and richness of disorder. And in this particular sample of the Buchan mythology, feminine power is unknown and irrelevant; David Crawfurd's task is to understand, acquire, and govern masculinity.

One of the most important trends in the adventure genre may therefore be its rejection of androgynous manliness and its replacement of the religion of femininity with the religion of manhood. As the twentieth century continues, the turn-of-the-century adventure hero is reborn again and again as the agent of a society by which he himself, by virtue of his perfect masculinity, remains untrammeled. As a great detective, as a war hero, as a lord of the elements such as W. E. Johns's Biggles, and as Superman, he fights for truth, justice, and the Anglo-American way with weapons that his creators claim are uniquely male, be they superior logic, superior skill, or superior strength.[80] As Victorian androgyny increasingly lost ground, masculinity and military strength gained it. Indeed, such was the force with which the adventure story rejected womanly values that after the Oscar Wilde scandal damaged the respectability of fin-de-siècle androgyny, there was a critical movement to redefine adventure tales as high culture: because they attacked Angelic mores, they must deserve serious attention.[81]

It is presumably this post-Victorian surge in the moral status of masculinist ideals that nourishes our own readiness to think of adventure stories as the archetype of Victorian children's literature. We are conditioned not to believe in Angels, precisely because adventure-tale authors were so conscious of the Angel that they constantly tried to redesign her. It was not Victorian storytellers but their postwar heirs, benefiting from the sexologists' redefinition of gender and morality, who finally won the struggle against femininity and re-created children's literature in their own image.

The Reforming Impulse
and the Fantasy

"Every one who has considered the subject," wrote Charles Dickens in his 1853 *Household Words* article "Frauds on the Fairies," "knows full well that a nation without fancy, without some romance, never did, never can, never will, hold a great place under the sun."[1] And with this opinion the majority of writers from midcentury onward heartily concurred. The pleas of eighteenth-century rationalists and preachers that fairy tales were no better than lies faded into silence as children and adults alike welcomed translations of Hans Christian Andersen and the brothers Grimm. Around 1850, fantasy writing became a pursuit of the eminent—and especially of the eminent social critics, as Dickens, William Makepeace Thackeray, and John Ruskin, followed by Charles Kingsley, George MacDonald, and other reformer/sages, tried their hand at combining serious messages with ornamental settings. The commitment to realism that struck early writers as essential to truth seemed to many mid-Victorians to be in fact inimical to it; as Sissy Jupe teaches in *Hard Times* (1854), there is more to a flower than its Latin name and botanical construction. To think only in terms of what is possible may make it impossible to understand what is important, for, according to the anonymous writer of "Children's Literature" in the *London Review* (January 1860), "there are duties of *being* as well as of doing. There are truths of imagination, as well as truths of fact."[2]

Thus, from its birth Victorian fantasy as a whole was less interested in escaping from reality than in criticizing it. Defending themselves against the charge that fantasy was untrue, authors attacked the values of fact—technical proficiency, acquisitiveness, practical utility—which coincided, significantly, with the values of the masculine public sphere. Unsentimental, money-minded, dominant, and virile, the Black Brothers of Ruskin's *The King of the Golden River* (1851; written in 1841) are perfect products of the Industrial Revolution; that they turn to stone while the powerless androgyne Gluck inherits the living gold of fertile and feminine Nature is typical of Victorian fantasy's happy endings. Perhaps more than any other type of children's literature in the nineteenth century, fantasy originated in the idealizing of childhood as a refuge from the excesses of adult masculinity. Postulating a reality impossible by the terms of Victorian (male) science, the genre could adopt ethics impossible within Victorian (male) laissez-faire capitalism. Because fantasy in general—and Victorian fantasy in particular—seeks "that which has been silenced, made invisible, covered over and made 'absent,'"[3] the influence of the Angel resonates throughout such stories.

In part, Victorian fantasy descends from the Romantic era's stress on the childlike imagination, as well as from such Romanticist studies as anthropology and folklore, which likewise often sought to locate virtue in the unsophisticated by arguing that savagery might be nobler than civilization. But the genre is also inseparable from the evangelical tradition. Not only did many religious writers see a connection between the literature of the impossible and the Christian didactic forms of allegory and parable; not only did the evangelical emphasis on one's "personal apprehension of God"[4] permit and even encourage the development of individual symbolic systems; but the entry of elements of the supernatural (the "above-nature") tended to induce in the reader a sense that what lies beyond our senses is what matters. More than any other fiction, fantasy requires our "willing suspension of disbelief," just as faith in God does; as George Landow observes, it therefore becomes the ideal vehicle for conveying such "essentially paradoxical" tenets of Victorian Christianity as the concept that death is the highest form of life.[5] Similarly, as apologists were quick to point out, since fantasy takes place in a world alien to that of the reader, it supports religion in discouraging egotism. The *London Review* comments that through fantasy, "the thoughts of a child are carried *out* from himself. . . . No unhealthy introspection, no personal vanity can possibly be stimulated."[6]

In keeping with the evangelical stress on the individual soul, fantasies in the late nineteenth and early twentieth centuries seem, far more frequently than does most children's fiction, to have had some particular child in mind. Not only did Ruskin write for Effie Gray and Lewis Carroll for Alice Liddell,[7] but Kingsley produced *The Water Babies* (1863) for his youngest son (since the older children shared a claim to *The Heroes*); Dinah Mulock Craik first told her fairy stories to her daughter; *The Wind in the Willows* (1908) initially found written expression as letters to little Alistair Grahame; and much of *Peter Pan* (1911) aims at the real-life Lost Boys, the Llewellyn-Davies family. Other writers—MacDonald, E. Nesbit—endow their childish heroes with the names or the characteristics of their own children, and while such twinning of fact and fiction occurs elsewhere in children's fiction, only in fantasy does it appear to be the rule rather than the exception. Fantasy seems to have a natural bias toward the private, toward traditions of orality and the rituals of family life, toward androgyny with the uniquely balanced gender ratios of its wider audiences.

And also, perhaps, toward subversion. Because of the importance of symbolism to this form, Victorian and Edwardian fantasies not only are able to create utopias where feminine values rule, but can permit the veiled expression of concerns about sexuality—even deviant sexuality. Like dreams, fantasy literature is a gold mine to the psychoanalytically inclined, and perhaps for the same reason: to label something "unreal" is to lower one's shield of inhibition; to create a world sacred to supposedly asexual childhood is to enable oneself to discuss the unspeakable without offending respectability.[8] The Jungian child, reconciling male and female through its androgyny, also reconciles conscious and unconscious through its nearness to primal innocence. Anticipating Jung, Victorian fantasists typically use their tales covertly to evade adult restrictions on gender and sexuality.

Discussing the role of the child in Victorian adult literature, Peter Coveney finds that the depiction of "innocent" childhood may have provided grown writers and readers with "a means of escape" from a complex and frightening world they weren't really mature enough to handle, "a means for coming to terms with the guilt created by a widely imposed repressive sexual morality" by denying, in effect, that sexuality existed.[9] Within the context of fantasies for children, however, this response is—paradoxically—more Edwardian than Victorian. Such modern critics as Susan Chitty, Maureen Duffy, and Ravenna Helson read *The Water Babies* as a parable about masturbation or childish sexual curiosity, in which the urges of the body may finally be vindicated, while Ruskin worried about the frankness of the erotic symbolism in MacDonald's "The Light Princess" (1862). But the fantasies of Barrie and Grahame, written at a time when sexual repression was beginning to seem increasingly inappropriate, suggest sex's dangers with all the horror of a mid-Victorian social-purity crusader. Simultaneously, fantasy seemed to be losing its didactic steam, so that in many Nesbit novels, for instance, the very structure of the narrative defuses the drive toward moral growth.[10] What began as a rejection of the adult male world ends as a rejection of maturity in any form; while Victorian fantasies may focus on the loving mother's likeness to God, their Edwardian equivalents often see her as monstrous because of her sexual knowledge.

Thus U. C. Knoepflmacher's contention that Victorian fantasy depends not only on adults' ambition to make children grown-ups, but on adults' longing to become children themselves,[11] convinces better with a chronological context; one thinks of the turn-of-the-century habit of writing children's books for adults (Grahame's *The Golden Age*, Nesbit's Bastable stories) and of the adult audience that first made *Peter Pan* a smash hit on stage. As children's fiction and the late-Victorian cult of the child increasingly established the child's separateness and superiority, fantasy literature, always spearheading the rejection of the marketplace's values, turned its subversive drive even against the adult Angel. Late fantasy may retain many of the tenets of mid-Victorian Angelhood, celebrating selflessness, conversion, and ideal death with all the fervor of its evangelical ancestors; but the Angel herself, adult and thus destructive, is barred from the childish paradise.

How to provide an adequate definition of fantasy is a vexed critical question. To C. N. Manlove fantasy is "a fiction evoking wonder and containing a substantial and irreducible element of the supernatural with which the mortal characters in the story or the readers become on at least partly familiar terms."[12] But a child's standards of the wonderful may differ from an adult's; a talking rabbit may seem no less probable than pirate treasure or tiger hunts, since the average child would classify all as things that happen only in books. Perhaps children's fantasy requires a definition that focuses more on the adult author's intent than on the child reader's response, such as: "Any fiction hinging on the deliberate amendment of universal physical laws." The wonder and the sense of rebellion evoked here seem to coincide with maturity; as most Victorians knew and many regretted, it is adults who have the best-developed sense of impossibility.

Nevertheless, definitions of fantasy and the fantastic designed for adult readers of, say, Kafka often prove provocative in considering some particular work for children. Thus Tzvetan Todorov's contention that "the fantastic is that hesitation experienced by a person who knows only the laws of nature, confronting an apparently supernatural event"[13] illuminates *The Water Babies*, a work that thrives on inducing the reader's "hesitation" through constantly contradicting its own premises.

Readers may have a hard time deciding whether *The Water Babies* is sophisticated or merely confused. Kingsley's tone may baffle; while the reader is always "my little man," naive and prepubescent, Kingsley's digressions are thoroughly adult in content, ranging from parodies of the dispute over the hippocampus major to disparagements of American culture and politics. Editors abridge, readers despair. The most common technique of dealing with the novel is to decide, perhaps arbitrarily, that it is "about" one particular theme: the "neurotic hatred of dirt," the resisting of illicit sexual temptation, redemption and purification, punishment and the need for discipline, or the search for faith.[14] Stephen Prickett offers a more illuminating solution, suggesting that the structure of the novel, accretive and heterogeneous, mirrors that of the book's setting Harthover House—described by Kingsley as having been "built at ninety different times, and in nineteen different styles . . . as if somebody had built a whole street of houses of every imaginable shape, and then stirred them together with a spoon"—which in turn mirrors that of Nature.[15] But while Nature is an obvious and constant preoccupation in *The Water Babies*, we may find it still more useful to view the structure and self-contradictions of the novel as an image of the Victorian subconscious.

Shorn of digressions, the story is straightforward enough: Tom, the sweep, comes with his cruel master, Grimes, to clean the chimneys of Sir John Harthover's mansion. Taking a wrong turn and ending up in the bedroom where Sir John's little daughter, Ellie, is sleeping, Tom flees the household, which assumes he intended thievery. He arrives at the house of a kindly schoolmistress (who turns out to be Grimes's mother) but succumbs to exhaustion and delirium, wandering out to the river, where he drowns. The female guiding spirit who appears as a mysterious Irishwoman, the punishing Mrs. Bedonebyasyoudid, the rewarding Mrs. Doasyouwouldbedoneby, and the nature goddess Mother Carey resurrects him as a water-baby, to learn "from the beasts which perish."[16] After his babyhood in the river, Tom swims to the ocean, where on displaying unselfishness he is allowed the company of other water-babies. Ellie, at the seaside with the pedantic Professor Ptthmlln-sprts, dies as a consequence of the professor's refusal to admit the existence of anything outside Victorian scientific knowledge and becomes Tom's moral tutor after Tom shames himself by stealing sweets. Finally Tom goes on a solitary quest to forgive and redeem Grimes (dead after a poaching exploit); grown up, he and Ellie are reunited.

The ethics of these bare bones are straightforwardly Angelic. The world of grown men is narrow, exploitive, filthy, and dangerous even at its most well meaning; Sir John bears responsibility for Tom's death and the professor for Ellie's. Real life occurs in the "unreal" world of supernatural womanhood, where male greed and hardheartedness are the chief sins and only the androgynous "dear, sweet, loving, wise, good, self-sacrificing people" will get to heaven. Those who will evolve spiritually "must go first where they do not like, and do what they do not like, and help somebody they do not like";[17] to think only of one's own comfort and preferences is to de-volve into eft or ape. And only women or their protégés have either hope or intention of cleaning up the mess men have made of the "real" world.

But the digressions, symbolic patterns, and asides considerably muddy this ethic. Kingsley instructs his "little man" to grow up into a hunting squire like Sir John, but reproves his water-baby for display-ing similar instincts: "I am sorry to say, he was too like some other little boys, very fond of hunting and tormenting creatures for mere sport. Some people say . . . that it is nature, and only a proof that we are all originally descended from beasts of prey. But whether it is nature or not, little boys can help it, and must help it." If instinct leads Tom astray in that passage, Mother Carey later advises him to complete his quest by following his dog, "who goes by instinct, and therefore can't go wrong." The plot, too, is deliberately inconsistent. By the world's standards, both Tom and Ellie die in childhood; nev-ertheless they grow up to rejoin earthly society. And for all Kingsley's dubiousness about Victorian science and technology, which create both chimney sweeps and narrowly learned professors, Tom's ten-ure as a water-baby makes him "a great man of science . . . [who] can plan railroads, and steam-engines, and electric telegraphs, and rifled guns, and so forth; and knows everything about everything, except . . . two or three . . . little things which no one will know till the coming of the Cocqcigrues."[18]

Finally, the novel is ambiguous about sexuality. Tom's intrusion into Ellie's bedroom, in which she is "an angel out of heaven" and he "a little black ape," suggests the customary mid-Victorian suspicion that men are highly sexed and therefore dirty and bestial, while women are virginal and unawakened and therefore pure and Angelic. Later Kingsley ties the novel's insistence on cold baths to the common cure for masturbation, which will render boys unfit to marry: the grown Ellie sits on a rock in the sea singing a siren song that is both tempting and good. Should the child reader wonder about the nature of the song, Kingsley tells him, "Ah, my little man, I am too old to sing that song, and you too young to understand it. But have patience, and keep your eye single, and your hands clean, and you will learn some day to sing it yourself, without needing any man to teach you"—so long as "you have plenty of cold water to wash in," for all will end happily "as long as you stick to hard work and cold water." As exemplified by the twin fairies, woman is both austerely forbidding and erotically maternal; Mrs. Doasyouwouldbe-doneby erases Tom's guilt over Ellie when "she took Tom in her arms, and laid him in the softest place of all, and kissed him, and patted him, and talked to him, tenderly and low, such things as he had never heard before in his life; and Tom looked up into her eyes, and loved her, and loved, till he fell fast asleep from pure love."[19] If the water world counteracts sexuality, it also suggests it, and as Tom discovers on his quest, Nature takes her revenge on those who, like the extinct Gairfowl, insist on maintaining their virginity from pride or prudery.

The contradictions in Kingsley's fable indicate the complexity of his attempt to unite the separate spheres of male and female, science and religion, adult and child, sexuality and purity into a whole that will comprise not only the dull competence of the adult Tom but also those "two or three little things" that remain outside the Victorian ken. His enthusiastic Darwinism is equally enthusiastically Christian. But Kingsley's private theology seems frequently to have struggled against itself. Thus he saw sex as defilement, suggesting to his fiancée that since he could not offer her his virginity perhaps he could not in good conscience become her true husband, but also as religious sacrament, the best road to cultural communion between married partners and indeed among all who share the secret knowledge.[20] Likewise, woman is man's civilizer and hope, but effeminacy is the great enemy; the famous quarrel with Newman seems to have sprung from Kingsley's simultaneous fascination and repulsion with what he saw as the homosexuality underlying Catholic Mariolatry.[21]

Much as *The Water Babies* wants to unite masculine energy with feminine unselfishness to build the ideal androgynous Christian, then, Kingsley consistently undercuts the idea. Androgyny both entrances and terrifies, offering a solution to all masculine problems but potentially creating dreadful new ones. Tom learns the feminine

7. *Sexuality and Motherhood.* Sated with orality, the water-babies return to the undersea womb in Noel Paton's illustration to Charles Kingsley's fable.

ethic of Thomas Hughes's Arthur, but remains as thoroughly masculine as a young Tom Brown in scuba gear, "a little dogged, hard, gnarly, foursquare brick of an English boy."[22] He can't remain in the feminine Eden but must enter the uninspiring realm of adult maleness because that is what men do. Like his creator, Tom flirts with a feminine religion and rejects it for an existence that seems at once more straightforward and less satisfying. The structure of Tom's underwater life, wavering between evangelical introspection and the anti-introspective release of male energy through work, suggests not only the conflict among the various elements of the novel but also that within Kingsley himself. Perennially seeking what he called "simply a healthy and manful Christianity, one which does not exalt the feminine virtues to the exclusion of the masculine,"[23] Kingsley may never have developed a consistent creed. Within his own science, Kingsley "identifies the principle of sacrifice, whereby a weaker life-form succumbs to a stronger, as the 'crowning lesson' of bio-geology and Christianity"; the oddity of this definition of sacrifice implies Kingsley's difficulties in reconciling his conceptions of morality and masculinity.[24] Tom, the "normal" masculine boy who must learn both male and female values in order to conform to two opposing worlds, has a difficult task.

For Kingsley as for Herbert Spencer, "the first requisite in life [although not the last], is to be a good animal."[25] Sound flesh implies sound spirit, because, as the primary lesson of *The Water Babies* has it, "your soul makes your body";[26] invalids are weak in two ways. In *At the Back of the North Wind* (1870), however, Kingsley's friend MacDonald creates a more positive version of the quest for androgynous purity; although like Kingsley he accepts Darwin's findings, he puts them in a moral (and thus un-Darwinian) context.[27] In fiction as in family life holding woman to be the more evolved,[28] MacDonald explores the moral evolution of one child toward physical frailty and spiritual strength.

Like *The Water Babies*, *North Wind* has both a real and a superreal dimension. London, where little Diamond lives with his cabman father and ever-growing family, is as bleak as the chimney-sweeping world of Tom and Grimes, being populated by drunkards, brutes, hags, and the dishonest nouveaux riches as well as the beleaguered good. The heavenly antechamber "at the back of the North Wind," however, is a community of peace, hope, and understanding. On the "realistic" level, we discover that the way from earthly poverty to spiritual richness lies through suffering; in one sense Diamond's journeys with North Wind, which bring him ever closer to sainthood and artistry, represent the bouts of illness that finally lead to his joyful death. Virtue, creativity, and trial all manifest God's love, because each encourages selflessness, which will unite the soul with its Creator. And since, as MacDonald writes in *Unspoken Sermons* (1885), "the final end is oneness,"[29] we gradually realize that to the understanding soul there is no difference between natural and supernatural; God's presence illuminates daily life and dream life alike. It is less that we all "live in two juxtaposed worlds," as Prickett suggests,[30] than that our world is far greater and more unified than most of us can understand.

Because the mundane world is so much with us, however, only the childlike can come to this insight, and then only in rare cases. Hence God apparently finds it necessary to strip people of power through North Wind, who is also Ruin, Bad Fortune, and Death. Weakness creates dependency, community, and a sense of ego's inadequacy. From childish helplessness and enforced dependence on providence, the dishonest businessman Mr. Coleman, whom financial failure saves from damnation, and the street waif Nanny, whom illness renders "so sweet, and gentle, and refined, that she might have had a lady and a gentleman for a father and mother," learn to think less of themselves. Nanny even learns to dream. The "trusting self-abnegation" Diamond needs before he can travel with North Wind is what makes the world work; for instance, in learning to ride, Diamond finds that "in order to guide the horse, he had in a measure to obey the horse first."[31] Abandonment of self equals both duty and Christianity.

The emphasis on selflessness, the inadequacy of the public world, and the need for wholeness suggest that Diamond will be a classic example of the boy Angel, and indeed he is. His first serious illness (or protracted trip to the back of the North Wind) leaves him aware of his housewifely duties: "Things go right there [the dream-country], and so I must try to get things to go right here." His mother appreciates his efforts at baby-sitting, cooking, and cleaning, exclaiming, "You're as good to your mother as if you were a girl." From girlhood, he widens his sphere to Angelhood, visiting the home of the drunken cabman next door to comfort the baby and bring peace into the house, like "an angel with a flaming sword, going out to fight the devil." But it is the feminine rather than the warlike angel Diamond most recalls; like Esther Summerson, he goes quietly to work instead of "leaving ill-bred though well-meant shabby little books for them to read, which they were sure to hate the sight of."[32] Personal influence is what counts.

Nursing babies, composing verses, discouraging evil language by his innocent presence, uniting lovers, finding homes for destitute children—even driving his father's cab during the older man's illness—all are part of a selfless motherly competence so alien to the aggressive errors of "reality" that the uncomprehending christen Diamond "God's baby" because they assume that he is "wanting." Ironically, Diamond is "God's baby" precisely because he is "wanting" in no sense of the word. MacDonald believed with F. D. Maurice that Christianity and capitalism are incompatible.[33] And in *North Wind* the thirst for possession is what causes all social evils, from the assumption that our friends are only those who give us things, to the havoc rich brewers wreak, to the "going against the will of God" implicit in get-rich-quick schemes. Rather, Diamond lives according to the feminine ethics North Wind encourages; to get to her own back (in other words, to reach heaven), she explains, "I have only to consent to be nobody, and there I am."[34] According to the Angelic theology for which MacDonald was a spokesman, Diamond's death is thus not tragedy but joy, and MacDonald's lifelong death wish is not the "hatred for mankind" Robert Lee Wolff has called it, but love.[35]

Although his realistic novels outnumber his fantasies, MacDonald seems to have felt that fantasy has the greater claim on truth. Because it deals more in symbol than in direct representation, it can mean more, becoming the best antiegotistic instrument of self-examination in the reader—who is the "aeolian harp" upon which the author plays; the quality of the music depends on the quality of the listener.[36] It takes more imagination to read fantasy than to read fact—more trust, more willingness to leave ourselves, more nearness to God. Thus imagination is the third element in a MacDonaldian Trinity composed not of Father, Son, and Holy Spirit (smacking too much of the rejected Calvinism of his boyhood), but of Angelic mother, child, and poetic truth. To MacDonald imagination is "she" and works less like the muses than like the Angel, curbing "selfishness, avarice, sensuality, cruelty" by "conceiving the noblest forms of action" and "devising how to make home blessed or to help the poor neighbour." And like the Angel, the squelched imagination may degenerate into a mere doll, "absorbed in the invention of the new dress, or worse, in devising the means of procuring it. For, if she be not occupied with the beautiful, she will be occupied by the pleasant; that which goes not out to worship, will remain at home to be sensual."[37] Diamond's androgyny is no accident; it signals his imagination, talent for poetry, and likeness to Christ. His simultaneous location within fantasy and realism bestows upon him the greatest possible Angelic influence, since he must engage the reader's imagination on an expanded level.

To Rosemary Jackson religious fantasy is a betrayal of subversive urges, a way to "defuse potentially disturbing, anti-social drives and retreat from any profound confrontation with existential dis-ease" by fleeing into mystical nostalgia; there is little of the flirtation with the nonsignifier that should be fantasy's main concern.[38] Yet although *The Water Babies* may not satisfactorily resolve its "anti-social drives," its multilevel contradictions surely argue an unconventional approach to meaning. Likewise, *North Wind* concentrates on the "nonsignifying" in several ways, from the sense of seemingly sense-less verse to the importance of apparently unimportant people; throughout, it emphasizes the need to rethink standard interpreta-tions of reality. That both novels are religious fantasies little differ-entiates them from other mid-Victorian fantasies, which typically partake at least to some extent of MacDonald's femininist message; Jackson might better level her complaint at the style of the age than the style of the subgenre. Thus Dinah Mulock Craik's *The Little Lame Prince* (1875) suggests no consciously religious intent, being rather a parable of woman's position and the inadequacy of male power. Its political (or antipolitical) content, however, strikingly resembles *North Wind's*.

Prince Dolor—named for his selfless, Angelic, and dead mother, Dolorez—acquires at one blow during his christening withered legs and a fairy godmother. His debility gives him feminine influence, since "the sight of him and his affliction made other people good, and, above all, made everybody love him," but deprives him of polit-ical power when his virile uncle usurps the throne. Just as his injury results from the public sphere's insistence on cold pomp and cere-mony, his confinement takes place in an environment notably male, an infertile plain, "barren, level, bare, except for short stunted grass," relieved only by a phallic symbol, "one large round tower which rose up in the centre of the plain, and might be seen all over it. . . . [It] rose, right up out of the ground, as if it had grown of itself, like a mushroom. But it was not at all mushroom-like; on the contrary, it was very solidly built."[39] Here Dolor grows to boyhood with no one to tend him but a convict nurse—until his godmother arrives.

The latter somewhat resembles North Wind in her association with imagination and travel; she gives him a flying cloak so that he can leave the tower, although he may not land. But she isn't Bad Fortune so much as its cheerful acceptance. "You must be content to stay just what you are," she instructs him; "Your life will be quite different to most people's lives: but it may be a happy life for all that. Do not be afraid." Dolor, who, "if he had been like other boys, would doubtless have grown up daring and adventurous—a soldier, a sailor, or the like," learns from her that he "could only show his courage morally." Feminine endurance, as usual, is better than mas-culine pluck, and "he showed more real valour than if he had had six pairs of proper legs." Deprived of "almost all the ordinary delights of boy-life," he finally regains his throne after learning to do house-work while his nurse undertakes a quest to establish his rights. And

Dolor becomes an ideal king, not in spite of but because of his femininity: "He [had] learned how to take advice before attempting to give it, to obey before he could righteously command." Patient and selfless, he is happy; wedded to his affliction, he is pure, for "no wife in all the world would have been found so perfect, so lovable, so tender to him in all his weaknesses, as his beautiful old godmother."[40] After transforming the country, he joyfully abdicates power and flies off into the sunset.

The story is subtitled "A Parable," and its underlying message seems to be a threefold comment on "the female situation":[41] in natural capacity although not in physical strength, men and women are similar; men use women's weakness to confine them and to steal their share of power; women's enforced subordination renders them men's moral superiors. And come the time when the Angel regains her own, society will enter a golden age. Dolor's injury relates to all that is best in him—his unselfconsciousness, his endurance, his longing for community and lack of class bias, his creativity (symbolized by the cloak), his asexual purity. Critized by the merely masculine for being less than a man, Dolor is actually the better for his debility. It is the male system of judgment, contaminated by ego and desire, that errs; to the seeing eye, Dolor's weakness is strength.

Dolor has other incarnations within Craik's works, not only in her realistic children's stories but in her fiction for adults; the best-known example is Phineas Fletcher of *John Halifax, Gentleman* (1856). Fletcher and his kind are wonderful for the strength of their love and the weakness of their passion. Unlike Kingsley, who somehow equated sex with true religion, and MacDonald, who saw sex as "the hold God has of us with His right hand, while death is the hold He has of us with His left,"[42] Craik accepted the more prevalent feminist view that sex is too animal to be Christian. While MacDonald's fairy tales often suggest that sexual union is the "golden key" to androgynous completion in God, Craik indicates rather that Christianity is the means by which humanity can escape Nature. As she writes in *A Woman's Thoughts About Women* (1858), "Nature herself has apparently decided for women . . . that their natural destiny should be *not* of the world"; but Christianity restores Dolor(ez), "rais[ing] the woman to her rightful and original place, as man's one help-meet . . . his equal in all points of vital moment." Home is not enough, whatever Nature may think. The sexual union of opposites that occurs in such MacDonald stories as "The Day Boy and the Night Girl" (1879) is not a Craik trope; she prefers to depict characters who, like Dolor, unite the feminine and the masculine in one asexual body. "Some of the finest types of character we have known among both sexes," she asks, "are they not often those who combine the qualities of both?"[43] When androgyny is perfect, sex is unnecessary.

Craik's conjunction of fortunate suffering, eradicated instinct, androgynous boys, and messages more overtly social than Christian appears again in Mary Louisa Molesworth's *Four Winds Farm* (1887), whose conception also closely resembles MacDonald's *North Wind*. Here too we have a solitary boy, Gratian Conyfer (again named for his mother, Grace), self-forgetful and the butt of his schoolfellows' teasing because his dreaminess makes him slow at lessons. He becomes the protégé of all four winds, who together comprise the ideal androgynous personality: the north wind apparently corresponds to courage, the east to conscience, the south to tenderness, and the west to imagination. Under their tutelage he becomes hardworking, forgiving, creative (as with Diamond, the winds blow stories into him), self-sacrificing, and at housework "as handy as a girl." These new qualities win him great chances; he becomes the companion of the rich invalid Fergus, and Fergus's parents offer to send him to school. But the winds also give hin the strength to refuse his opportunity, since he can't leave his sick mother—he promises, indeed, like the perfect Victorian daughter, that should she need him "I would never marry or go about in the world. I'd stay at home to be a comfort to you." The price of real education is deprivation, and "the lessons he learnt in that winter of patient waiting, of quiet watching and self-forgetfulness, bore their fruit."[44]

For all the plot's MacDonaldisms, Molesworth appears to intend her story more as an explication of woman's plight than as a parable of the soul's absorption into God. Thus Gratian tells Fergus a tale about a seagull named Quiver, who "was very brave, almost too brave" and whose "discontent and impatience" betray him into the hands of people who clip his wings, until having become "so patient that no one would have thought he was the same discontented bird," he rediscovers flight. But Fergus approves the modification of the traditional Christian ending: "I was just a little afraid at the end that you were going to say that Quiver had grown so good that he went 'up, up, up' straight into heaven. I shouldn't have liked that—at least not till he had lived happily by the sea first." For birds, children, and women, self-actualization satisfies better than self-annihilation, and the ending of Fergus's story recalls that of Quiver's; though he will always be lame, he regains a measure of health, and will be able to learn to play the organ, which creative freedom "makes up for all."[45] Molesworth's boys discover the back of the north wind not in death but at home.

Lacking the upper-class male privileges of schooling, camaraderie, and carelessness, Gratian—who serves "instead of a daughter" to his mother—enjoys instead the privilege of learning from feminine sorrow. While Fergus's unseen father is generous but arbitrary and "a little peculiar," the child's mother reminds Gratian of south and west winds combined, since her loveliness derives not only from her "sunny brightness" but from her "look of pitying sadness, almost sweeter."[46] Fergus's mother's example of sympathy and melancholy enables Gratian to interpret his own mother, who, trapped by the bleak moor and the rheumatism she inherits from Gratian's grandmother, suggests north and east winds. As usual, men control the practical realm of physical labor, learning, and money; but women dominate imagination and empathy. So while Gratian must gain some competence in the male sphere (he must succeed in school before he can enter the female world), womanliness is the ultimate goal.

Molesworth's novels, most of which are realistic tales of nursery life, may strike the modern reader as sickeningly cute. The amount of baby talk they contain suggests a longing for irresponsibility, and when we hear that in 1884 Swinburne compared Molesworth to George Eliot, declaring that a chapter of "the enchanting *Adventures of Herr Baby* is worth a shoal of the very best novels dealing with the characters and fortunes of mere adults,"[47] we take it as additional evidence of the poet's mental instability. But in fact Molesworth's obsession with childhood seems to have had its roots not in a rejection of adulthood but in the feeling that adult power was dangerously undependable. Separated from an insane husband and forced to support her family, she had an invincible sense that adults must draw on their childhood "innocence and happiness" if they are to surmount "their own struggles and difficulties." As with Gratian, the obedience, femininity, and relinquishment that compose the good child furnish the only means of survival for the good adult; "in so many, many ways, we would all do well to resemble" the "'little ones.'"[48] While Molesworth often uses her realistic domestic tales as spiritual palate-cleansers, enabling readers "to see through child-eyes; to hear with child-ears—above all, to feel with child-heart,"[49] her fantasies paradoxically suggest the practical use to which adults may put childish experience; except you become as a little child, you shall not survive the kingdom of adulthood. Fantasy, femininity, innocence, and imagination may not transform society, but they will save its individual members.

By Edwardian times, indeed, society was coming to seem less and less salvageable. Nesbit's fantasies emphasize the lure not only of the individual past of middle-class childhood, but of the general past of England or the world. In Nesbit's cosmos almost all magic derives from long ago; her Psammead is a prehistoric fairy, her Phoenix has classical antecedents, her Amulet is described as coming from the "dawn of time," and even the magic charm at the heart of *The Enchanted Castle* commemorates an ancient love. Similarly, all long agos are comparatively magic periods. Thus Babylonian slaves are happier than London's deprived and sullen back-street dwellers, unwanted slum children can find a real home in pre-Roman Britain, Atlantis is prettier than modern England, and Greek gods are more understanding and jolly than mortal grown-ups. Not surprisingly, Nesbit prefers those children, and those rare adults, who have not sold out—who can escape the toils of adulthood through imagination or reading or their logical extension, magic. Her ideal children neither have nor expect to have any effect on the adult sphere. The efforts of the Bastables or the Railway Children to benefit the mature poor always flop; children can only help other children.

Thus Nesbit's favorite among her books for young readers, *Harding's Luck* (the 1909 sequel to *The House of Arden*), stars a hero who in many ways, as Julia Briggs has observed, reworks the classic ministering waif of Hesba Stretton/George MacDonald fame[50]—but with a key difference. Dickie Harding, a lame slum child who is really the rightful Lord Arden, can do good, but only outside the social context. The adult he helps, the dishonest tramp Beale, is as much a romantic rebel against society as Dickie himself ("Please do not be too shocked," Nesbit comments; "Remember that neither of them knew any better"). Enchanted by nonconformity, they live the life of a wild rabbit, who "gets 'is own meals and larks about on 'is own,"[51] and Dickie can only change Beale by continuing this pattern of animal or childish freedom—he must remove the man from adulthood. The unreformed Beale has unsavory Bill Sikes–like associates; Dickie surrounds the new Beale only with the dogs, setting him up as a puppy breeder and restoring his past by returning him to his father in the country. Similarly, renouncing his title for the modern Ardens' sake, Dickie—who has spent much of the novel traveling in time—achieves literal self-abnegation by turning his back on 1909 and taking over the identity of the 1609 Richard Arden he has heretofore been only sporadically.

Flickering between the centuries, Dickie has long recognized the seventeenth century's superiority over the twentieth. In Jacobean times he is strong and whole; his own society has lamed him, having left him in the power of a careless foster mother who dropped him as a baby. Nor does physical powerlessness confer upon him moral force, as would happen in a Victorian evangelical novel; all Dickie's power comes from the world of the past, either through reading or through direct experience. And while the Edwardian poor are doomed, the Jacobean social system teaches him that "he had duties of kindness and protection to the servants; that he was expected to grow up brave and noble and generous and unselfish, to care for those who called him master." Modern laissez-faire economics leave him outcast and forgotten, but under the bygone paternalism "he was a person of consequence."[52] Others are better off as well. The Thames is clean and surrounded by gardens; there is no unemployment.

Most of all, the values of the Angel are at work—and instead of being subdued by the selfish power structure of masculine capitalism, they rule. Richard, "called to a destiny of power and helpful kindness," learns an androgynous ideal within which male and female values harmonize. Honor, industry, selfless love, are all connected; manly emotion is no contradiction in terms, so that under the ethics of 1609, Richard can part from his Edwardian cousin Edred with a kiss. And although taking money into the magic makes awkward changes in the rules (since money "always does upset everything"[53]), importing intangibles like morality and skill from past into future can only improve modern times.

In *The House of Arden* femininity is better than masculinity; Elfrida is Edred's superior not only in patience and courtesy but in courage and enterprise. But in *Harding's Luck*, where the three children correspond to the three Mouldiwarps (the magic moles that are the heraldic badges of the family), the androgynous Richard is the truest Arden of them all. Edred and Elfrida lose their magic at the end of the first novel, succumbing to the bonds of time, which only Elfrida regrets; Richard retains his enchanted freedom until he enters voluntary exile. Likewise, the magic assigns moral tasks on the basis of their difficulty. Precisely because he doesn't want to, Edred must rescue Richard from the clutches of the evil foster mother and Beale's former associate: "It will cost you more to do it than it would cost Elfrida, because she is braver than you are. . . . Every soul has one such chance, a chance to be perfectly unselfish, absolutely noble and true. . . . [Elfrida] will have a thousand chances to be good and noble. And she will take them all." But Richard, as the best of the three, has the greatest challenge: "It would be very bitter—it would be like leaving home never to return. It was exile" to abandon the twentieth century. Nesbit explicitly aligns such achievements with those of the heroes and heroines of childish historical fiction, which began the unlocking of the past by making "a new world for Dickie."[54] Because Richard actually stays within the past, he becomes one of these heroes, partaking of the great androgynous society and forever escaping the Edwardian adulthood that will soon engulf Elfrida and Edred.[55]

The extent of Nesbit's iconoclasm has always been a matter for critical debate. Personally she seems to have been "radical and anarchistic" (the description is H. G. Wells's)[56]—her unconventional sex life, her position among the founders of Fabian Socialism, her attraction to the *Yellow Book* contributors and other practitioners of the shocking certainly suggest an antipathy to the status quo. The ethics of her novels, however, tend to be confused, so that Knoepflmacher can contend that she "neither radically challenges a patriarchal order nor sharply departs from the more pronounced moralism of earlier nineteenth-century women writers," Manlove that she is "not largely concerned with moral issues and the instruction of a juvenile readership," and Alison Lurie that her stance is one of "implicit feminism."[57] The problem seems to be not only that Nesbit hovers between two conceptions of herself, as daring bohemian and as child who never grew up—tradition requires the one to have strong social notions, the other to have none—but that she hovers between the nineteenth-century morality of the Angel and the new twentieth-century urge toward the masculine. Thus she argues alternately that children should seek to transform (as in the Arden series, where the family treasure will build model housing for the Arden villagers), to acquire, and to re-create a broken family circle. Nor can we be sure whether she values dash and enterprise above unselfishness and kindness. The best children have the virtues of both genders, and succeed in giving, getting, and regressing all at the same time. Nesbit's vision of androgyny takes on the often-contradictory tones of an older tradition that transcends childhood and a new one that seeks to prolong it.

The late-Victorian longing for innocence ensured that Swinburne would have company in considering children's books the best adult reading; it also ensured that any transgressions against innocence in such stories would find a censorious audience. Sophistication in fantasy had always had its Victorian critics—reviewing Thackeray's *The Rose and the Ring* (1854), for instance, William Caldwell Roscoe had found disgusting "the thorough child-about-town air of which the whole is redolent."[58] But by the 1890s any confluence of child and adult values seemed downright sacrilegious. Even the "bad" child charmed, since its badness usually signaled blissful uncontamination by adult rules; bourgeois, miniaturized, and contained, Huckleberry Finn crossed the Atlantic to appear in middle-class British nurseries as Molesworth's Carrots or Nesbit's Bastables. Because bad children could not be bad in the same way as adults, they must be good.

Thus early critical reaction was favorable to Oscar Wilde's fairy tales, contained in *The Happy Prince* (1888) and *A House of Pomegranates* (1891). The morals of all the stories are unimpeachably opposed to selfishness and egotism; the values at stake are spirituality, gentleness, and art not for art's sake but for love's. Reviewers of the first volume generally approved it, reading it as a children's book and so defining its sensuality as innocent. Indeed, it was the publication of this group of stories that established Wilde's authorial reputation.[59]

When the second volume appeared, however, Wilde announced that the stories were not aimed at children at all but expressed his deliberately antipopular aestheticism; he also implied that they professed no morality save that of beauty. So *A House of Pomegranates* took a critical savaging. The *Athenaeum* and the *Saturday Review*, which had cautiously liked *The Happy Prince*, damned the second volume for exclusivity, while the *Speaker* of 2 January 1892 found it "'precious,'" its moral message "sicklied over with detail and cloying to the taste."[60] What had leaped into the foreground on the stories' redefinition as adult reading was their homoeroticism. Full of illicit loves, "slim, fair-haired Court pages," and devils with lips "like a proud red flower,"[61] the tales seemed newly dangerous. Certainly children's fantasy had mixed eroticism and Angelic ethics before Wilde came along, but adult fantasy couldn't afford this luxury. In an adult context and in the 1890s, homoeroticism implied homosexuality. The Christian and social-reform aspects of stories such as "The Young King" paled beside their invocation of Adonis and Endymion and Roman slave boys. As he was about to do with still greater effect in a nonliterary context, Wilde had cast doubt on the innocence of androgyny.

Edwardian fantasy, set within a cultural context that placed more and more boundaries between childhood and adulthood and signposted adulthood as dangerous, is therefore especially likely to play with sexuality only to reject it. Sex destroys childhood; sex in fantasy brings the world of childish imagination too near the world of adult fact. Mid-Victorian writers might, like Kingsley and MacDonald, hymn sexuality as a symbol of wholeness and of unifying androgyny, or like Craik damn it as a bar to feminine maturity; Edwardian fantasists agreed that it signaled maturity but rejected it on just that ground. Wilde's blend of youth and eroticism was not so much ahead of its time as behind it. By the end of the century fantasy was pursuing its rebellious course by sealing off childhood from adulthood instead of integrating the two. Such a separation provides the happy ending to one of the most characteristic of Edwardian fantasies, Kenneth Grahame's *The Wind in the Willows*.

Ten years before the publication of Grahame's masterpiece, the *Pall Mall Gazette* polled "What Children Like to Read"; *Alice in Wonderland* won, with the Andersen and Grimm tales and other fantasies traditional and new also scoring well. The editor commented on this "victory of fairy tales," implying that the true victory lay with the antididactic: "Aesop's absence from the elect is perhaps to be attributed to the pernicious trick of printing morals that nobody wants along with the fables."[62] This urge to believe that the truest children's books don't socialize was to linger; Grahame is very much a man of his time in writing to Teddy Roosevelt (who arranged for the novel's publication) that the "qualities [of *The Wind in the Willows*], if any, are mostly negative—i.e.—no problems, no sex, no second meaning—it is only an expression of the simplest joys of life as lived by the simplest beings."[63] Edwardian childhood was to be an arcadian age, free from trouble, free from duties, free from conflict. Subsequent critics, however, find the novel turbulent,[64] and far from being absent, problems, sex, and second meanings are at the root of it all.

From the beginning, Grahame establishes an opposition between the "dark and lowly little house" and "divine discontent and longing"—between domesticity and adventure. At first we may assume that he prefers adventure, as Mole abandons spring cleaning in favor of pursuing experience. But just as domesticity unalloyed by adventure stultifies, adventure unbounded by domesticity imperils. As Rat says, "Beyond the Wild Wood comes the Wide World. . . . And that's something that doesn't matter, either to you or to me. I've never been there, and I'm never going, nor you either, if you've got any sense at all. Don't ever refer to it again, please."[65] Both Wood and World attract; Mole risks the one, the other nearly seduces Rat. But sensible animals restrict their desires to the legitimate ones of "messing about in boats" and, especially, eating. It is the unsensible Toad who demonstrates the true nature of the danger beyond the River: sexual adulthood.

Of all the animals, Toad has the greatest affinity with the human (adult and—worse—female) world. He lives in a human-type house, alone mixes with human people, and even talks in pompous and unnatural locutions quite unlike Mole's or Rat's or Badger's "common way" of speaking: "I've discovered the real thing, the only genuine occupation for a lifetime. I propose to devote the remainder of mine to it, and can only regret the wasted years that lie behind me, squandered in trivialities." Condescending, puffed-up, and uncomprehending, he is the child's view of an adult, and he finds himself the slave of strange adult passions. His addiction to the excessive adventure of motoring puts him continually at risk of the over-domesticity of confinement by way of a counterbalance, first as he spends "weeks in hospital, being ordered about by female nurses,"[66] next as he becomes his friends' prisoner as they try to break him of his habit, again in jail under the benevolent eye of the turnkey's daughter, and finally within the washerwoman's dress, which as Lois Kuznets points out, "becomes virtually a flirtatious woman who castrates him: 'a strange uncanny thing that seemed to hold his hands, turn all muscular strivings to water, and laugh at him all the time.'"[67]

By going too far in his adventurings, in fact, Toad has betrayed himself into the enemy feminine hand. The motoring instinct, it transpires, is really a sexual instinct. Toad falls in love at first sight with "that swan, that sunbeam, that thunderbolt," the oddness of his metaphors suggesting a reference to that thunderbolt-wielding sexual force that mastered Leda and Danaë. And when deprived of the object of his passion, his behavior takes on a peculiarly biological cast, as he builds a dummy car out of bedroom chairs in his "violent paroxysms" and climbs on board, "bent forward and staring fixedly ahead, making uncouth and ghastly noises, till the climax was reached, when, turning a complete somersault, he would lie prostrate amidst the ruins of the chairs, apparently completely satisfied for the moment."[68] Appropriately, circumstances can only redeem Toad by converting him into at least the outward shell of the asexual Angel, hair evangelically straight and conversation modest, to whom auto-eroticism is forever denied.

The conflict between freedom and enslavement, individuality and community,[69] can only find resolution in the bonding of upper-class males. Femininity, Kuznets observes, is the Other;[70] the panic Wild Wood and Wide World create, the fear of the unknown and the alien, connect to the male's fear of the female in a realm in which even beneficent Nature and companionable River are masculine. In Grahame's world, "panic" has no association with the male god but with proles and women. And if Zeus leads Toad astray for a time, the other animals remain faithful to Pan—who stood for Grahame's homosexual contemporaries as a god of male love, as he appears, for instance, in certain of E. M. Forster's tales. But Grahame's Pan has no sexuality.[71] He is the father, not the lover.

Modern critics frequently associate Toad with Wilde, finding irresistible the confluence of girth, recklessness, and illicit sexuality.[72] In this interpretation, Grahame appears as a repressed homosexual. Still, it seems more likely that his hatred of corruption and his miserable marriage connect to a rejection of sexuality and adulthood in general rather than to any specific brand of sexuality. Grahame's animals are free to remain within the confines of childhood innocence forever, if only they take care to curb natural instincts that urge escape and expansion. The only safe instinct is the craving for food, which serves throughout as a mechanism for bonding and comfort—because food is the childish drive, a quest males may indulge in together with no fear of losing their innocence or finding too untamable an adventure. Food is the sexual surrogate to cement agreeable male domesticity.[73]

The back-and-forth swing between change and stasis thus ends in the unification of heroism and home.[74] In other words, each animal joins the pattern first set by Badger, the natural bachelor who in everything is Toad's opposite and who alone feels no "divine discontent" because his community responsibilities provide him with adventure enough within the domestic setting; adventures literally trip over his front door. Like Badger, Toad and his friends must learn to temper instinct with sense, aggression with pacifism, egotism with altruism. Thus the values of the novel are ultimately the androgynous ones of the Angel but occur within an exclusively masculine environment.[75] Sexual woman is too often the root of both desire and entrapment. To maintain perfect security, Grahame had to rewrite her as male child and even to devalue religion lest it "overshadow mirth and pleasure."[76]

The pattern of opposing tensions that animates Grahame's fantasy appears again in that strangest of twentieth-century children's tales, *Peter Pan*. Organized around odd separations and odder correspondences, the story derives its force less from its theatrical magic than from its ambiguity: we are fascinated because we never know who the villain is and what the crime. For the characters range along two different axes, adult-child and female-male; the oppositions thus keep changing without notice, much like the Lost Boys' battle with the Indians in which Boys suddenly decide to be Indians for the day, and vice versa. Ultimately Mrs. Darling, maternal, selfless, and sexual, is both what the novel yearns toward and what it abhors.

When the chief conflict is that between adult and child, it seems easy to tell good guys from bad at first glance—but at second glance the task gets harder. The Darling family initially assumes the typically Edwardian configuration of stuffy parents and imaginative children. Adults stick fast in the public realms of money-making (inevitably, Mr. Darling is a stockbroker) and of conformity: "Mrs. Darling loved to have everything just so, and Mr. Darling had a passion for being exactly like his neighbours." Because so much children's fiction hinges on the assumption that any child must wish to leave dull adult convention, we side with the children, shoving aside the suspicion that this family must be more magical than most or it wouldn't have a dog for a nurse. But the narrator introduces a new view of childhood, in which children are not simply amoral but heartbreaking, and in which their charm depends on their cruelty: "Off we skip like the most heartless things in the world, which is what children are, but so attractive; and we have an entirely selfish time; and then when we have need of special attention we nobly return for it, confident that we shall be embraced instead of smacked." Except that they do get embraced instead of smacked, children bear an uncomfortable resemblance to the pirate crew. Indeed, adult selflessness, as personified by Mrs. Darling, is sometimes the ethical focus of the novel; as the narrator informs us, "Some like Peter best and some like Wendy best, but I like her best."[77]

At the same time, it's often hard to tell where child leaves off and adult begins. We can draw a line between the young John, who can fly and dream, and his old ghost, a "bearded man who doesn't know any story to tell his children." But such lines blur. For all his stodginess, Mr. Darling often seems like a child forced into a boring game, so that when Nana gets hair on his trousers, which "were not only new trousers but . . . the first he had ever had with braid on them . . . he had to bite his lip to prevent the tears coming." Hook's status as an Old Etonian, source not only of his occasional gentlemanly scruples but of his ruthless discipline toward inferiors and even, perhaps, of his longing for a mother, is the key to his personality; all men are boys who have never grown up. Even the audience, the narrator implies, consists entirely of adults longing for their lost childhood: "We too have been there [the Neverland]; we can still hear the sound of the surf, though we shall land no more."[78]

This fuzzing of adult and child makes possible the greater, if more subtle, opposition in the novel—that between female and male. In this dialogue, even female children are to some extent adult and dangerous, even adult males childlike and endangered. Just as all mothers are the same, stretching from Mrs. Darling to Wendy to Jane to Margaret into infinity, all women want the same thing: motherhood. Tink, Tiger Lily, and Wendy instinctively understand the sexuality that no males (especially Peter) have an inkling of; thus the female inhabitants of the Neverland are forever at war instead of forming a cooperative tribe like boys or pirates, since sexuality creates jealousy. Each wants Peter to be something more than "a devoted son."[79] And as the pirates finally realize, no ship can run smoothly with a woman aboard, because male bonding doesn't jibe with the female desire for marriage.

Here then is the secret of how the little boy who is Mr. Darling has been entrapped into interminable tedious games of house and stockbroker—it is the fault of Mrs. Darling's maternal urge. She can't produce free and selfish children without someone to play the confined and selfless role of father. Wendy displays just the same sinister drive, inventing a new role for Peter which "consisted in pretending not to have adventures" and in acting as stuffy paterfamilias to the Lost Boys.[80] This is the stuff of Barrie's nightmares as a student at Edinburgh, when he kept a dream notebook to record such jottings as "Greatest horror—dream I am married—wake up shrieking."[81] Peter's danger is not Hook, whose role he indeed toys with after the pirate's demise, getting Wendy to make him a suit out of Hook's clothes and sitting "long in the cabin with Hook's cigarholder in his mouth and one hand clenched, all but the forefinger, which he bent and held threateningly aloft like a hook."[82] Nor is it Mr. Darling, who inherits Peter's role as leader of the Lost Boys, suggesting games of hide-and-seek and housing his tribe in the imaginary drawing room instead of the Neverland house—even though in the stage version the actor who plays Mr. Darling traditionally also plays Hook. Both adult men are more victims than villains. Peter's true enemy is Wendy.

Her weapon is sex, which both saves her own life and threatens Peter's identity. The acorn "kiss" he gives her after she has "made herself rather cheap by inclining her face towards him" deflects Tootles's arrow and wins her a house of her own. Since "it would not

8. *The Angel as Enemy.* "Pointing upward," Wendy hypnotizes both
Lost Boys and Indians with stultifying tales of domesticity; only
Peter is immune to the danger she represents. Illustration by F. D.
Bedford to the American edition of J. M. Barrie's *Peter and Wendy*
(AKA *Peter Pan*, 1911).

be sufficiently respectful" to touch Wendy in what the narrator terms "her present delicate state of health," the boys must build a home around her for her confinement. And confinement it is: "Really there were whole weeks when, except perhaps with a stocking in the evening, she was never above ground." But she enjoys her domestic slavery because she sees in it a snare to catch Peter; when she finally lures all the boys out of fairyland into incipient adulthood, it is Peter whom she is really after. Here Peter runs a grave risk of turning into Mr. Darling, who "might have passed for a boy again if he had been able to take his baldness off" and who like the boy possesses "a noble sense of justice and a lion courage to do what seemed right to him." But the younger male sees his danger. He denies any intention of saying "anything to my [i.e., Wendy's] parents about a very sweet subject"; and when she tells him that "I should love you in a beard" and her mother tries to embrace him, he stands firm: "Keep back, lady, no one is going to catch me and make me a man." Wendy, "one of the kind that likes to grow up,"[83] is the enemy of boyish freedom.

But for all their dangerousness, mothers are good. With sexual desire comes the possibility of selflessness; thus Tink can consume the poison Hook has left for Peter, facing death because she loves him. Living adventures, boys can never recount them, for story is the province of mothers. Indeed Wendy, who constantly recounts the Darling saga for the benefit of her "children," is an aspect of the narrator; like her he professes the values of femininity and worries about Peter's "cockiness" and the effect of the Indians' adulation, which "was not really good for him."[84] The feminine ethic opposes the joyous irresponsibility that characterizes Peter, but it has its own worth. Barrie customarily referred to Peter as "the tragic boy,"[85] and we see what his tragedy consists of as we watch him watching the Darling family reunion: "He had ecstasies innumerable that other children can never know; but he was looking through the window at the one joy from which he must be for ever barred."[86]

Peter Pan serves as a prism separating Victorian constellations of childhood, femininity, and morality into their component parts, leaving them free to recombine at will. Women can be vain, selfless, dangerous, nurturing, sexual, and innocent all at once; children can be delightful, cruel, masterful, and meek. The values of the Angel become incompatible with each other, so that sexuality causes selflessness and amorality lurks at community's roots. The radicalism of *Peter Pan* and its Edwardian predecessors, rewriting the Angel to be what she was supposed most not to be—sexual, punitive, threatening—suggests the enormous cultural force she had come to wield by the early twentieth century. Her intrinsic ambiguity as a power that rejected power was her chief weapon; but it was a weapon that turned in her hand, as more and more writers and genres began to deconstruct what she stood for and to claim internal inconsistencies. Thus Victorian fantasy, which works by creating utopias and by questioning reality, increasingly came to question the utopia's major Victorian symbol, dividing gender from virtue and virtue from happiness.

The debate over the Angel by both opponents and proponents animates each major genre of children's literature, from the mid-Victorian era to the First World War. Complicated by changing attitudes toward sexuality, each tradition re-created her in its own image. Newly iconoclastic school stories retained the values but not the femininity; historical novels conducted an endless tug-of-war between Angel and anti-Angel; adventure tales tried to replace the female Angel with a sexualized or masculine equivalent; fantasies restructured priorities to separate not male and female but adult and child. But in each genre, once we approach the end of the nineteenth century it becomes harder and harder to find an example of classically uncomplicated Angelic ethics. Nothing Edwardian is so straightforward as *Tom Brown*, *The Caged Lion*, *The Island Queen*, or *The Little Lame Prince*, even though themes, ethics, and explorations of androgyny continue unabated.

Ultimately, in fact, it may have been the emphasis on androgyny as much as the new cultural emphasis on sexuality and strength that undid the Angel. Androgyny was an essential tenet of evangelical books for boys, or for boys and girls, because the same system of values had to apply to both genders; religion was not for women only. If egolessness would save one soul, it must save two. And even while first Darwinism and later growing homophobia insisted on the value of strict demarcations between male and female, social reformers drew on evangelical and Angelic fervor to increase women's power in the public world. Yoked together, feminine virtue and masculine know-how could eradicate the sexual and economic abuses that preoccupied earnest Victorian minds. In this Victorian formulation we have a perfect example of femininism at work, which anthropologist Michelle Zimbalist Rosaldo has described in general terms as follows: "In those societies where domestic and public spheres are firmly differentiated, women may win power and value by stressing their differences from men. By accepting and elaborating upon the symbols and expectations associated with their cultural definition, they may goad men into compliance, or establish a society unto themselves."[87] But what then happens when women's difference—in Rosaldo's terms the source of their strength—lessens, as the separate spheres drift together under feminist pressure? To a Victorian eye, the achieving of public power has permitted the crumbling of the private influence that was the Angel's chief weapon. Ultimately, instead of conquering men, the Angel may have conquered herself.

Biographical Appendix
of Children's Authors

A.L.O.E. [Charlotte Maria Tucker] (1821–1893). • Daughter of an Indian civil servant, she herself became a missionary to India at age fifty-four, after writing some 150 evangelical tales for children from 1851 onward. Like many of her fellows, her stated goal in writing was not "earthly remuneration" but "God's blessing upon my attempts to instruct His lambs."[1]

Anstey, F. [Thomas Anstey Guthrie] (1856–1934). • Anstey's father, a military tailor, sent him to the original of *Vice Versa*'s Crichton House and then to King's College School. The younger man read law at Cambridge but abandoned his practice for full-time writing when *Vice Versa* won acclaim. He became a humorous writer for *Punch*, but in more than two dozen subsequent novels, collections of sketches and comic verses, and dramatizations of his own works and those of Molière for the British stage, he never repeated his early success.

Ballantyne, Robert Michael (1825–1894). • The representative of a Scottish literary family—his father owned a newspaper, his uncle published Sir Walter Scott—Ballantyne early met disappointment when Scott's bankruptcy ruined the family fortunes, and the boy went to Canada as a clerk at age sixteen. Returning home to support his mother and five unmarried sisters, he began to publish accounts of the wilderness and gradually became one of the most popular boys' authors of the nineteenth century, producing more than a hundred books. Strongly religious, he married a teenage girl when he was forty but never quite escaped the guilt of early sexual escapades; when he suffered from dizzy spells before his death, for instance, he secretly underwent tests for ataxia, which was often considered to have sexual causes.

Barrie, Sir James Matthew (1860–1937). • A leader of the Kailyard School, Barrie was the son of a handloom weaver, a graduate of Edinburgh University, and eventually a baronet, with some thirty-eight plays and a smaller number of novels to his credit. His fifteen-year marriage to an actress, Mary Ansell, ended when he divorced her for adultery in 1909; his relationships with women were always problematic (as a young man he assumed that his height—five feet one inch—would forever preclude romance, and most critics assert that he was impotent), and it appears to have been his Carrollian friendships with young boys that dominated his emotional life after his adored mother's death.

Bowman, Anne (Fl. 1837–1867). • Bowman wrote some twenty-four books; besides adventures, they included a cookbook, collections of charades and acrostics, a reading primer, and a poetry anthology, almost all of which were published in America as well as in Britain.

Brereton, Frederick S. (1872–1957). • A physician and an army officer, Brereton was a cousin and imitator of G. A. Henty. Married, with two children, he produced more than forty novels for boys, centering on wars from the Boer War to the Great War and on the more militant bits of history.

Buchan, John (1875–1940). • Buchan was the son of a Scottish Free Church minister and began to publish even before matriculating at Oxford. His varied career included stints as a lawyer, as the private secretary to the high commissioner for South Africa after the Boer War, as a literary advisor to the publisher Thomas Nelson, and finally as Canada's governor-general; he was eventually created Baron Tweedsmuir. His publications were also various, ranging from literary criticism to biography to children's fantasy, but he is best known today for his adult adventure novels. Buchan's marriage seems to have been particularly successful—hence, perhaps, the importance to most of his novelistic plots of his daring and competent heroines.

Bullen, Frank T. (1857–1915). • Having left school at age nine, Bullen was at sea from 1869 to 1883, finally becoming chief mate before taking a shore job as a junior meteorological clerk between 1883 and 1899. The author of twenty-four books, mostly on nautical topics, he also wrote stories, essays, and articles for papers that included the *Boy's Own Paper.*

Burnett, Frances Hodgson (1849–1924). • The Hodgson family emigrated from Manchester to Tennessee in 1865, and Hodgson Burnett was to use both British and American settings for her fifty-odd novels and plays, just as she divided much of her adulthood between the two countries. While her novels for adults early won her comparisons to Eliot and Gaskell, it was her works for children that most snared public favor. Twice unhappily married, a feminist whose unconventionality offended critics, she often used her writings for children to create worlds where feminine values could triumph outside political reality.

Clare, Austin [Wilhelmina Martha James] (Fl. 1860s–1900s). • After beginning her forty-year authorial career in 1868, Clare produced at least forty-six works, many of which were published through the Society for Promoting Christian Knowledge. Her biggest hit, however, was unquestionably *The Carved Cartoon*, which was twice dramatized (in 1932 and 1958) and has been reprinted as recently as 1972.

Craik, Dinah Maria Mulock (1826–1887). • The author of more than fifty books, including volumes of poetry and short stories, Mulock Craik's greatest success was the best seller *John Halifax, Gentleman*. Married late in life, she adopted a foundling girl and signed over her Civil List pension to less fortunate authors. As a publisher's reader, she helped establish George MacDonald's reputation.

Doyle, Sir Arthur Conan (1859–1930). • Educated at Stonyhurst and Edinburgh, Doyle was the nephew of the illustrator Richard Doyle. Between 1882 and 1890 he practiced medicine. Besides his Sherlock Holmes stories and historical novels, he wrote the Professor Challenger series, books on spiritualism and military history, and a one-act play. His 1902 knighting was a recognition not of his literary achievements but of his services to a field hospital in South Africa.

Edgar, John George (1834–1864). • Despite his early death, Edgar produced some eighteen books, divided among boys' history, biography, and historical novels. His writing is strongly didactic.

Ewing, Juliana Horatia Gatty (1841–1885). • The daughter of Margaret Gatty, who founded *Aunt Judy's Magazine* (named for the young Juliana, the family storyteller), and wife of an army major, Ewing was one of the most widely admired of Victorian children's novelists and was particularly influential upon Kipling. Her collected works occupy seventeen volumes; besides her novels, she published many collections of verses and short stories.

Farrar, Frederic William (1831–1903). • Born to missionaries in India, Farrar attended King William's School—immortalized in *Eric* as Roslyn—and Cambridge. He wrote *Eric* as a master at Harrow; after marrying in 1860 (the union would yield ten children), he produced his final novel of school life. There was also a handful of college and historical novels for adults, but most of his writings were theological and scholarly. He rose from headmaster of Marlborough to canon of Westminster and finally to dean of Canterbury.

Fenn, George Manville (1831–1909). • Friend of Henty and father of seven, Fenn began his career as a private tutor but moved on to newspaper work, eventually editing *Cassell's Magazine* and becoming both editor and owner of *Once a Week*. His more than a thousand tales, articles, and sketches appeared in such periodicals as *Chambers's Journal* and *All the Year Round*, and he produced over a hundred novels and stories for boys, although he never matched Henty's popularity.

Grahame, Kenneth (1859–1932). • Barred by a practical uncle from attending Oxford, Grahame led a double life in the *Yellow Book* set and in the Bank of England, of which he became secretary in 1898. His unhappy marriage produced one son, who would commit suicide as an undergraduate, but like his animal creations Grahame's most intense instinct seems to have been the gastronomic. *The Golden Age* (1895) and *Dream Days* (1898) won him many adult admirers, among them Swinburne and Nesbit, but *The Wind in the Willows* had trouble finding a publisher and was long in achieving popularity.

Grant, Mrs. G. Forsyth (Fl. 1890s–1900s). • The mother of at least one son, Grant wrote a handful of novels—most of them school stories—that were popular on both sides of the Atlantic.

Grierson, Miss (Fl. 1820s–1830s). • Author of at least ten works with a strong evangelical bias, among them tracts, religious histories, biographies, and travel narratives, Grierson seems to have been a Scottish Presbyterian with a particular admiration for Henry Martyn, the missionary to India who also influenced Sherwood. *Lily Douglas* was one of her best-known stories and was still being reprinted into the 1850s.

Haggard, Sir Henry Rider (1856–1925). • Sixth son of a squire, Haggard was regarded as the family dunce and not worth educating. Instead he went to Natal at nineteen as the governor's secretary; returning in 1879, he married and became a writer, eventually producing several children and more than seventy books on topics ranging from gardening to the Salvation Army. His friends included Kipling and Andrew Lang, with whom he collaborated on one of his thirty-four adventure novels, but owing to his tactlessness his enemies were also many and influential.

Hemyng, S. Bracebridge (1841–1901). • Hemyng, a nonpracticing London barrister and the son of the registrar of the Calcutta Supreme Court, not only researched for Henry Mayhew but wrote more than thirty books on his own account, some for adults; most were boys' adventure stories such as the Dick Lightheart and Jack

Harkaway tales. He wrote for E. J. Brett and, during an American sojourn, for Frank Leslie. The two-shilling yellow-backs he published in the 1860s are the sort of reading that frequently proves the downfall of boys within the rival *Boy's Own Paper* tradition.

Henty, George Alfred (1832–1902). • Henty's father, a stockbroker and mine owner, sent him to Westminster and Cambridge. Henty then joined the army and became a war correspondent in the Crimea. He wrote eleven unsuccessful novels for adults, but his eighty-odd books for boys dominated the field from 1880 until his death; he also edited the short-lived *Union Jack* and Samuel Beeton's *Boy's Own Magazine*. He married twice (his second marriage shocked his friends because the bride had been his housekeeper) and had four children.

Hope, Ascott R. [A. R. Hope-Moncrieff] (1846–1927). • After initial success with *Oudendale* (1865), a school story, Hope produced more than a hundred more books for boys, including school stories in the Farrar tradition, as well as adventure novels and historical tales.

Hughes, Thomas (1822–1896). • The son of a country gentleman, Hughes attended Arnold's Rugby (where the boy was cricket and football captain) and Oxford. His marriage to a clergyman's daughter increased his moral earnestness; he became a Christian Socialist because of F. D. Maurice's influence and taught night school and boxing while he practiced law. He entered Parliament as a Radical in 1865 and became a judge in 1882. In 1879 Hughes founded Rugby, Tennessee, as a community for Tom Browns, but the project failed owing to the inhabitants' indolence. Hughes's publications include speeches and political commentary.

Kingsley, Charles (1819–1875). • Kingsley's father was in orders, and on graduating from Cambridge the young Kingsley also became a minister, marrying in 1844 and taking a rectorship. His subsequent career included the professorship of modern history at Cambridge (1860–1869), the canonries of Chester and Westminster, and over sixty published works. His novels for adults exhibit the strong polemic tendency and the dogmatism about the nature of Englishness, true religion, and sexuality that would culminate in the famous feud with Newman in 1864.

Kingston, William Henry Giles (1814–1880). • Kingston grew up in Portugal, the son of a businessman, and began writing for boys in 1850; his more than a hundred novels usually feature foreign travel and adventure as well as a strong religious message. Shortly before his death he founded *The Union Jack*, the fourth journal under his editorship; his dying message to his readers was widely held up as a pattern of Christian resignation.

Kipling, Rudyard (1865–1936). • Born in India, where his father was principal of the Bombay Art School, Kipling was sent to England in 1871, where he spent some unhappy years before attending the United Services College and returning to India as a journalist in 1882. Arriving in London in 1889, he soon became the poet of empire and, in 1907, the first Englishman to win the Nobel Prize for literature. He married an American and wrote most of his stories for children with his own children in mind.

MacDonald, George (1824–1905). • Philosopher, mystic, and miller's son, MacDonald studied science but became a Congregationalist minister, until his parishioners rejected him for heresy. Thereafter he taught, lectured, and wrote some sixty works of fiction and nonfiction, all of which exhibit his blend of Romanticism, radicalism, and religion. He was married and the father of eleven children, some of whom succumbed to his own lifelong ailment, tuberculosis.

Marryat, Frederick (1792–1848). • Son of an M.P., Marryat commanded his own ship while still in his twenties and won the Royal Humane Society's gold medal for heroic rescues; he retired from the Navy in 1829 after the success of his first novel. He published nearly thirty books of fiction and nonfiction, his work winning Dickens's admiration, and he also owned and edited the *Metropolitan Magazine* from 1832 to 1836. Of his novels for children, the best known today is *The Children of the New Forest* (1847).

Molesworth, Mary Louisa Stewart (1839–1921). • Upon her separation from her mentally damaged soldier-husband, Molesworth turned to writing to support her family and became one of the most admired children's authors of the late nineteenth century. She worked in both realistic and fairy-tale genres; it is for the latter that she is chiefly remembered today, with fantasies like *The Cuckoo Clock* (1877) and *The Tapestry Room* (1879).

Nesbit, E[dith] (1858–1924). • Marrying Hubert Bland shortly before the birth of her first child, Nesbit entered "advanced" circles as an early member of the Fabian Society and a friend of H. G. Wells, George Bernard Shaw, and other notables. The Bland-Nesbit ménage also included Bland's mistress and her three children, whom Nesbit took as her own; after her first husband's death, however, the family fell apart and Nesbit married a working-class former sailor. She wrote many potboilers and adult novels, but her present reputation derives from her children's books.

Reed, Talbot Baines (1852–1893). • The chronicler of boys' boarding-school life was actually a day boy at the City of London School.

Son of an M.P., Reed became the manager of the family's type-foundry and also produced a dozen novels, most of them school stories but one a historical work. One of the most popular of all *Boy's Own Paper* writers, he sold his copyrights to the Religious Tract Society for nominal amounts.

Reid, Thomas Mayne (1818–1883). • The son of a Presbyterian minister in Northern Ireland, Reid emigrated to America in his twenties and served in the Mexican War. Returning to England as a captain and self-conscious frontiersman, he married a teenage girl and wrote boys' stories and books on natural history; he produced at least a book a year from 1851 until his death.

Sherwood, Mary Martha Butt (1775–1851). • A clergyman's daughter, Sherwood married a military cousin in 1803 and accompanied him to India, where she taught school and came under the influence of the evangelical missionary Henry Martyn. Over 350 stories, pamphlets, and tracts from her pen demonstrate the gradual evolution of her religion from Puritanism to something gentler after her 1816 return to England. The three parts of *The Fairchild Family* (1818, 1842, 1847) were almost universal reading for Victorian children.

Stables, W. Gordon (1840–1910). • Author of 150 books, Stables was born in Scotland and began his career as a doctor, serving for nine years in the navy and two on a polar whaler. After being invalided out of the service in the 1870s, he began writing for boys, enjoying a long connection with the *Boy's Own Paper*, whose advice column he wrote. Stables was married and the father of six but spent much of his time on the road, touring Britain in a gypsy caravan like Grahame's Toad.

Stevenson, Robert Louis (1850–1894). • Stevenson was the son of a civil engineer in Edinburgh; frail health kept him from entering his father's profession. Instead he read law at Edinburgh, abandoning this career to become a writer. Restlessly poised between bohemianism and Calvinism, he spent much of his life traveling for his health's sake, from France to California to the South Seas. He married a divorced American ten years his senior, whose son became his playmate and collaborator. Stevenson's collected works occupy twenty-eight volumes of fiction, travel narratives, essays, and poetry.

Stretton, Hesba [Sarah Smith] (1832–1911). • A founder of the London Society for the Prevention of Cruelty to Children and the product of a Dissenting family, Stretton wrote some sixty evangelical stories—many of them on the waif theme—and a few novels for adults. Although she disliked the ostentatious piety of many of its members, she published most of her works through the Religious Tract Society, combining keen business sense with genuine social concern.

Vachell, Horace Annesley (1861–1955). • Vachell was educated at Harrow and Sandhurst. He produced two children and more than a hundred published works, among them a number of plays; he was also a fellow of the Royal Society of Letters.

Waugh, Alexander Raban (1898–1981). • Elder brother of Evelyn, Waugh and his father were removed from the alumni lists of their public school after the publication of *The Loom of Youth* (they were later reinstated). Waugh became a successful novelist and travel writer, with more than fifty books to his credit, but never again reached the level of notoriety his first novel achieved.

Welldon, James Edward Cowell (1854–1937). • Welldon's father, a master at a public school, sent him to Eton and Cambridge, where he won many honors. In 1885 he became headmaster of Harrow, and in 1892 chaplain to the queen; his tenure of both positions ended in 1898, when he was discovered to have compromised himself with a schoolboy. He subsequently became bishop of Calcutta, canon of Westminster, and dean of Manchester and finally of Durham, retiring in 1933 and remaining unmarried throughout his life. His sixteen books are mostly on philosophical and religious topics.

Wilde, Oscar (1854–1900). • Son of a Dublin surgeon and his literary wife, Wilde won the Newdigate prize at Oxford and quickly became known for his provocative aestheticism, which brought him an American lecture tour and a lampooning in Gilbert and Sullivan's operetta *Patience*. He married in 1884 and wrote *The Happy Prince* shortly after the birth of his first son; at about the same time he began to explore homosexuality (at first under the guidance of the seventeen-year-old Robert Ross) and was soon producing his most enduring works. Wilde's 1895 conviction for homosexual offenses had wide repercussions for the sexual mores of his day.

Wodehouse, Sir Pelham Grenville (1881–1975). • Wodehouse wrote some 120 books and the lyrics for eighteen musicals but began his career by publishing school stories in *The Captain* magazine because he didn't want to become a banker. Psmith's success as a character contributed largely to Wodehouse's crossing over into adult fiction. Caught behind enemy lines in France in 1940, he and his wife were interned by the Germans; his good-humored but ill-advised broadcasts from captivity aroused much bad feeling in Britain, and he became an American citizen in 1955.

Yonge, Charlotte Mary (1823–1901). • The daughter of an army officer cum country squire, Yonge was raised on Edgeworthian principles and religious enthusiasm; she taught Sunday school from age seven. John Keble became the local priest in 1835 and encouraged her to write Christian novels, which she began publishing in 1844— always contributing the profits to worthy causes, at her father's behest, and keeping her name off the title pages. She founded the Anglican magazine the *Monthly Packet*, serving as its editor for forty years, and wrote nearly 180 books, including textbooks, plays, catechisms, and collections of verse. *The Heir of Redclyffe* (1853) was particularly popular among soldiers in the Crimea.

Notes

INTRODUCTION

1. Carol Dyhouse, *Girls Growing Up in Late Victorian and Edwardian England* (London: Routledge & Kegan Paul, 1981), 144; Deborah Gorham, *The Victorian Girl and the Feminine Ideal* (Bloomington: Indiana University Press, 1982), 18.

2. Throughout, I shall follow such critics as Elisabeth Jay in using "evangelical" in its broad sense, to refer not to some specific Dissenting sect but to any British Christians who accepted the call to religious enthusiasm, an introspective "personal relationship with God," justification by faith, and the authority of the Bible over that of the Church. Similarly, "Darwinism" is intended as shorthand not only for the pronouncements of Darwin himself, but for the generalized Victorian conception of what evolutionary pronouncements were and what they implied.

3. Barbara Ehrenreich and Deirdre English, *For Her Own Good: 150 Years of the Experts' Advice to Women* (Garden City, N.Y.: Anchor Books, 1979), 26.

ONE

1. F. J. Harvey Darton, *Children's Books in England: Five Centuries of Social Life*, 3d ed. revised by Brian Alderson (Cambridge: Cambridge University Press, 1982), 141.

2. *A Cup of Sweets That Can Never Cloy; or, Delightful Tales for Good Children*, in Andrew W. Tuer, ed., *Stories from Old-Fashioned Children's Books* (1899; reprint, London: Bracken Books, 1985), 57, 58.

3. *Tales Uniting Instruction with Amusement*, in Tuer, *Stories*, 147.

4. See Gillian Avery, *Childhood's Pattern: A Study of the Heroes and Heroines of Children's Fiction 1770–1950* (London: Hodder and Stoughton, 1975), 22.

5. *Tales of the Hermitage; written for the Instruction and Amusement of the Rising Generation*, in Tuer, *Stories*, 250.

6. Nancy Armstrong, *Desire and Domestic Fiction: A Political History of the Novel* (New York: Oxford University Press, 1987), 63, 21.

7. David Grylls, *Guardians and Angels: Parents and Children in Nineteenth-Century Literature* (London and Boston: Faber and Faber, 1978), 97.

8. Mrs. [Mary Martha] Sherwood, *The History of the Fairchild Family; or, The Child's Manual: Being a Collection of Stories Calculated to Show the Importance and Effects of a Religious Education*, vol. 1, 14th ed. (London: J. Hatcherd and Son, 1841), 260, 37.

9. J. S. Bratton, *The Impact of Victorian Children's Fiction* (London: Croom Helm, 1981), 56.

10. Sarah Stickney Ellis, *The Daughters of England: Their Position in Society, Character, and Responsibilities* (New York: D. Appleton, 1843), 6, 8.

11. Ibid., 76, 176, 156, 214.

12. Nina Auerbach, *Woman and the Demon: The Life of a Victorian Myth* (Cambridge: Harvard University Press, 1982), 73.

13. Ellis, *Daughters of England*, 125, 3.

14. Dinah Maria Mulock Craik, *A Woman's Thoughts about Women* (New York: Rudd & Carleton, 1858), 22, 140–141, 20.

15. Elaine Showalter, "Dinah Mulock Craik and the Tactics of Sentiment: A Case Study in Victorian Female Authorship," *Feminist Studies* 2 (1975): 5–23, 6.

16. Grylls, *Guardians and Angels*, 29, 39.

17. [Miss Grierson], *Lily Douglas; A Simple Story. Humbly Intended as a Pattern for Sabbath Scholars*, 7th ed. (Edinburgh: William Oliphant, 1824), 10, 20.

18. Ibid., 70.

19. Especially in the early part of the century, it is not always possible to differentiate boys' books from girls'; as with historical tales and fantasy novels later in the period, much of this literature is simply meant for children. Still, one useful if not invariably reliable indication of the expected audience is the protagonist's gender.

20. Avery, *Childhood's Pattern*, 35.

21. Frederick Marryat, *Masterman Ready* (1841; reprint, London: J. M. Dent, 1970), 28, 39.

22. Ibid., 207, 226–227, 213, 333.

23. Ibid., 333. To be sure, the startling contrast between the didacticism of Marryat's works for children and the cheerful picaresqueness of such of his works for adults as *Mr. Midshipman Easy* (1836) might suggest some doubt on the author's part as to the mature reader's ability or inclination to absorb moral teachings.

24. [Lady Eastlake], "Books for Children," *Quarterly Review* 71 (1842–1843): 54–83, 63.

25. "Childhood," *Blackwood's Magazine* 12, no. 67 (August 1822): 139–145, 143.

26. "Children," *Chambers's Journal of Popular Literature* 19, no. 481 (21 March 1863): 177–180, 177, 178.

27. Richard D. Altick, *The English Common Reader: A Social History of the Mass Reading Public, 1800–1900* (Chicago: University of Chicago Press, 1957), 389.

28. Hesba Stretton [Sarah Smith], *Jessica's First Prayer* (1867; reprint, New York and London: Garland, 1976), 58, 88–89.

29. Juliet Dusinberre, *Alice to the Lighthouse: Children's Books and Radical Experiments in Art* (London: Macmillan, 1987), 31.

30. [Alexander Innes Shand], "Children Yesterday and Today," *Quarterly Review* 183 (1896): 374–396, 390.

31. Catherine Sandbach-Dahlström, *Be Good Sweet Maid: Charlotte Yonge's Domestic Fiction: A Study in Dogmatic Purpose and Fictional Form* (Stockholm: Almqvist & Wiksell International, 1984), 7, 169.

32. Charlotte Yonge, *The Trial: More Links of the Daisy Chain* (1864; reprint, London: Macmillan, 1908), 41–42.

33. Charlotte Yonge, *The Daisy Chain, or Aspirations: A Family Chronicle* (1856; reprint, London: Macmillan, 1904), 552, 563.

34. Quoted in Gorham, *Victorian Girl*, 49; Farningham edited the *Sunday School Times*.

35. Juliana Horatia Ewing, *The Story of a Short Life* (1882; reprint, New York: A. L. Burt, n.d.), 1, 6, 68, 74, 95.

36. Correspondence, *Girl's Own Paper* 1 (21 February 1880): 127.

37. "Beauty on Crutches," *Girl's Own Paper* 1 (21 February 1880): 120.

38. *Wild Kathleen*, *Girl's Own Paper* 1 (22 May 1880): 333; 1 (25 September 1880): 622.

39. Edward G. Salmon, "What Girls Read," *Nineteenth Century* 20 (October 1886): 515–529, 521, 522, 516.

40. Dyhouse, *Girls Growing Up*, 136.

41. Anna Davin, "Imperialism and Motherhood," *History Workshop* 5 (Spring 1978): 9–65, 50.

42. Grant Allen, "The New Hedonism," *Fortnightly Review* n.s., 55, no. 327 (1 March 1894): 377–392, 379, 392.

43. Lucy Bland, "Marriage Laid Bare: Middle-Class Women and Marital Sex 1880–1914," in Jane Lewis, ed., *Labour and Love: Women's Experience of Home and Family, 1850–1940* (Oxford: Basil Blackwell, 1986), 135. Other women, Yonge among them, took a more conservative stance, fearing that women might "lower themselves" from Angelhood by too much emulation of male behaviors. Thus, L. M. Montgomery's response to the new feminism was "I have no desire to be equal to man. I prefer to maintain my superiority" (quoted in Mary Cadogan and Patricia Craig, *You're a Brick, Angela! A New Look at Girls' Fiction from 1839 to 1975* [London: Victor Gollancz, 1976], 27, 97). Still, both conservative and radical positions relied largely on the concept of the Angel.

44. Frances Hodgson Burnett, *The Secret Garden* (1911; reprint, Philadelphia: J. B. Lippincott, 1962), 147.

45. Humphrey Carpenter, *Secret Gardens: A Study of the Golden Age of Children's Literature* (Boston: Houghton Mifflin, 1985), 189.

46. Burnett, *Secret Garden*, 90–91.

47. Phyllis Bixler, *Frances Hodgson Burnett* (Boston: Twayne, 1984), 99.

48. Burnett, *Secret Garden*, 28, 167.

49. Fred Inglis, *The Promise of Happiness: Value and Meaning in Children's Fiction* (Cambridge: Cambridge University Press, 1987), 111.

TWO

1. Quoted in Eric Trudgill, *Madonnas and Magdalens: The Origins and Development of Victorian Sexual Attitudes* (New York: Holmes and Meier, 1976), 242.

2. Deborah Gorham, "The 'Maiden Tribute of Modern Babylon'

Re-Examined: Child Prostitution and the Idea of Childhood in Late-Victorian England," *Victorian Studies* 21 (Spring 1978): 353–379, 360.

3. Josephine Butler, "Letter to My Countrywomen, Dwelling in the Farmsteads and Cottages of England" (1871), in Sheila Jeffreys, ed., *The Sexuality Debates* (New York and London: Routledge & Kegan Paul, 1987), 157.

4. Ibid., 173–174.

5. J. Hirst Hollowell, *Brotherly Honour versus Selfish Passion, an Address to Young Men and to Citizens, on Social Purity* (London: Moral Reform Union, 1889), 7.

6. Quoted in Angus McLaren, "The Early Birth Control Movement: An Example of Medical Self-Help," in John Woodward and David Richards, eds., *Health Care and Popular Medicine in Nineteenth Century England: Essays in the Social History of Medicine* (New York: Holmes & Meier, 1977), 92.

7. Cited in Trudgill, *Madonnas and Magdalens*, 63.

8. McLaren, "Early Birth Control," 97.

9. [W. R. Greg], "Prostitution," *Westminster Review* 52 (June 1850): 448–506, 457, 459, 452, 457, 473.

10. See M. Jeanne Peterson, "Dr. Acton's Enemy: Medicine, Sex, and Society in Victorian England," *Victorian Studies* 29 (Summer 1986): 569–590, 582–584.

11. Excerpted in Jeffreys, *Sexuality Debates*, 61, 63.

12. Peter Gay, *Education of the Senses*, vol. 1 of *The Bourgeois Experience: Victoria to Freud* (New York: Oxford University Press, 1985), 468.

13. Quoted in Patricia Branca, *Silent Sisterhood: Middle-Class Women in the Victorian Home* (London: Croom Helm, 1975), 125.

14. Social Purity Alliance, *Some Medical Opinions on Social Purity* (London, 1889), 3.

15. George H. Napheys, *The Transmission of Life: Counsels on the Nature and Hygiene of the Masculine Function* (1871; reprint, Philadelphia: H. C. Watts Co., 1882), 173–174.

16. Patrick Geddes and J. Arthur Thomson, *The Evolution of Sex* (London: Walter Scott; New York: Charles Scribner's Sons, 1897), 271.

17. Jean L'Esperance, "Doctors and Women in Nineteenth-Century Society: Sexuality and Role," in Woodward and Richards, *Health Care*, 106.

18. Quoted in Fraser Harrison, *The Dark Angel: Aspects of Victorian Sexuality* (New York: Universe Books, 1977), 9.

19. "Feigned Insanity," *Journal of Mental Science* 18 (July 1872): 232–233, 233.

20. Richard von Krafft-Ebing, *Psychopathia Sexualis: With Especial Reference to the Antipathic Sexual Instinct; A Medico-Forensic Study*, trans. Franklin S. Klaf (New York: Bell, 1965), 48.

21. Excerpted in Jeffreys, *Sexuality Debates*, 29.

22. Quoted in Gay, *Education of the Senses*, 156.

23. McLaren, "Early Birth Control," 91.

24. Thomas Laycock, "An Inquiry into the Influence of Libidinous Excess on the Causation of Locomotor Ataxy or Tabes Dorsalis," *Dublin Quarterly Journal of Medical Science* 47, no. 94 (1 May 1869): 257–269, 265.

25. Alfred S. Dyer, *Facts for Men on Moral Purity and Health: Being Plain Words to Young Men upon an Avoided Subject; with Safeguards against Immorality and Facts that Men Ought to Know* (London: Dyer Brothers, 1884), 20.

26. J. H. Kellogg, *Plain Facts for Old and Young* (1885; reprint, New York: Arno Press, 1974), 136–137, 211.
27. Excerpted in Jeffreys, *Sexuality Debates*, 325.
28. Nancy F. Cott, "Passionlessness: An Interpretation of Victorian Sexual Ideology, 1790–1850," in Cott and Elizabeth H. Pleck, eds., *A Heritage of Her Own: Toward a New Social History of American Women* (New York: Simon and Schuster, 1979), 173.
29. Lionel S. Beale, *Our Morality and the Moral Question: Chiefly from the Medical Side* (London: J. & A. Churchill; Philadelphia: Presley Blakiston and Son, 1887), 41.
30. James Foster Scott, *The Sexual Instinct: Its Uses and Dangers as Affecting Heredity and Morals* (New York: E. B. Treat, 1900), 77.
31. Henry C. Wright, *Marriage and Parentage* (1855; reprint, New York: Arno Press, 1974), 24. A child conceived during an act of lust would be degenerate; its counterpart conceived during a deliberate attempt to procreate would be Angelic, Wright asserted, implying that he practiced what he preached by printing a frontispiece that showed the author with his arm around an idealized golden-haired girl child, the scene captioned, "My Wee Darling."
32. Thomas Hughes, *Tom Brown's Schooldays* (1857; reprint, New York: Puffin Books, 1983), 288.
33. David Newsome, *Godliness and Good Learning: Four Studies on a Victorian Ideal* (London: John Murray, 1961), 26–27.
34. Thomas Hughes, *The Manliness of Christ* (1879; reprint, Boston: Houghton, Osgood, 1880), 19, 17–18, 30–31.
35. George J. Worth, "Of Muscles and Manliness: Some Reflections on Thomas Hughes," in James R. Kincaid and Albert J. Kuhn, eds., *Victorian Literature and Society: Essays Presented to Richard D. Altick* (Columbus: Ohio State University Press, 1984), 310.
36. Hughes, *Manliness of Christ*, 73.
37. Quoted in Ronald Pearsall, *The Worm in the Bud: The World of Victorian Sexuality* (New York: Macmillan, 1969), 219.
38. Napheys, *Transmission of Life*, 128, 277.
39. Rev. R. Ashington Bullen, *Our Duty as Teachers with Reference to Social Purity Work: An Address to Clergy, Day and Sunday School Teachers, and Others, at Carlisle, May 20th, 1884* (London: J. & F. Ward, 1886), 20, 21, 19.
40. Grylls, *Guardians and Angels*, 33.
41. Kellogg, *Plain Facts*, 22.
42. Stephen Kern, "Freud and the Discovery of Child Sexuality," *History of Childhood Quarterly* 1 (Summer 1973): 117–141, 137.
43. Greg, "Prostitution," 479.
44. Milton Rugoff, *Prudery and Passion* (New York: G. P. Putnam's Sons, 1971), 36–37.
45. Quoted in Steven Marcus, *The Other Victorians: A Study of Sexuality and Pornography in Mid-Nineteenth-Century England* (New York: Basic Books, 1964), 13–14.
46. Marcus, *Other Victorians*, 15.
47. Peterson, "Dr. Acton's Enemy," 581.
48. Henry Maudsley, "Illustrations of a Variety of Insanity," *Journal of Mental Science* 14 (July 1868): 149–162, 153, 157, 160.

49. Krafft-Ebing, *Psychopathia Sexualis*, 36.

50. Napheys, *Transmission of Life*, 17.

51. Bratton, *Victorian Children's Fiction*, 112.

52. Kenneth Allsop, "A Coupon for Instant Tradition: On *Tom Brown's Schooldays*," *Encounter* 25, no. 5 (November 1965): 60–63, 61, 63.

53. Bratton, *Victorian Children's Fiction*, 112.

54. Henry R. Harrington, "Childhood and the Victorian Ideal of Manliness in *Tom Brown's Schooldays*," *Victorian Newsletter*, Fall 1973, 13–17, 15.

55. Worth, "Of Muscles and Manliness," 302.

56. Hughes, *Tom Brown's Schooldays*, 166.

57. Norman Vance, *The Sinews of the Spirit: The Ideal of Christian Manliness in Victorian Literature and Religious Thought* (Cambridge: Cambridge University Press, 1985), 144, 73.

58. Hughes, *Manliness of Christ*, 20–21.

59. Hughes, *Tom Brown's Schooldays*, 180, 177, 236.

60. Ibid., 279, 280.

61. [Fitzjames Stephen], "Tom Brown's Schooldays," *Edinburgh Review* 107, no. 217 (January 1858): 172–193, 176.

62. Hughes, *Tom Brown's Schooldays*, 174, 185.

63. Harrington, "Childhood," 17.

64. Thomas Hughes, *Tom Brown at Oxford* (1861; reprint, New York and Boston: H. M. Caldwell, n.d.), 3, 53, 113, 64; *Manliness of Christ*, 58.

65. Hughes, *Tom Brown at Oxford*, 171, 170, 236.

66. Ibid., 295–296, 473, 505, 548.

67. Ibid., 222.

68. Hughes, *Tom Brown's Schooldays*, 182.

69. Bram Dijkstra, *Idols of Perversity: Fantasies of Feminine Evil in Fin-de-Siècle Culture* (New York: Oxford University Press, 1986), 65.

70. Annie Besant, *The Law of Population: Its Consequences, and Its Bearing upon Human Conduct and Morals* (1877), reprinted as pp. 149–201 in S[ripati] Chandrasekhar, *"A Dirty, Filthy Book": The Writings of Charles Hamilton and Annie Besant on Reproductive Physiology and Birth Control and an Account of the Bradlaugh-Besant Trial* (Berkeley: University of California Press, 1981), 158, 182, 193.

71. [George Drysdale], *The Elements of Social Science; or, Physical, Sexual, and Natural Religion*, 4th ed., enl. (London: E. Truelove, 1861), 80.

72. Allen, "New Hedonism," 391, 392.

73. Stephen Kern, *Anatomy and Destiny: A Cultural History of the Human Body* (Indianapolis: Bobbs-Merrill, 1975), 95.

74. [Henry] Havelock Ellis, "Auto-Erotism," in *Studies in the Psychology of Sex* (1900; reprint, Philadelphia: F. A. Davis, 1905), 174–175.

75. Emmeline Pethick Lawrence, "Education in Love" (1912), in Jeffreys, *Sexuality Debates*, 461.

76. Jeffrey Weeks, *Sexuality and Its Discontents: Meanings, Myths, and Modern Sexualities* (London: Routledge & Kegan Paul, 1985), 67.

77. J. Matthews Duncan, *On Sterility in Women* (London: J. & A. Churchill, 1884), 121, 97.

78. Beale, *Our Morality*, 61, 58.

79. Stephen Bourne, *Plain Thoughts on Purity* (London: Kegan Paul, Trench, 1885), 13.

80. Richard A. Armstrong, *Our Duty in the Matter of Social Purity: An Address to Young Men* (London: Social Purity Alliance, 1885), 9.

81. Edward Lyttelton, *The Causes and Prevention of Immorality in Schools* (London: Privately printed for Rev. R. A. Bullen, 1887), 21.

82. J. M. Wilson, "Morality in Public Schools and Its Relation to Religion," *Journal of Education* 148 (1 November 1881): 253–259, 253.

83. Vox in Solitudine Clamantis, "Our Public Schools: Their Methods and Morals," *New Review* 9, no. 50 (July 1893): 34–44, 44.

84. Michel Foucault, *An Introduction,* vol. 1 of *The History of Sexuality* (New York: Vintage Books, 1980), 43.

85. See David Hilliard, "Un-English and Unmanly: Anglo-Catholicism and Homosexuality," *Victorian Studies* 25 (Winter 1982): 181–210, 182.

86. Those specialists who were themselves homosexual, however, tended to assert that homosexuality was permanent. Edward Carpenter, for one, holds that *"sexual inversion . . . is in a vast number of cases quite instinctive and congenital, mentally and physically, and therefore twined in the very roots of individual life and practically ineradicable"* (*Homogenic Love, and Its Place in a Free Society* [Manchester: Labour Press Society, 1894], 18). Thus legal and medical remedies alike would have seemed inappropriate.

87. [Henry] Havelock Ellis, *Studies in the Psychology of Sex: Sexual Inversion* (1897; reprint, Philadelphia: F. A. Davis, 1908), 162, 167.

88. Scott, *Sexual Instinct,* 430–431, 40.

89. J.E.C. Welldon, "Our Public Schools: A Defence of Their Methods and Morals," *New Review* 9 (September 1893): 248–256, 252–253.

90. John Addington Symonds, *A Problem in Greek Ethics: Being an Inquiry into the Phenomenon of Sexual Inversion Addressed Especially to Medical Psychologists and Jurists* (New York: Haskell House Publishers, 1971), 3, 18. The book was written in 1873; ten copies were printed in 1883.

91. Quoted in Ronald Pearsall, *Public Purity, Private Shame: Victorian Sexual Hypocrisy Exposed* (London: Weidenfeld and Nicolson, 1976), 20.

92. Krafft-Ebing, *Psychopathia Sexualis,* 223.

93. Hughes, *Tom Brown's Schooldays,* 171, 181, 221.

94. Dr. B[enjamin] Tarnowsky, *The Sexual Instinct and its Morbid Manifestations from the Double Standpoint of Jurisprudence and Psychiatry* (Paris: Charles Carrington, 1898), 46–47.

95. Krafft-Ebing, *Psychopathia Sexualis,* 253.

96. Hilliard, "Un-English and Unmanly," 187.

97. Quoted in Jeffrey Richards, "'Passing the Love of Women': Manly Love and Victorian Society," in J. A. Mangan and James Walvin, eds., *Manliness and Morality: Middle-Class Masculinity in Britain and America 1800–1940* (Manchester: Manchester University Press, 1987), 111.

98. Armstrong, *Desire and Domestic Fiction,* 40.

99. R. Murray Leslie, "Woman's Progress in Relation to Eugenics," *Eugenics Review* 2, no. 4 (January 1911): 282–298, 285, 291.

100. Ellis, *Sexual Inversion,* 147.

101. In actual practice, of course, when feminine behavior became inappropriate for boys many girls rejected it also; in fiction, E. Nesbit's heroines often acquire male or neuter aliases (Bobbie, Phil, Panther) and announce their longing to be boys.

102. Excerpted in Jeffreys, *Sexuality Debates,* 485.

103. Armstrong, *Desire and Domestic Fiction*, 227.
104. Lillian Faderman, *Surpassing the Love of Men: Romantic Friendship and Love Between Women from the Renaissance to the Present* (New York: William Morrow, 1981), 239.

THREE

1. Jonathan Gathorne-Hardy, *The Old School Tie: The Phenomenon of the English Public School* (New York: Viking Press, 1978), 63.
2. Stephen, "Tom Brown's Schooldays," 172, 178, 186.
3. Frederic W. Farrar, *Eric; or, Little by Little: A Tale of Roslyn School* (1858; reprint, London: Hamish Hamilton, 1971), 15, 24.
4. Terence Wright, "Two Little Worlds of School: An Outline of a Dual Tradition in Schoolboy Fiction," *Durham University Journal* 75 (December 1982): 59–71, 59, 62.
5. Robert Lee Wolff, *Gains and Losses: Novels of Faith and Doubt in Victorian England* (London: John Murray, 1977), 222; Jeffrey Richards, *Happiest Days: The Public Schools in English Fiction* (Manchester: Manchester University Press, 1988), 14.
6. Richards, *Happiest Days*, 91.
7. Farrar, *Eric*, 42.
8. Ibid., 10.
9. Ibid., 269, 279.
10. P. G. Scott, "The School Novels of Dean Farrar," *British Journal of Educational Studies* 19, no. 2 (June 1971): 163–182, 178.
11. Farrar, *Eric*, 81.
12. Ibid., 76.
13. Hughes, *Tom Brown's Schooldays*, 271; Farrar, *Eric*, 153.
14. John Chandos, *Boys Together: English Public Schools 1800–1864* (London: Hutchinson, 1984), 300.
15. See Newsome, *Godliness and Good Learning*, 37; P. W. Musgrave, *From Brown to Bunter: The Life and Death of the School Story* (London: Routledge & Kegan Paul, 1985), 82; A. Jamieson, "F. W. Farrar and Novels of the Public Schools," *British Journal of Educational Studies* 16, no. 3 (October 1968): 271–278, 275.
16. Avery, *Childhood's Pattern*, 184. One index of the impression Farrar's work made on the working class was the dramatic rise in the number of boys christened Eric after 1858. Among the namesakes was Eric Blair, later to propose the need for left-wing school stories under his pen name of George Orwell.
17. Quoted in Musgrave, *From Brown to Bunter*, 109.
18. [Edward] G. Salmon, "What Boys Read," *Fortnightly Review* 39 (February 1886): 248–259, 251, 250.
19. [W. Lucas Collins], "School and College Life: Its Romance and Reality," *Blackwood's Edinburgh Magazine* 89, no. 544 (February 1861): 131–148, 137, 139–140.
20. Farrar, *Eric*, 16.
21. Hughes, *Tom Brown's Schooldays*, 141.
22. Dominic Hibberd, "Where There Are No Spectators: A Rereading of

Tom Brown's Schooldays," Children's Literature in Education 21 (Summer 1976): 64–73, 66; J. R. de S. Honey, *Tom Brown's Universe: The Development of the Victorian Public School* (London: Millington, 1977), 149.

23. Ian Watson, "Victorian England, Colonialism, and the Ideology of *Tom Brown's Schooldays," Zeitschrift für Anglistik und Amerikanistik* 29, no. 2 (1981): 117–129, 125, 128.

24. Vance, *Sinews of the Spirit*, 72.

25. Isabel Quigly, *The Heirs of Tom Brown: The English School Story* (London: Chatto & Windus, 1982), 7.

26. Excerpted in Nigel Temple, ed., *Seen and Not Heard: A Garland of Fancies for Victorian Children* (London: Hutchinson, 1970), 115.

27. Quigly, *Heirs of Tom Brown*, 106.

28. Excerpted in Temple, *Seen and Not Heard*, 190; quoted in Brian Simon, Introduction to Simon and Ian Bradley, eds., *The Victorian Public School: Studies in the Development of an Educational Institution* (Dublin: Gill and Macmillan, 1975), 3.

29. J. A. Mangan, *Athleticism in the Victorian and Edwardian Public School: The Emergence and Consolidation of an Educational Ideology* (London and New York: Falmer Press, 1986), 27.

30. Bruce Haley, *The Healthy Body and Victorian Culture* (Cambridge: Harvard University Press, 1978), 82–83.

31. Richards, *Happiest Days*, 120.

32. Mangan, *Athleticism*, 30.

33. Gathorne-Hardy points out that despite this insistence on the group, team spirit offered a way to contain, and thus to express, aggression and the will to win, by providing "a cloak under which individual achievement could seem less glaring and therefore less upsetting" (*Old School Tie*, 150).

34. Quoted in J. A. Mangan, *The Games Ethic and Imperialism: Aspects of the Diffusion of an Ideal* (New York: Viking, 1986), 55.

35. Quoted in Honey, *Tom Brown's Universe*, 114.

36. Quoted in Haley, *Healthy Body*, 167.

37. See Jeffrey Richards, Introduction to Richards, ed., *Imperialism and Juvenile Literature* (Manchester: Manchester University Press, 1989), 7.

38. W. Gordon Stables, "Doings for the Month," *Boy's Own Annual* 26 (1902–1903): 287. In a charmingly ironic twist, however, the financial health of both the *Boy's Own Paper* and the *Girl's Own Paper* caused some Religious Tract Society committee members to worry about the papers' souls; the climbing circulations suggested that the magazines had become too secular (Patrick A. Dunae, "*Boy's Own Paper*: Origins and Editorial Policies," *Private Library*, 2d ser., 9 (Winter 1976): 123–158, 135).

39. Bratton, *Victorian Children's Fiction*, 192.

40. Jack Cox, *Take a Cold Tub, Sir! The Story of the "Boy's Own Paper"* (Guildford, Surrey: Lutterworth Press, 1982), 44.

41. Richards, *Happiest Days*, 105.

42. Quigly, *Heirs of Tom Brown*, 79.

43. [Talbot Baines Reed], *The Adventures of a Three-Guinea Watch*, serialized in *Boy's Own Annual* 3 (1880–1881), 87, 88, 138.

44. Ibid., 150, 151, 199.

45. Ibid., 303, 319, 403, 448.

46. Ibid., 367.

47. "Mazeppa: A School Story in Six Chapters," serialized in *Boy's Own Annual* 3 (1880–1881), 82, 99, 131.

48. Ascott R. Hope [A. R. Hope-Moncrieff], "Toby: A School Story," serialized in *Boy's Own Annual* 3 (1880–1881), 746. I say "sociointellectual" because Mr. Brooks's nonaristocratic background and his low-status specialty are inseparable here; Toby would forgive the master his ignorance of the classics if the man were an Old Etonian, or even vice versa—but together the two deficiencies are both insult and injury.

49. Ibid., 779; cf. Mrs. Fairchild's similarly couched lecture to her offspring.

50. Ibid., 794.

51. Ibid., 794, 796.

52. Quoted in Chandos, *Boys Together*, 338.

53. Honey, *Tom Brown's Universe*, 223, 338–339.

54. Mangan, *Athleticism*, 135.

55. J.E.C. Welldon, *Gerald Eversley's Friendship: A Study in Real Life* (London: Smith, Elder & Co., 1895), 88, 75, 352.

56. He later left Harrow for a colonial bishopric, in secret disgrace over a romantic liaison with a pupil.

57. J.E.C. Welldon, *Sermons Preached to Harrow Boys in the Years 1885 and 1886* (New York: Thomas Whittaker, 1887), 50, 253, 125.

58. Richards, *Happiest Days*, 206.

59. Mrs. G. Forsyth Grant, *The Hero of Crampton School* (1895; reprint, Edinburgh: W. P. Nimmo, Hay & Mitchell, n.d.), 9, 10, 22.

60. Ibid., 87, 104, 102.

61. "The Boy's Own Club Room," *Boy's Own Annual* 35 (1913): 264.

62. Horace Annesley Vachell, *The Hill: A Romance of Friendship* (London: John Murray, 1907), 39, 95.

63. Ibid., 154, 147.

64. Quigly, *Heirs of Tom Brown*, 139.

65. Vachell, *The Hill*, 236, 318.

66. [Charles] Harold Avery, *An Old Boy's Yarns: or, School Tales for Past and Present Boys* (London: Cassell, 1895), 4.

67. Quoted in Mangan, *Games Ethic*, 48.

68. This suggestion that the only good soldier is a dead soldier surely informs the chilling irony of the final episode of *Stalky*, in which Stalky uses the corpse of one of his fallen (and orthodox) comrades to conceal his escape route from a besieged fort.

69. F. Anstey [Thomas Anstey Guthrie], *Vice Versa* (1882; reprint, New York: Puffin Books, 1985), 25, 71, 119–120.

70. Grant, *Hero of Crampton School*, 97.

71. Anstey, *Vice Versa*, 155, 299.

72. [Andrew Lang], "Vice Versa," *Saturday Review* 54, no. 1394 (15 July 1882): 88–89, 89.

73. Rudyard Kipling, *Stalky & Co.* (1899; reprint, New York: Puffin Books, 1987), 81, 151, 25.

74. Ibid., 197, 144.

75. Ibid., 106–107, 182.

76. Steven Marcus, "Stalky & Co.," in Elliot L. Gilbert, ed., *Kipling and the Critics* (London: Peter Owen, 1966), 155, 156, 159.

77. Robert F. Moss, *Rudyard Kipling and the Fiction of Adolescence* (London: Macmillan Press, 1982), 112.

78. Marcus, "Stalky & Co.," 155.

79. Musgrave, *From Brown to Bunter*, 171.

80. Richards, *Happiest Days*, 134–135.

81. P. G. Wodehouse, *Mike and Psmith* (1909), in *The World of Psmith* (London: Barrie & Jenkins, 1974), 15, 11, 115.

82. Ibid., 132.

83. Edward Lyttleton of Eton, panning the novel as "uniformly dull, occasionally unpleasant, and . . . almost wholly untrue," fought back against Waugh's charges by implying that the boy author could have done with more athleticism, not less: giving too much thought to intellect gives the adolescent mind "an unhealthy precocity" characterized by "a kind of egoistic superficiality." It is Waugh and Swinburne, not Fernhurst and football, who fail the Angel ("*The Loom of Youth*," *Contemporary Review* 112, no. 624 (December 1917): 658–664, 658, 662, 661.

84. Alec Waugh, *The Loom of Youth* (London: Grant Richards, 1918), 60, 141, 335.

FOUR

1. A. Dwight Culler, *The Victorian Mirror of History* (New Haven: Yale University Press, 1985), 26.

2. James C. Simmons, *The Novelist as Historian: Essays on the Victorian Historical Novel* (The Hague: Mouton, 1973), 20; "The Novelist as Historian: An Unexplored Tract of Victorian Historiography," *Victorian Studies* 14 (March 1971): 293–305, 296.

3. Nicholas Rance, *The Historical Novel and Popular Politics in Nineteenth-Century England* (London: Vision, 1975), 62.

4. John Clive, "The Use of the Past in Victorian England," *Salmagundi* 68/69 (Fall 1985–Winter 1986): 48–65, 49.

5. Valerie Chancellor, *History for Their Masters: Opinion in the English Historical Textbook: 1800–1914* (Bath: Adams & Dart, 1970), 66, 67.

6. J. G. Edgar, *The Young Crusaders* (London: Gall and Inglis, n.d.), 28. Originally published as *The Boy Crusaders*, 1865.

7. Ibid., 65.

8. Ibid., 193, 196.

9. Charlotte Yonge, *What Books to Lend and What to Give* (1887; reprint, London: National Society's Depository, n.d.), 55, 6.

10. Charlotte Yonge, *The Caged Lion* (1870; reprint, London: Macmillan, 1892), 3.

11. Ibid., 127, 135, 95, 209, 217.

13. Ibid., 5, 251.

14. Mark Girouard, *The Return to Camelot: Chivalry and the English Gentleman* (New Haven: Yale University Press, 1981), 146, 198.

15. Alice Chandler, *A Dream of Order: The Medieval Ideal in Nineteenth-Century English Literature* (London: Routledge & Kegan Paul, 1971), 5.

16. Girouard, *Camelot*, 164.

17. Ibid., 146; Avrom Fleishman, *The English Historical Novel: Walter Scott to Virginia Woolf* (Baltimore: Johns Hopkins University Press, 1971), 57.

18. Fleishman, *English Historical Novel*, 155.

19. Harry R. Shaw, *The Forms of Historical Fiction: Sir Walter Scott and His Successors* (Ithaca, N.Y.: Cornell University Press, 1983), 49.

20. Eveline C. Godley, "A Century of Children's Books," in Lance Salway, ed., *A Peculiar Gift: Nineteenth-Century Writings on Books for Children* (Harmondsworth, Middlesex: Kestrel Books, 1976), 102.

21. John Henry Raleigh, "What Scott Meant to the Victorians," *Victorian Studies* 7 (September 1963): 7–34, 16.

22. Culler, *Victorian Mirror*, 24.

23. Austin Clare [Wilhelmina Martha James], *The Carved Cartoon: A Picture of the Past* (1873; reprint, London: Society for Promoting Christian Knowledge, n.d.), ix.

24. Ibid., 27, 31, 111, 108–109.

25. Ibid., 172, 258.

26. W.H.G. Kingston, *Exiled for the Faith: A Tale of the Huguenot Persecution* (London: Sunday School Union, n.d. [1898]) 181, 40. (The original title of the book is *Villegagnon*; the earliest known edition—a posthumous one—is dated 1886; an 1870s original publication date seems probable.) Note the intertwining of "sensual[ity]" and "carnal weapons"; in a novel that rarely mentions biology, Kingston yet arranges his adjectives to suggest a sexuality that is both despicable and anti-Protestant.

27. Ibid., 146, 161, 71.

28. Quoted in Andrew Noble, "Highland History and Narrative Form in Scott and Stevenson," in Noble, ed., *Robert Louis Stevenson* (London: Vision; Totowa, N.J.: Barnes & Noble, 1983), 139.

29. Leslie A. Fiedler, "R.L.S. Revisited," in *No! in Thunder: Essays on Myth and Literature* (Boston: Beacon Press, 1960), 81, 79.

30. Robert Louis Stevenson, *The Black Arrow: A Tale of the Two Roses* (1888; reprint, New York: Charles Scribner's Sons, 1925), 25, 81, 64.

31. Ibid., 100.

32. Ibid., 135, 179.

33. Ibid., 235.

34. Ibid., 271.

35. Paul Binding, *Robert Louis Stevenson* (London: Oxford University Press, 1974), 14, 25, 15.

36. Noble, "Highland History," 138.

37. Sir Arthur Conan Doyle, *The White Company* (1891; reprint, London: John Murray, 1968), 10, 55, 202, 81, 10.

38. Ibid., 125.

39. Ibid., 115–116, 124.

40. Ibid., vii, 311, 363.

41. W. G. Blackie, Henty's publisher, estimated that "he was the most popular Boys' author of his day. . . . The figure of 150,000 [copies] a year in the days of his popularity I do not think can be under the mark . . . I know that with our figure [some 3,514,000 printed and presumably sold], Scribner's and Donohue's plus an unknown quantity for other pirated editions, it looks as if 25,000,000 is not impossible" (quoted in Guy Arnold, *Held Fast for England: G. A. Henty, Imperialist Boys' Writer* [London: Hamish Hamilton, 1980], 17).

42. Peter Newbolt, "G. A. Henty: The Earlier Books for Boys, 1871–1885," *Antiquarian Book Monthly Review* 4 (November 1977): 438–447, 440.

43. G. A. Henty, *The Young Franc-Tireurs: And Their Adventures in the Franco-Prussian War* (1871; reprint, London: Griffith Farran Okeden & Welsh, 1891), 3.

44. Quoted in William Allan, "G. A. Henty," *Cornhill Magazine* 1082 (Winter 1974–1975): 71–100, 98–99.

45. Quoted in John Cargill Thompson, *The Boys' Dumas: G. A. Henty: Aspects of Victorian Publishing* (Cheadle, Cheshire: Carcanet Press, 1975), 8.

46. André Rault, "George Alfred Henty, Romancier de la Jeunesse," in Marie-Claire Hamard, ed., *Home, Sweet Home or Bleak House? Art et Littérature à l'Époque Victorienne* (Paris: Les Belles Lettres, 1985), 168, 172.

47. Ibid., 176.

48. J. S. Bratton, "Of England, Home, and Duty: The Image of England in Victorian and Edwardian Juvenile Fiction," in John M. MacKenzie, ed., *Imperialism and Popular Culture* (Manchester: Manchester University Press, 1986), 83.

49. Jeffrey Richards, "Spreading the Gospel of Self-Help: G. A. Henty and Samuel Smiles," *Journal of Popular Culture* 16 (Fall 1982): 52–65, 53.

50. G. A. Henty, *The Young Carthaginian: or, A Struggle for Empire* (London: Blackie & Son, 1887), 38.

51. Robert A. Huttenback, "G. A. Henty and the Vision of Empire," *Encounter* 35 (July 1970): 46–53, 48; Rault, "Henty," 179.

52. Arnold, *Held Fast*, 66.

53. Roy Turnbaugh, "Images of Empire: George Alfred Henty and John Buchan," *Journal of Popular Culture* 9 (Winter 1975): 734–740, 736.

54. Henty, *Franc-Tireurs*, 34.

55. Patrick A. Dunae, "Penny Dreadfuls: Late-Nineteenth-Century Boys' Literature and Crime," *Victorian Studies* 22 (Winter 1979): 123–158, 146.

56. Quoted in Huttenback, "G. A. Henty," 47.

57. Martin Green, *Dreams of Adventure, Deeds of Empire* (London: Routledge & Kegan Paul, 1980), 220, 98.

58. Quoted in Allan, "G. A. Henty," 80.

59. G. A. Henty, *Bonnie Prince Charlie: A Tale of Fontenoy and Culloden* (1888; reprint, Chicago: Donohue Brothers, n.d.), 350.

60. G. Manville Fenn, *George Alfred Henty: The Story of an Active Life* (London: Blackie & Son, 1907), 321, 314.

61. Ibid., 1, 334.

62. G. A. Henty, "True Heroism: A Talk with the Boys," *Home Messenger* 12 (March 1903): 54–56, 56.

63. Captain F. S. Brereton, *In the King's Service: A Tale of Cromwell's Invasion of Ireland* (London: Blackie & Son, 1901), 176, 279, 17, 182–183, 340.

64. Ibid., 17.

65. G. Manville Fenn, *Marcus: The Young Centurion* (1904; reprint, London: E. Nister, n.d.), 10, 12.

66. Ibid., 329, 117.

67. Ibid., 329, 134, 149, 367, 309, 391, 392.

68. Patrick A. Dunae, "Boys' Literature and the Idea of Empire, 1870–1914," *Victorian Studies* 24 (Autumn 1980): 105–121, 110.

69. Cited in Girouard, *Camelot*, 226; Chancellor, *History for Their Masters*, 127.

70. Dunae, "Boys' Literature," 112–114.

71. Green, *Dreams of Adventure*, 396.

72. John Coates, "Thor and Tyr: Sacrifice, Necessary Suffering, and the Battle against Disorder in *Rewards and Fairies*," *English Literature in Transition* 29 (1986): 64–75, 66.

73. Ibid., 67.

FIVE

1. Darton, *Children's Books*, 252–253.

2. Green, *Dreams of Adventure*, 54, 57.

3. Mayne Reid, *The Boy Slaves* (1865; reprint, New York: E. P. Dutton, 1927), 6.

4. Dunae, "Boys' Literature," 109.

5. Ian Bradley, *The Call to Seriousness: The Evangelical Impact on the Victorians* (London: Jonathan Cape, 1976), 84, 74.

6. Brian V. Street, *The Savage in Literature: Representations of "Primitive" Society in English Fiction 1858–1920* (London and Boston: Routledge & Kegan Paul, 1975), 26, 49.

7. Lynda Nead, *Myths of Sexuality: Representations of Women in Victorian Britain* (New York and Oxford: Basil Blackwell, 1988), 83.

8. Anne Bowman, *The Boy Voyagers; or, The Pirates of the East* (London: Routledge, Warne & Routledge, 1859), 2, 4, 61, 400, 66.

9. Ibid., 167, 255.

10. Ibid., 405, 194.

11. Ibid., 4.

12. A.L.O.E. [Charlotte M. Tucker], *The Light in the Robber's Cave: A Story of Italy* (London: T. Nelson & Sons, 1862), 8, 15.

13. Ibid., 99.

14. Ibid., 118, 147, 155, 171–172, 222, 223.

15. Darton, *Children's Books*, 253.

16. Bratton, *Victorian Children's Fiction*, 147.

17. Yonge, *What Books to Lend*, 30.

18. Salmon, "What Boys Read," 255.

19. Eric Quayle, *Ballantyne the Brave: A Victorian Writer and His Family* (London: Rupert Hart-Davis, 1967), see pp. 88, 91; Jacqueline Rose, *The Case of Peter Pan: or, The Impossibility of Children's Fiction* (London: Macmillan, 1984), 79.

20. R. M. Ballantyne, *The Island Queen; or, Dethroned by Fire and Water: A Tale of the Southern Hemisphere* (London: James Nisbet, 1885), 98, 105, 106, 110, 120.

21. Ibid., 143, 202, 153.

22. Ibid., 181, 130.

23. Peter Haining, ed., *The Penny Dreadful: or, Strange, Horrid, and Sensational Tales!* (London: Victor Gollancz, 1975), 302.

24. Marjory Lang, "Childhood's Champions: Mid-Victorian Children's Periodicals and the Critics," *Victorian Periodicals Review* 13 (Spring/Summer 1980): 17–31, 22.

25. Quoted in Dunae, "Penny Dreadfuls," 143.

26. Louis James, "Tom Brown's Imperialist Sons," *Victorian Studies* 18

(September 1973): 89–99, 92; Ralph Rollington [H. J. Allingham], *A Brief History of Boys' Journals with Interesting Facts about the Writers of Boys' Stories* (Leicester: H. Simpson, 1913), 21.

27. Quoted in Dunae, *"Boy's Own Paper,"* 125.

28. James, "Tom Brown's Imperialist Sons," 96–97.

29. [Bracebridge Hemyng], *Jack Harkaway's Adventures Afloat and Ashore* (1888; reprint, Chicago: Donohue Brothers, n.d.), 222.

30. Kirsten Drotner, *English Children and Their Magazines, 1751–1945* (New Haven: Yale University Press, 1988), 104, 107.

31. E. S. Turner, *Boys Will Be Boys: The Story of Sweeney Todd, Deadwood Dick, Sexton Blake, Billy Bunter, Dick Barton, et al*, rev. ed. (London: Michael Joseph, 1975), 105.

32. Dunae, "Boys' Literature," 109–110.

33. Robert Louis Stevenson, letter to W. E. Henley, in Paul Maixner, ed., *Robert Louis Stevenson: The Critical Heritage* (London: Routledge & Kegan Paul, 1981), 125.

34. John Rowe Townsend, *Written for Children: An Outline of English-Language Children's Literature*, 2d ed., rev. (New York: J. B. Lippincott, 1983), 64.

35. Binding, *Robert Louis Stevenson*, 150.

36. Review of *Treasure Island*, in *Dial* (Chicago; May 1884), in Maixner, *Robert Louis Stevenson*, 142.

37. David H. Jackson, *"Treasure Island* as a Late-Victorian Adults' Novel," *Victorian Newsletter* 72 (Fall 1987): 28–32, 28, 29.

38. Robert Louis Stevenson, *Treasure Island* (1883; reprint, Boston: Houghton Mifflin, 1962), 107, 171, 165, 85, 147.

39. Ibid., 191, 116.

40. Ibid., 42, 43, 40, 65.

41. Review of *Treasure Island* in *Academy* (1 December 1883), in Maixner, *Robert Louis Stevenson*, 129.

42. Armstrong, *Desire and Domestic Fiction*, 52.

43. Stevenson, *Treasure Island*, 59.

44. Roger Lancelyn Green, *Tellers of Tales: Children's Books and Their Authors from 1800 to 1968*, rev. ed. (London: Kay and Ward, 1969), 156.

45. Quoted in Peter Berresford Ellis, *H. Rider Haggard: A Voice from the Infinite* (London: Routledge & Kegan Paul, 1978), 98.

46. Morton Cohen, *Rider Haggard: His Life and Work*, 2d ed. (London: Macmillan, 1968), 95, 90.

47. Norman Etherington, *Rider Haggard* (Boston: Twayne, 1984), 41, 42.

48. Hartwig A. Vogelsberger, *"King Romance": Rider Haggard's Achievement, Romantic Reassessment* 92, no. 3 (1984), 142.

49. R. M. Ballantyne, *The Gorilla Hunters* (1861; reprint, London: Peal Press, n.d.), 67, 120.

50. Ibid., 72, 65, 169.

51. Ibid., 144, 143, 255.

52. H. Rider Haggard, *She* (1887; reprint, New York: Airmont, 1967), 100, 121.

53. Ibid., 172, 130, 126, 198.

54. H. Rider Haggard, *Ayesha: The Return of She* (1905; reprint, New York: Ballantine Books, 1978), 269, 282, 330.

55. Etherington, *Rider Haggard*, 62.

56. Quoted in Ellis, *H. Rider Haggard*, 111.
57. Sandra Gilbert, "Rider Haggard's Heart of Darkness," *Partisan Review* 50 (1983): 444–453, 449–450.
58. Cohen, *Rider Haggard*, 224.
59. Wendy R. Katz, *Rider Haggard and the Fiction of Empire: A Critical Study of British Imperial Fiction* (Cambridge: Cambridge University Press, 1987), 31.
60. H. Rider Haggard, "Sex and the Short Story," *Bystander* 9 (18 January 1911): 113.
61. Frank T. Bullen, *Frank Brown: Sea Apprentice* (London: James Nisbet, 1906), 3.
62. Ibid., 19, 48, 66, 100.
63. Ibid., 55, 159, 160.
64. Ibid., 313, 224, 194.
65. Ibid., 294, 328.
66. W. W. Mayland, "Dr. Gordon Stables, R.N.: His Life and Work," *Captain* 3 (September 1900): 483–488, 483.
67. [W. Gordon Stables], Correspondence Column, *Boy's Own Annual* 26 (1903): 48.
68. W. Gordon Stables, *From Slum to Quarter-Deck* (1908; reprint, London: Religious Tract Society, n.d.), 31.
69. Ibid., 25, 38, 53.
70. Ibid., 192, 243.
71. Frances Hodgson Burnett, *The Lost Prince* (London: Hodder and Stoughton, 1915), 8, 47, 55.
72. Ibid., 136, 128, 132, 145–146.
73. Ibid., 35, 44, 103, 107.
74. Ibid., 115.
75. Bixler, *Frances Hodgson Burnett*, 113.
76. Burnett, *Lost Prince*, 197, 269, 311, 275.
77. David Daniell, "Buchan and 'The Black General,'" in David Dabydeen, ed., *The Black Presence in English Literature* (Manchester: Manchester University Press, 1985), 141, 147.
78. John Buchan, *Prester John* (1910; reprint, London: Thomas Nelson and Son, n.d.), 138, 38.
79. Ibid., 365, 364.
80. As all young addicts to juvenile mystery stories know, girl detectives of the Nancy Drew type succeed by means of feminine intuition and an unfair share of good luck.
81. Green, *Dreams of Adventure*, 321.

SIX

1. Charles Dickens, "Frauds on the Fairies," in Salway, *Peculiar Gift*, 111.
2. "Children's Literature," *London Review* 13, no. 26 (January 1860): 469–500, 480.
3. Rosemary Jackson, *Fantasy: The Literature of Subversion* (London and New York: Methuen, 1981), 4.
4. Elisabeth Jay, *The Religion of the Heart: Anglican Evangelicalism and the Nineteenth-Century Novel* (Oxford: Clarendon Press, 1979), 51.

5. George P. Landow, "And the World Became Strange: Realms of Literary Fantasy," in Roger C. Schlobin, ed., *The Aesthetics of Fantasy Literature and Art* (Brighton: Harvester Press; Notre Dame, Ind.: University of Notre Dame Press, 1982), 140.

6. "Children's Literature," 481. Paradoxically, more traditional evangelical fiction could not always say the same. Writing in *Longman's Magazine* in April 1893, L. B. Lang complained of the "self-consciousness" of *The Fairchild Family*: "The children are eternally watching themselves, probing themselves, writing down their bad thoughts, talking about themselves. It is Self, Self, Self from morning till night, and the more they talk about Self the more delighted their parents are" ("The Fairchild Family and Their Creator," in Salway, *Peculiar Gift*, 465).

7. The combination of female protagonist and female listener places the *Alice* books outside the bounds of my study—much to my relief, since others have so well analyzed them elsewhere.

8. See Fiedler, "The Eye of Innocence: Some Notes on the Role of the Child in Literature," in *No! in Thunder*, 256, 266.

9. Peter Coveney, *The Image of Childhood: The Individual and Society; a Study of the Theme in English Literature*, rev. ed. (Baltimore: Penguin Books, 1967), 240, 302.

10. Isabelle Jan, *On Children's Literature*, ed. Catherine Storr (London: Allen Lane, 1973), 67. For the linkage between *The Water Babies* and sexuality, see Ravenna Helson, "The Psychological Origins of Fantasy for Children in Mid-Victorian England," *Children's Literature* 3 (1974): 66–76, 71, and works by Chitty and Duffy cited below.

11. U. C. Knoepflmacher, "The Balancing of Child and Adult: An Approach to Victorian Fantasies for Children," *Nineteenth-Century Fiction* 37 (March 1983): 497–530, 497.

12. Colin N. Manlove, *Modern Fantasy: Five Studies* (Cambridge: Cambridge University Press, 1975), 1.

13. Tzvetan Todorov, *The Fantastic: A Structural Approach to a Literary Genre* (Ithaca, N.Y.: Cornell University Press, 1975), 25.

14. Respectively the views of Tony Tanner, "Mountains and Depths—An Approach to Nineteenth-Century Dualism," *Review of English Literature* 3, no. 4 (October 1962): 51–61, 54; Maureen Duffy, *The Erotic World of Faery* (London: Hodder and Stoughton, 1972), 283; Townsend, *Written for Children*, 99; Gillian Avery with Angela Bull, *Nineteenth-Century Children: Heroes and Heroines in English Children's Stories 1780–1900* (London: Hodder and Stoughton, 1965), 48; Jerome Hamilton Buckley, *The Victorian Temper: A Study in Literary Culture* (1951; reprint, Cambridge: Cambridge University Press, 1981, 102.

15. Charles Kingsley, *The Water Babies* (1863; reprint, New York: E. P. Dutton & Co., 1910), 14; Stephen Prickett, *Victorian Fantasy* (Hassocks, Sussex: Harvester Press, 1979), 158. See also Manlove, *Modern Fantasy*, 24ff., for a convincing discussion of natural theology in Kingsley's fable.

16. Kingsley, *Water Babies*, 38.

17. Ibid., 140.

18. Ibid., 40, 16, 59, 171, 207.

19. Ibid., 18, 206, 209, 128.

20. Susan Chitty, *The Beast and the Monk: A Life of Charles Kingsley* (London:

Hodder and Stoughton, 1974, 57); Henry R. Harrington, "Charles Kingsley's Fallen Athlete," *Victorian Studies* 21 (Autumn 1977): 73–86, 77.

21. Allan John Hartley, *The Novels of Charles Kingsley: A Christian Social Interpretation* (Folkestone: Hour-Glass Press, 1977), 9; Chitty, *Beast and the Monk*, 236–237.

22. Kingsley, *Water Babies*, 174–175.

23. Quoted in Haley, *Healthy Body*, 215.

24. Charles H. Muller, "Spiritual Evolution and Muscular Theology: Lessons from Kingsley's Natural Theology," *University of Cape Town Studies in English* 15 (March 1986): 24–34, 27. See Vance, *Sinews of the Spirit*, especially pp. 110 and 120, for an interesting discussion of Kingsley's views on manliness and its relation to womanliness. Kingsley may be the best example of what Vance terms the "inevitable" uneasiness of juxtaposed muscularity and Christianity (p. 7).

25. Quoted in Bruce Haley, "Sports and the Victorian World," *Western Humanities Review* 22 (Spring 1968): 115–125, 118.

26. Kingsley, *Water Babies*, 57.

27. Stephen Prickett, *Romanticism and Religion: The Tradition of Coleridge and Wordsworth in the Victorian Church* (Cambridge: Cambridge University Press, 1976), 243.

28. See William Raeper, *George MacDonald* (Tring, Hertfordshire: Lion Publishing, 1987), 345; Greville MacDonald, *George MacDonald and His Wife* (London: George Allen & Unwin, 1924), 300. "None of us four [boys]," George MacDonald's son Ronald remembered in 1932, "could hope ever to become as good as our sisters"; in 1924 Greville MacDonald confessed to feeling "still crushed at times by the conviction . . . that I, as a male, am still a worm."

29. Quoted in Colin N. Manlove, *The Impulse of Fantasy Literature* (London: Macmillan, 1983), 92.

30. Stephen Prickett, "The Two Worlds of George MacDonald," *North Wind* 2 (1983): 14–23, 15.

31. George MacDonald, *At the Back of the North Wind* (1870; reprint, London: Octopus, 1979), 201, 49.

32. Ibid., 120–121, 125, 142–143.

33. Greville MacDonald, *George MacDonald*, 402.

34. George MacDonald, *North Wind*, 196, 83.

35. Robert Lee Wolff, *The Golden Key: A Study of the Fiction of George MacDonald* (New Haven: Yale University Press, 1961), 374.

36. George MacDonald, "The Fantastic Imagination," in Glenn Edward Sadler, ed., *The Gifts of the Child Christ: Fairytales and Stories for the Childlike by George MacDonald*, vol. I (1893; reprint, London: A. R. Mowbray, 1973), 27–28.

37. George MacDonald, "The Imagination: Its Functions and Its Culture," in *Orts* (London: Sampson Low, Marston, Searle & Rivington, 1882), 26, 29–30.

38. Jackson, *Fantasy*, 9.

39. Dinah Maria Mulock Craik, *The Little Lame Prince and His Travelling Cloak: A Parable for Young and Old]* (1875; reprint, Garden City, N.Y.: Children's Classics, 1956), 28, 30–31.

40. Ibid., 46, 47, 54, 63, 108, 110.

41. Sally Mitchell, *Dinah Mulock Craik* (Boston: Twayne, 1983), 88.

42. George MacDonald, *The World of George MacDonald: Selections from His Works of Fiction*, ed. Rolland Hein (Wheaton, Ill.: Harold Shaw, 1978), 80; MacDonald finds that both activities require abandoning the self.

43. Craik, *Woman's Thoughts*, 198, 30.

44. Mrs. [Mary Louisa] Molesworth, *Four Winds Farm* (London: Macmillan, 1887), 158, 156, 176.

45. Ibid., 139, 145, 146, 148, 179.

46. Ibid., 170, 173, 100.

47. Quoted in Roger Lancelyn Green, *Mrs. Molesworth* (London: Bodley Head, 1961), 44.

48. Mrs. [Mary Louisa] Molesworth, "Story-Writing," *Monthly Packet* 88 (August 1894): 158–165, 163, 165.

49. Mrs. [Mary Louisa] Molesworth, "Story-Reading and Story-Writing," *Chambers's Journal* 1, 6th ser. (5 November 1898): 772–775, 774.

50. Julia Briggs, *A Woman of Passion: The Life of E. Nesbit, 1858–1924* (London: Hutchinson, 1987), 289.

51. E. Nesbit, *Harding's Luck* (London: Hodder and Stoughton, 1909), 35, 32.

52. Ibid., 84, 83.

53. Ibid., 84, 278, 164.

54. Ibid., 236, 238, 275, 240, 8.

55. It's tempting to connect Richard, best of the three children and irretrievably exiled in the past, with Nesbit's favorite son, Fabian, dead at fifteen.

56. Quoted in Briggs, *Woman of Passion*, 318.

57. U. C. Knoepflmacher, "Of Babylands and Babylons: E. Nesbit and the Reclamation of the Fairy Tale," *Tulsa Studies in Women's Literature* 6 (Fall 1987): 299–325, 302; Colin N. Manlove, "Fantasy as Witty Conceit: E. Nesbit," *Mosaic* 10 (Winter 1977): 109–130, 111; Alison Lurie, "E. Nesbit: Riding the Wave of the Future," *New York Review of Books* 31, no. 16 (25 October 1984): 19–22, 19.

58. William Caldwell Roscoe, "Fictions for Children," in Salway, *Peculiar Gift*, 42.

59. Richard Ellmann, *Oscar Wilde* (London: Hamish Hamilton, 1987), 282.

60. "*A House of Pomegranates*," *Speaker* 5, no. 105 (2 January 1892): 26–27, 27.

61. Oscar Wilde, *The Faity Stories of Oscar Wilde* (London: Victor Gollancz, 1976), 97, 188.

62. "What Children Like to Read: The Verdict," *Pall Mall Gazette* 67, no. 10,378 (1 July 1898): 1–2, 2.

63. Quoted in Lois R. Kuznets, "Kenneth Grahame and Father Nature; or, Whither Blows *The Wind in the Willows*?" *Children's Literature* 16 (1988): 175–181, 175.

64. See Michael Mendelson, "*The Wind in the Willows* and the Plotting of Contrast," *Children's Literature* 16 (1988): 127–144, 127; Carlee Lippman, "All the Comforts of Home," *Antioch Review* 41 (Fall 1983): 409–420, 412.

65. Kenneth Grahame, *The Wind in the Willows* (1908; reprint, London: Methuen, 1959), 9, 20.

66. Ibid., 271, 37, 127.

67. Kuznets, "Kenneth Grahame," 178.
68. Grahame, *Wind in the Willows*, 51, 127–128.
69. Mendelson, "*Wind in the Willows*," 135, 140.
70. Kuznets, "Kenneth Grahame," 179.
71. Peter Green, *Beyond the Wild Wood: The World of Kenneth Grahame* (Exeter: Webb & Bower, 1982), 96.
72. Ibid., 109; Carpenter, *Secret Gardens*, 158. Maureen Duffy goes one better (or worse) by identifying all three central characters as phallic symbols (*Erotic World of Faery*, 305).
73. Food and fantasy seem to be natural affinities, judging by the prominence of eating in the works of such later male fantasists as C. S. Lewis and J.R.R. Tolkien. But while Lewis and Tolkien use food to indicate character, making divisions among the homely, the exotic, and the unwholesome according to "racial" boundaries (animal, human, witch; hobbit, elf, orc) Grahame's obsession with food allows no moral distinctions. Adventurers and stay-at-homes may have slightly different diets, but all food is good, satisfying, and unifying. Appropriately, a major source of marital conflict in Grahame's later life was his wife's refusal to permit him foods his doctor had forbidden.
74. Mendelson, "*Wind in the Willows*," 142.
75. Kuznets, "Kenneth Grahame," 179.
76. Grahame, *Wind in the Willows*, 153.
77. J. M. Barrie, *Peter Pan* (1911; reprint, New York: Puffin Books, 1986), 15, 139, 197.
78. Ibid., 210, 30, 19.
79. Ibid., 132.
80. Ibid., 102.
81. Quoted in Carpenter, *Secret Gardens*, 172.
82. Barrie, *Peter Pan*, 192.
83. Ibid., 42, 88, 99, 195, 206, 210.
84. Ibid., 127.
85. Quoted in Roger Lancelyn Green, *J. M. Barrie* (London: Bodley Head, 1960), 49.
86. Barrie, *Peter Pan*, 202. Harry M. Geduld explores another dimension of Peter's tragedy by linking him with Barrie's elder brother David, dead in childhood, with whom Barrie thereafter forever competed for their mother's love (*Sir James Barrie* [New York: Twayne, 1971], 30). The ensuing resentments would indeed help to explain Barrie's ambiguity about mothers, who appear in such late plays as *The New Word* (1915) and *A Well-Remembered Voice* (1918) as stifling and as unfair to fathers.
87. Michelle Zimbalist Rosaldo, "Woman, Culture, and Society: A Theoretical Overview," in Rosaldo and Louise Lamphere, eds., *Woman, Culture, and Society* (Stanford, Cal.: Stanford University Press, 1974), 37.

APPENDIX

1. Quoted in Avery, *Nineteenth-Century Children*, 100–101.

Index